# The I.R.A. a ...

# The I.R.A.
# at War
# 1916–1923

*Peter Hart*

OXFORD
UNIVERSITY PRESS

*This book has been printed digitally and produced in a standard specification*
*in order to ensure its continuing availability*

# OXFORD
UNIVERSITY PRESS

Great Clarendon Street, Oxford OX2 6DP
United Kingdom

Oxford University Press is a department of the University of Oxford.
It furthers the University's objective of excellence in research, scholarship,
and education by publishing worldwide. Oxford is a registered trade mark of
Oxford University Press in the UK and in certain other countries

British Library Cataloguing in Publication Data
Data available

Library of Congress Cataloguing in Publication Data
Data available

ISBN 978-0-19-927786-5

*To the memory of*
*Lucien Karchmar, Ralph Pastore,*
*Stuart Pierson, and Peter Young*

# PREFACE

When did the Irish revolution start and when did it end?
Why was the I.R.A. so much stronger in some counties than others?
Why was the Irish revolution so violent?
Did the I.R.A. want to establish a military dictatorship?
What kind of people became guerrillas?
Were the I.R.A. terrorists?
How did the Thompson gun get to Ireland?
Did Michael Collins order the assassination of Sir Henry Wilson?
Were Protestants ethnically cleansed from southern Ireland?
Did a pogrom take place against Belfast Catholics?

The answers to these questions, all raised in the course of this book, illustrate three things: the endless capacity of Irish history to surprise; the extraordinary volume and variety of evidence available concerning the Irish revolution; and the necessity for historians to challenge all assumptions made about it. Systematic information is available on every aspect of the revolution; it can often be quantified and a huge range of variables charted and compared. Thousands of witness testimonies can be consulted—and cross-examined using the files of their organizations, or those of their enemies. We must push the research as far as we can and follow where it leads us. Good data must drive out bad. New interpretations must override politicized labels, cross the Northern Irish border and the Irish Sea, discard selective definitions and chronologies. New questions must pursue all the implications of their answers.

These essays represent sixteen years' work on the history of the Irish revolution. When I began I would meet very few people doing related research, but now the pace has picked up to the point where it is possible to speak of an active field of revolutionary history emerging around a series of key debates. Among them: the social origins and nature of the revolutionary movement; the origins and dynamics of violence; and the role of ethnic identity and conflict in shaping both. These are the central problems that most of the following essays seek to define, quantify, and explain.

The twenty-one tables presented here provide the foundations for a statistical history of the revolution. In them, I have compiled the first full accounting of revolutionary casualties—those killed and wounded, divided into cities, counties, provinces, and various time periods, as well as by the affiliation of the victims (Chapters 2, 3, and 10). Many other types of violence can be quantified, including riots and arson (Chapters 2 and 3). The same methodology has been applied to revolutionary activity in Britain (Chapter 6). I have also charted the occupations, ages, and landholdings of a large sample of I.R.A. members, along with their family and neighbourhood networks (Chapter 5). Examining demographic and communal change, it is possible to track church attendance and membership as well as school enrolments to pinpoint when southern Protestants left Ireland (Chapter 9). Declan Martin has done an extraordinary job of doing the same for those displaced by violence in Belfast (Chapter 10). Moving down to the front lines of guerrilla war, we can even measure the impact of the Thompson gun on the southern Civil War (Chapter 7). Given the extraordinary volume of information at our disposal, the possibilities for further quantification are numerous. Any assertion or conclusion that can be tested, *must be tested*.

Along the way I have also became intrigued by some of the mysteries of the revolution—who shot whom and why—and by the possibility of puzzling out the clues Columbo-style. My attempts to unravel assassinations and gun-running can be found in Chapters 7 and 8. Playing detective is always part of historical enquiry (often the best part), and it can also tell us a great deal about the revolution. Detailed reconstructions of particular chains of events provide a necessary counterpoint to quantification and pattern-seeking, and the two kinds of analysis are ultimately complementary. For example, the assassination of Sir Henry Wilson appears singular in its London context, and therefore seems more likely to be the product of a conspiracy or invisible hand. Set against the backdrop of Irish chaos, however, it can be seen as just one more revenge killing. Of course, another possible context is Michael Collins's 'northern policy' of aiding republicans across the border, in which Wilson was cast as a leading antagonist. Choosing between them, assessing relevance, brings us back to the actual—and abundant—evidence of documents, witnesses, and the sequence of events. If you are curious, turn to Chapter 8.

I hope my findings are intriguing to all readers of revolutionary history and useful to those thinking about the same issues. This work is intended to contribute to a larger debate about the nature of the Irish revolution. How and why did it happen? What do we call it and its various episodes? Why was it so violent? How did events in southern counties relate to those in the north? The essays in Part I discuss these questions and suggest some ways of conceptualizing and explaining the course of events. Chapter 1 is a general analysis of the framework of revolutionary history. Chapters 2 and 3 address revolutionary violence and attempt to describe and analyse it using the statistics I have assembled from newspapers, police reports, and other sources. Part II explores the character of the I.R.A. in Ireland. Chapter 4 tackles the phenomenon of republican paramilitarism and its place in the Irish political system; Chapter 5 uses occupation, age, property, and family data to anatomize the membership of the I.R.A. and associated organizations.

Part III concerns the neglected revolutionaries in Britain, who mounted their own considerable campaign (Chapter 6), were responsible for most of the I.R.A. and Irish Republican Brotherhood gun-running in concert with their comrades in the United States (Chapter 7), and nearly caused a second Anglo-Irish war in 1922 with the Wilson assassination (Chapter 8). Part IV turns finally to the question of ethnic violence and its consequences for the southern Protestant minority (Chapter 9) and for northern Catholics (Chapter 10).

Six of these studies have been published before in articles or books, and remain intact except for occasional corrections or additions where new work or data has been taken into account. Three—Chapters 5, 6, and 7—began many years ago as research papers at Yale University under the supervision of Paul Kennedy, Brian Sullivan, and James Scott, whom I must thank for allowing me to follow my peculiar interests. At the same institution, Edward Tufte taught me applied statistics, the results of which can be found herein—although any shortcomings are entirely my responsibility. Many people deserve thanks for improving these essays: Joost Augusteijn, Fergus Campbell, Richard English, David Fitzpatrick, Anne Hart, Keith Jeffery, Greg Kealey, Patrick Maume, Graham Walker, Robin Whitaker, and the anonymous readers at the *English Historical Review*, *Historical Journal*, *Past and Present*, and Oxford University Press. I have spent my working life at two universities, Memorial University of Newfoundland and Queen's University, Belfast. At Memorial, I have been helped by (among others): Louise Dawe, Andy den Otter, Tom Evans, Beverly Evans-Hong, David Facey-Crowther, Eleanor Fitzpatrick, Greg Kealey, Linda Kealey, Roxanne Millan, Terry Murphy, Rosemary Ommer, Bill Reeves, Bob Sweeny, and Fran Warren. Martin Howley has put all scholars in Newfoundland in his debt by making Memorial's Irish studies collection into one of the finest in North America. Queen's provided an extraordinarily supportive and stimulating environment—for which I will always be grateful to Paul Bew, Tim Bowman, Sean Connolly, Colm Crean,

Enda Delaney, Bob Eccleshall, Richard English, Gordon Gillespie, Ian Green, Judith Green, David Hayton, Alvin Jackson, Peter Jupp, Liam Kennedy, Patrick Maume, Margaret O'Callaghan, Mary O'Dowd, Ian Packer, Una Short, Brian Walker, and Rick Wilford. For support and friendship throughout my research career, I am indebted to Donald Akenson, Tom Garvin, Kevin Herlihy, Michael Hopkinson, Jane Leonard, Ben Levitas, Mary Murray, Kevin Myers, Eunan O'Halpin, Chris Morash, Peter Neary, and Martin Staunton. For their hospitality in Toronto I must thank Stephen Barnard and Maureen Ridzick, Jeremy Stolow and Danielle Filion, Jordan Berger and Marit Stiles, Carol Musselman, Uri Shafrir and Masha Etkind. I, like so many others, am deeply in debt to Roy Foster for all his help and kindness. And what would I have done without Anne, David, Stephen, and Susan Hart, Stephenson Yang and Peter Hart Yang, and Linda Siegel? One thing for sure, I would never have made it this far without Robin Whitaker.

In the course of my research I have visited and revisited a number of archives whose exemplary services must also be acknowledged. Seamus Helferty and the staff at the Archives Department of University College Dublin, Victor Laing and the much-missed Peter Young at the Irish Military Archives, Patricia McCarthy and others at the Cork Archives Institute, the staffs at the Imperial War Museum, National Archives of Ireland, National Library of Ireland, and Public Record Office in London have made research a pleasure and should get much of the credit for the growth of modern Irish history. I must also record my appreciation for the support given to me by the British Academy, the Institute of Social and Economic Research at Memorial University, and the Social Sciences and Humanities Research Council of Canada. Finally, thanks to Ruth Parr, Anne Gelling, and Kay Rogers at Oxford University Press for all their help, and to Jeff New for his superb copyediting.

The following chapters first appeared (with slightly different titles and contents) in the following journals and book: Chapter 2 in *Past and Present* (1997); Chapter 5 in *The Historical Journal* (1999); Chapter 6 in the *English Historical Review* (2000); Chapter 7 in *The Irish Sword* (1995); Chapter 8 in *Irish Historical Studies* (1992); and Chapter 9 in Richard English and Graham Walker (eds.), *Unionism in Modern Ireland: New Perspectives on Politics and Culture* (Macmillan, 1996). Parts of Chapter 1 appeared in Joost Augusteijn (ed.), *The Irish Revolution, 1913–1923* (Palgrave, 2002). My thanks to the publishers and editors of the above for permission to reprint.

# CONTENTS

# LIST OF FIGURES AND MAPS

# LIST OF TABLES

# Abbreviations

| | |
|---|---|
| Adj. | Adjutant |
| A/G | Adjutant-General |
| A.F.I.L. | All For Ireland League |
| Bn. | Battalion |
| Bde. | Brigade |
| C/S | Chief of Staff |
| C.I. | County Inspector |
| Coy. | Company |
| D/E | Director of Engineering |
| D/I | Director of Intelligence |
| D.I. | District Inspector |
| Div. | Division |
| D.M.P. | Dublin Metropolitan Police |
| DORA | Defence of the Realm Act |
| G.A.A. | Gaelic Athletic Association |
| G.H.Q. | General Headquarters |
| I.G. | Inspector-General |
| I/O | Intelligence Officer |
| I.R.A. | Irish Republican Army |
| I.R.B. | Irish Republican Brotherhood |
| I.S.D.L. | Irish Self-Determination League |
| O/C | Officer in Command |
| Org. | Organizer |
| R.I.C. | Royal Irish Constabulary |

*Archives*

| | |
|---|---|
| CAI | Cork Archives Institute |
| HLRO | House of Lords Records Office, London |
| IWM | Imperial War Museum, London |
| MA | Military Archives of Ireland, Dublin |
| NA | National Archives of Ireland, Dublin |
| NLI | National Library of Ireland, Dublin |
| PRO | Public Record Office, London |
| PRONI | Public Record Office of Northern Ireland, Belfast |
| SRO | Scottish Record Office, Edinburgh |

UCD          University College Dublin Archives

*Records*

CAB          British Cabinet Office
CO           Colonial Office
CSO          Chief Secretary's Office
DE           Dail Eireann
FIN          Irish Department of Finance
GPB          General Prisons Board
HO           Home Office
RRO          Reports on Revolutionary Organizations
SIC          Special Infantry Corps
WO           War Office

# PART I
# The Structure of Revolution

# 1

# A New Revolutionary History

The essays in this volume investigate and interpret the revolution that took place in Ireland, and the forces that shaped it both there and in Britain. They focus on violence, its practitioners, and its victims. Guerrilla warfare, terrorism, communal conflict, displaced people, assassins, gunmen, and gun-runners: the storyline and cast are familiar to any initiate in Irish history—1916: failed rebellion sparks emotional response from nationalist population seeking oft-denied self-government; 1917–18: separatist movement arises, combats incompetently oppressive government, and wins majority of Irish seats at general election; 1919: revolutionary assembly is formed, claims sovereignty, is suppressed by government but retains mass support; 1920: revolutionary army wages war of liberation. Official counter-insurgency policies further alienate nationalists; 1921: military stalemate leads to truce, negotiation, and compromise treaty delivering functional independence; 1922: movement splits as many revolutionaries are ideologically opposed to treaty terms. Intranationalist civil war follows between adherents and enemies of the new state; 1923: pro-state forces win; 1920–2: country partitioned to satisfy counter-revolutionary anti-nationalist ethnic minority. Regional anti-nationalist state established, accompanied by extensive ethnic violence.

This narrative arc is equally familiar to anatomists of revolution. At least it should be: Irish republicans invented modern revolutionary warfare, with its mass parties, popular fronts, guerrilla warfare, underground governments, and continuous propaganda campaigns. What Michael Collins and company did in post-Great War Ireland, Mao, Tito, and

Ho Chi Minh would do during and after the next world war. Irish rebels didn't know they were doing this, however, so no patent was claimed. The formula for success had to be reinvented and would be exported by more programmatic strategists. Thus, comparative students of revolution have passed Ireland by as well. It has not found its place alongside France, Russia, China, Cuba, and Iran in the analytical pantheon.

The events of 1916–23 are not usually referred to as a revolution— rarely referred to collectively at all in fact, except vaguely as 'the troubles'. There was a Rising, an election, a war of independence (with various alternate names), a Truce, a Treaty, another election, a Civil War. None of these terms describes more than a couple of years, and most implicitly refer only to the twenty-six counties with large Catholic majorities that became the 'southern' Free State. Northern Irish history is typically segregated as a separate topic and has no title for this period, apart from the 'pogroms' afflicting the Catholic population of Belfast in 1920–2.

This is an essentially nationalist narrative in terms of its periodization, focus, and plot. The republican movement *was* the plot in effect, driven by the cause of national freedom, itself an expression of the national will, itself the product of a united, homogenous, self-identifying nation. This cause was in accordance with universal democratic ideals, self-government being a collectively rational political choice. Further legitimacy and motive force came from historic ethnic and economic grievances on the one hand, and cultural nationalism on the other. The revolution was thus also an outgrowth of national self-discovery. Given these predicates, British government and its policies were inherently oppressive. The indigenous anti-nationalist (Unionist) movement was the creature of British interests, not of a separate ethnic (let alone national) consciousness, and therefore did not have a legitimate or genuinely competitive claim to self-determination. So much would, I think, be agreed by most nationalists. Not so the ending. Those in favour of the Anglo-Irish Treaty would see it and the consequent Free State as the realization of national liberation. Those opposed demanded republican popular sovereignty to satisfy this goal. All would believe that the nation-state is incomplete without the territory and population of Northern Ireland. Further liberation required.

The nationalist paradigm is overwhelmingly dominant, but a unionist—or at least anti-revolutionary—version of events does exist. Where nationalists saw popular will at play, its enemies saw manipulation and intimidation. One man's democratic mandate is another's electoral fraud. For republicans, violence was a symptom of political repression and popular resistance to aggression; for others, it was the product of conspiracy and terrorism. For nationalists, their cause was inclusive of all Irish people; for non-nationalists or non-republicans, it often appeared as coercive, sectarian, and ethnically aggrandizing.

These arguments have been rehearsed many times, and have been renewed in a modified form in the so-called revisionism debate of the 1970s, 1980s, and 1990s.[1] They are not usually encountered as arguments, though, but rather as articles of belief justifying current political positions or animating yet another historical chronicle. The irrational element in each—and their deployment in contemporary politics—do not mean they should be attacked or ignored, however. At the very least, the fact that these interpretations were shared by many of the actual historical actors makes them significant. And, rendered into approximate hypotheses, they can be tested. This requires a new approach, defined not by nationalist or anti-nationalist ideology but by extensive empirical research and a comparative, sociological method.

It has partly been this method that has inspired some of the hostility towards 'revisionism'. The very categories of inquiry—class, status, gender, ethnicity, social psychology and structure—threaten the necessary nationalist (or unionist) concepts of nation- and people-hood and proffer explanations for collective action other than a national desire for freedom. Patriotic leaders and heroes become psychological case studies or social constructs. Movement activists are judged by their behaviour, not by their intentions or ideals. Governmental actions are determined by bureaucratic inertia or disorganization rather than imperial malevolence or interest. What of it? If nationalist explanations for the course of events fail to meet empirical and logical tests, they should be discarded. The same is true for unionist or any other models (that of social revolution, for example).

We do have the materials for a new revolutionary history. Ireland's may be the best-documented modern revolution in the world. Dozens of daily and weekly newspapers provide a detailed local and national record for every city and county. Police, prison, military, and I.R.A. documents survive in marvellous abundance, as do departmental files and correspondence from all governments. Thousands of memoirs and reminiscences have been recorded in published or unpublished form—many

[1] For a variety of perspectives on 'revisionism', see Ciaran Brady (ed.), *Interpreting Irish History: The Debate on Historical Revisionism* (Dublin, 1994) and D. George Boyce and Alan O'Day (eds.), *The Making of Modern Irish History: Revisionism and the Revisionist Controversy* (London, 1996).

solicited for an official archive, the Bureau of Military History (now in the Irish Military Archives in Dublin). Manuscript household census returns and land valuation, ownership, and occupation records exist for nearly every individual and family involved. Church records provide data on congregations, parishes, and individuals, their lives, deaths, and movements. Official and economic information and statistics continued to be collected for much of this period, on matters ranging from crime to prices to emigration. A great array of personal diaries and letters have been collected. Tens of thousands of otherwise unrecorded episodes and experiences are preserved in swathes of compensation claims. Hundreds of voluntary organizations, trade unions, and businesses operating through the period have left documentary remains. All can be brought to bear on analytical problems. Almost any actor can be identified, profiled, and tracked through time. Events can be reconstructed through the eyes of multiple observers. A great range of social and political phenomena can be accurately quantified. Practically the only limit to inquiry is that created by the historian's imagination.

We also have the methodological tools to test established hypotheses and formulate new questions. The comparative study of revolutions has largely ignored Ireland, and historians of the Irish case have generally returned the compliment. The two should meet more often.[2] Irish sources allow for an unrivalled depth and breadth of inquiry and historical surveillance, penetrating into communities and families and encompassing entire populations. The study of how and why revolutions occur and how social movements behave has recently opened up into a remarkably creative debate, based on well-grounded case studies as well as subtle theoretical modelling. There is no necessary conflict here between empiricism and abstraction. There is instead a new set of questions, along with new frameworks for formulating both questions and answers.[3] Generalizations are not our enemies: unquestioned assumptions are, along

---

[2] Historians of the Land War of 1879–82 have already applied such techniques and theories: see James Donnelly, *The Land and the People of Nineteenth-Century Cork* (London, 1975); Samuel Clark, *Social Origins of the Irish Land War* (Princeton, 1979); Paul Bew, *Land and the National Question in Ireland, 1858–82* (Dublin, 1979); Andrew Orridge, 'Who Supported the Land War? An Aggregate Data Analysis of Irish Agrarian Discontent, 1879–1882', in *Economic and Social Review*, 12 (1980–1), 203–33.

[3] For some recent work, see John Foran (ed.), *Theorizing Revolutions* (London, 1997); Jeff Goodwin, *No Other Way Out: States and Revolutionary Movements, 1945–1991* (Cambridge, 2001); Doug McAdam, Sidney Tarrow, and Charles Tilly, *Dynamics of Contention* (Cambridge, 2001); Sidney Tarrow, *Power in Movement: Social Movements and Contentious Politics* (Cambridge, 1998).

with inadequately framed research. An effective new revolutionary history should seek to assert models and theories, and to test them just as aggressively.

Such work has already begun—indeed, it began in the 1970s with the work of David Fitzpatrick, Charles Townshend, and Tom Garvin. These researchers originated some of the key models now in circulation. David Fitzpatrick adopted the county as his unit of study in *Politics and Irish Life* in order to anatomize the revolution and its impact on life (in Clare) between 1913 and 1921.[4] He pioneered the use of many now-familiar sources (including those of oral history) for investigating the inner workings and social character of participant organizations, and set the agenda for much subsequent work on group membership and motivation, political factionalism, and revolutionary practice. Charles Townshend's *The British Campaign in Ireland* used similarly untapped sources to examine the British government and army's response to the rise of republicanism between 1916 and 1921.[5] His was the first proper institutional and policy study of this aspect, and the first to register bureaucratic and political structures and decision-making as a systematic focus of investigation. As such it was followed by Eunan O'Halpin's book on the Irish government, *The Decline of The Union*, which also emphasized organizational problems and scarce resources as key determinants of governmental behaviour.[6] Townshend's subsequent work took much the same tack in deconstructing the I.R.A.'s campaign.[7] Tom Garvin followed Erhard Rumpf in setting the revolutionary period in a longer framework and, along with David Fitzpatrick, began the quantitative analysis of nationalist political behaviour in Ireland using the plentiful data available.[8] Ruth Dudley Edwards's brilliant and infuriating (to partisans) biography of Patrick Pearse, *The Triumph of Failure*, must also be mentioned for the depth of its research

[4] Fitzpatrick, *Politics and Irish Life 1913–21: Provincial Experiences of War and Revolution* (Dublin, 1977).

[5] Townshend, *The British Campaign in Ireland 1919–1921* (Oxford, 1975). See also his 'Historiography: Telling the Irish Revolution' in Joost Augusteijn (ed.), *The Irish Revolution, 1913–1923*, (London: 2002), 1–17.

[6] O'Halpin, *The Decline of the Union: British Government in Ireland, 1892–1920* (Dublin, 1987).

[7] Charles Townshend, 'The Irish Republican Army and the Development of Guerrilla Warfare, 1916–21', *English Historical Review*, 94 (1979), 318–45. See also his *Political Violence in Ireland: Government and Resistance Since 1848* (Oxford, 1983).

[8] Erhard Rumpf and A. C. Hepburn, *Nationalism and Socialism in Twentieth-Century Ireland* (Liverpool, 1977); David Fitzpatrick, 'The Geography of Irish Nationalism, 1910–21', *Past and Present*, 78 (1978), 113–44; Tom Garvin, *The Evolution of Irish Nationalist Politics* (Dublin, 1981). For a detailed analysis of this work, see Ch. 2.

and its still-rare psychological perspective.[9] These new perspectives are reflected in some recent general histories: in R. F. Foster's masterful *Modern Ireland*, in David Fitzpatrick's innovative comparative study, *The Two Irelands 1912–1939*, and in Alvin Jackson's comprehensive *Ireland 1798–1998* (although for many writers in what is a popular field outside the academy, this body of work may as well have never been written).[10]

These historians have laid the foundation for a new revolutionary history built around the detailed reconstruction of movements and institutions, an intensively local perspective, and a quantitative and comparative national perspective, all drawing on primary sources from both Ireland and Britain. Several standard research models have been established, the main vehicle for advancing debate being studies of one county or comparing counties.[11] What has yet to happen is a conceptual discussion of how these interpretations are framed. Even if nationalist and unionist frameworks are no longer explicitly endorsed, they are still implicitly obeyed in many respects. The dominant narrative remains that of the nationalist movement in conflict with British rule. Periodization is generally segmented by movement events: the 1916 Rising; the 1918 election; the 1919–21 War of Independence; the 1921 Truce and Treaty; the 1922–3 Civil War. But why should the 1922–3 conflict between nationalists be called *the* civil war? Violent deaths in the six counties of Northern Ireland between July 1920 and July 1922 come close to matching those in the other twenty-six counties between June 1922 and June 1923, and property losses likely did as well—despite a much smaller population. Was this not an ethnic or sectarian civil war? If we include the Protestant civilians attacked and killed in the south, we could argue it was a island-wide phenomenon. If we want to categorize events by their social impact, the most obvious measurable change attributable to the revolution was massive population displacement, partly due to the victims' loyalties but primarily due, again, to their ethnicity—whether they were

---

[9] Ruth Dudley Edwards, *Patrick Pearse: The Triumph of Failure* (London, 1977). Two other biographies important for their approach as well as for their insights, are: Alvin Jackson, *Sir Edward Carson* (Dundalk, 1993) and Richard English, *Ernie O'Malley: I.R.A. Intellectual* (Oxford, 1998).

[10] Foster, *Modern Ireland 1600–1972* (London, 1988); Fitzpatrick, *The Two Irelands 1912–1939* (Oxford, 1998); Alvin Jackson, *Ireland 1798–1998: Politics and War* (London, 1988).

[11] See Oliver Coogan, *Politics and War in Meath 1913–23* (Maynooth, 1983); Joost Augusteijn, *From Public Defiance to Guerrilla Warfare: The Experience of Ordinary Volunteers in the Irish War of Independence, 1916–1921* (Dublin, 1996); Terence Dooley, *The Plight of Monaghan Protestants, 1912–1926* (Dublin, 2000); Michael Farry, *The Aftermath of Revolution: Sligo 1921–23* (Dublin, 2000); and Marie Coleman, *County Longford and the Irish Revolution, 1910–1923* (Dublin, 2002).

Belfast Catholics or Cork Protestants. These population events occurred in 1920–2 in the north and in 1921–4 in the south, regardless of 'wars' beginning and ending. On this basis, it might be better to think of the Irish revolution as an ethnic power struggle at least as much as a national war of liberation—and without such clear chronological dividing lines. We could even go further and point out that in the War of Independence, also known as the Anglo-Irish War, possibly the majority of the I.R.A.'s victims were Irish policemen and civilians. Another civil war? And can we call the surge of popular anti-Catholic violence in Belfast a loyalist rising to match Dublin's republican original? It was undoubtedly more popular and spontaneous. If we take the presence of crowds as an index of mobilization and confrontation, riots between rival nationalist parties, or between republicans and the police, were frequent before 1920. After June 1920, however, such street politics was mostly confined to the sectarian battle-grounds of urban Ulster.[12] The southern civil war of 1922–3 was an all-gunman affair, generating no real popular response. If we follow the crowd, it is a many-sided struggle we are describing.

Geographical distinctions can be as misleading as periodization and nomenclature. The Irish border cuts through the historiography, with historians working on the south often ignoring the north and vice-versa. 'North' and 'south' change meanings after partition but are used as if this was not the case. Donegal, Monaghan, and Cavan suddenly become southern in 1921, despite the fact that in many ways they have much more in common with parts of Ulster. Conversely, western Ulster counties are lumped together with Belfast as if they formed an organic political or social unit when this was not the case. In many ways, Belfast's revolutionary experience was unique, while Fermanagh can be classed with Leitrim and Monaghan. If we zoom outwards, a United Kingdom-wide perspective is often helpful or necessary—in dealing with the I.R.B., the I.R.A., violence, and gun-running, or with questions of revolutionary identity and motivation.

The new revolutionary history should focus on process and dynamics, on mobilization and its constituents, on the nature of political identities and relationships. What follows, therefore, is a series of propositions, based on the theory of revolutions and on recent local research, regarding the origins, nature, structure, and dynamics of the revolutionary movement, process, and outcomes. They are not intended to end discussion but

---

[12] See Table 8.

to begin it. Debates have indeed begun on a number of key issues concerning republicanism and the revolution: the social background and motives of the revolutionaries; the nature of violence; the radical potential of social conflict; and sectarianism north and south. However, there has been little critical consideration of equally or more fundamental factors such as gender and ethnicity, or of the conceptual terms of the debate itself. What do we call the events of 1916–23? Or should it be 1912–22 or 1917–21? Do these events form a unity or are they better understood discretely, as a succession of crises, rebellions, and wars? Was there a revolution and if so, what kind of revolution was it?

## Revolution?

General definitions of revolution are many and various. I prefer the simple, useful, and broadly inclusive model put forward by Charles Tilly (and widely endorsed in its essence by other writers):

A revolution is a transfer of power over a state in the course of which at least two distinct blocs make incompatible claims to control the state, and some significant portion of the population subject to the state's jurisdiction acquiesces in the claims of each bloc. A full revolutionary sequence thus runs from a sundering of sovereignty and hegemony through a period of struggle to reestablishment of sovereignty and hegemony under new management. We can usefully distinguish between revolutionary situations and outcomes. A revolutionary *situation* consists of an open division of sovereignty, while a revolutionary *outcome* entails a definitive transfer of power.[13]

I would put equal emphasis on the revolutionary struggle or *process* as a component of analysis.

The main point here is Tilly's concept of 'multiple sovereignty', whereby incompatible claims on the state and popular loyalty acquire powerful support and split the polity.[14] Situations that do not meet this definition are not revolutionary; revolutionary outcomes that do not arise from such circumstances are not 'full-fledged revolutions'. This excludes social movements, rebellions, and *coups d'état* as such from the definition (although in practice, the distinctions are often blurred).

---

[13] Charles Tilly, *Popular Contention in Great Britain 1758–1834* (Cambridge, Mass., 1995), 237. For a much fuller analysis, see his *From Mobilization to Revolution* (Reading, Mass., 1978).

[14] Tilly, *European Revolutions, 1492–1992* (Oxford, 1993), 5–15.

By these criteria the United Irishmen of the late 1790s constituted a revolutionary movement and the 1798 rebellion may have created a genuinely revolutionary situation—although only marginally so, given the poor record of the rebels and the weakness of their support at a national level. Since their efforts fell far short of shifting those in power, however, we cannot speak of a revolution as such occurring. The Land War of 1879–82 accompanied the rise and fall of a powerful social movement—the Land League—but neither it, nor the crisis it produced, nor its resolution, could be deemed revolutionary in the absence of a serious threat to the state. The Easter Rising was the product of a revolutionary movement (albeit a very small one), but it produced neither a situation nor an outcome of a revolutionary nature as it lacked national strength or support.

From the above follows my first proposition: that the events surrounding the transfer of power from Britain to its Irish successor states constitute the only real revolution in modern Irish history. The legitimacy and existence of the British state was directly and forcibly challenged, this challenge was supported by a large proportion of the Irish population, and sovereignty in the twenty-six counties was ultimately transferred to a new polity and government. This is not the same as saying the rebels were victorious, however, as the actual outcomes were not the ones envisioned—as is most often the case in revolutions.

When did this Irish revolution begin and end? While it might be useful in some respects to speak of a revolutionary decade falling more or less between 1912 and 1922, I do not think the home rule crisis of 1912–14 was even potentially revolutionary by itself. Ulster's unionists did raise an army and contemplated a local provisional government, but neither was intended to overthrow the existing state. Quite the opposite. Even if fighting had broken out, insofar as it pitted the unionist paramilitary Ulster Volunteer Force against the nationalist Irish Volunteers, it would have been little more revolutionary than the periodic Belfast riots. If the U.V.F. had faced the Royal Irish Constabulary or the British army in combat, we could speak of a local rebellion, but not a revolution proper.[15] Only if matters had escalated into either a war of separation from both Britain and Ireland, or a UK-wide Conservative–Liberal conflict, would a true state crisis have been born. On the other hand, the appearance of

---

[15] For such counterfactual scenarios, see Alvin Jackson, 'British Ireland: What if Home Rule Had Been Enacted in 1912?', in Niall Ferguson (ed.), *Virtual History: Alternatives and Counterfactuals* (London, 1998). For a contrary argument that Ulster unionism constituted a second revolutionary movement, see David Fitzpatrick, *The Two Irelands 1910–1939* (Oxford, 1998).

paramilitaries and the rejection of constitutional authority did pave the way for the subsequent revolutionary challenge.

It was the Great War that added the causal momentum to start the revolutionary clock ticking with the 1916 Easter Rising. It is true that the Rising itself was not a revolution, and that a situation of genuine multiple sovereignty did not arise until early 1920, when real power and legitimacy began to shift to the Dáil ministries while the I.R.A. was defeating the old R.I.C. This revolutionary moment could be shifted back a year to the formation of the putatively sovereign Dáil by the majority of Irish MPs, but no earlier.

On the other hand, in 1916 we do see a preliminary sketch of the revolution to be, complete with a claim to exclusive sovereignty by the insurgent government and army. Also, the continuous history of the republican movement, its leadership and ideology, and of revolutionary violence, begins here. This, and not 1912, is Ireland's 1789 or 1917, the Dublin GPO its Bastille or Winter Palace.[16]

If the revolution started in 1916, when did it end? Not with the Truce or Treaty of 1921, nor with the formal establishment of a sovereign Free State and self-governing Northern Ireland in 1922. What began in 1916 did not come to a close until the republican armed struggle, having lost most of its popular support, gave up its attempt to resist the Treaty settlement in the spring of 1923. Only then was the era of multiple sovereignty clearly over.

One other thing: the use of the term 'revolution' to describe political and social events over several generations—between the late 1870s and the early 1920s, for example—is not analytically useful. It may be worthwhile to take this period as a unit when examining changes in land-ownership or the Irish political system, but legal and gradual changes of this kind do not constitute a revolution in the sociological or political sense of the word.

How much of what happened can be categorized as 'civil war'? The term is not very well defined as yet, but since it is used some thought should be given to it. When are revolutions also civil wars? When there is massive fatal violence between well-organized forces fighting for control of a territory within a state, for one (revolutions don't have to to be violent). Another prerequisite suggested by Stathis Kalyvas is the presence, not just

---

[16] Not in every sense of course; 1789 and 1917 saw great shifts in power and authority—1916 did not.

of two or more armies, but also of clearly demarcated multiple territories under their full control—that is, the at least temporary division of the state into multiple *de facto* governments, as in the Spanish or American civil wars:

Civil war alters the nature of sovereignty in a fundamental way. At its core lies the breakdown of the monopoly of violence by way of armed internal challenge. The effective *territorial* challenge of sovereignty fragments it. This is the fundamental reality of civil war, which is often disregarded, especially by studies inspired by social movement theories... Sovereignty is segmented, in the sense that two political actors (or more) exercise full sovereignty over *distinct parts* of what used to be the pre-civil war territory of the state. At the same time, sovereignty in a civil war is also fragmented, in the sense that two political actors (or more) exercise *simultaneously* varying degrees of sovereignty over the *same parts* of what used to be the pre-civil war territory of the state.[17]

This condition applied to southern Ireland for several months before the start of the fight between Provisional Government and anti-Treaty forces in June 1922, and for two months afterwards. Otherwise, the revolution produced only guerrilla or communal wars.

Another possible defining feature of civil war, proposed by Patrick Maume,[18] is of multiple mobilizations. That is, there would have had to be a significant, popular, and public counter-revolutionary response to revolutionary violence. This did happen in the twenty-six counties in 1922, as shown in votes for pro-Treaty candidates, recruits to the new army and police, and a widespread pro-Treaty campaign within civil society. In 1917–18 there had been a strong if scattered challenge to Sinn Féin and the I.R.A. from partisans of the Irish Party—but this was in the absence of serious violence. In 1920–1 the guerrillas and the revolutionary state met with almost no popular resistance from outside Ulster, and fought an increasingly anglicized state apparatus thanks to the native constabulary's inability to recruit enough Irishmen. So while Irishmen were often killing Irish men and women after 1918, those in the employ of the British state had very little popular support and most were recruited before the revolution. Of course, there was such a popular anti-republican mobilization in Ulster. There local armed groups sprang up to take on the guerrillas, crowds attacked what they saw as rebel supporters and neighbourhoods, and the new state was able to recruit tens of thousands of enthusiastic

---

[17] Stathis Kalyvas, *The Logic of Violence in Civil War* (forthcoming).
[18] In private discussion.

defenders. By this reckoning, what happened in the six counties in 1920–2 was very much a civil war.

## Why Was There a Revolution?

Revolutions are never monocausal. A conjunction of necessary conditions is required to break an existing state and make a new one.[19] Theorists mostly agree on three fundamentals: a (fiscally, politically, or militarily) weakened state, alienated or divided elites, and the effective mobilization of a challenging movement or coalition with widespread popular support. Different studies emphasize different factors but, generally speaking, all are necessary and none are sufficient.

Rebellions are usually doomed by the odds against them. Governments simply wield too much power to lose. In the Irish case, the failure to defeat the republican movement has been convincingly analysed by Charles Townshend and Eunan O'Halpin in particular.[20] A liberal regime in Dublin Castle, and an Irish Party equally distracted by war, left the Irish Republican Brotherhood free to produce the Rising, and the R.I.C. and Dublin Metropolitan Police incapable of preventing it. From 1916 to 1920 followed the oft-described sequence of failed conciliation and coercion, undermining the police forces and empowering the republican militant tendency. The end result, in 1920–1, was the ceding of initiative to the I.R.A. which could only be regained by a politically costly military campaign.

The government's failure was also political, in that it alienated potentially supportive elites and granted popular legitimacy to its enemies. Crucial in this regard was its maladroit handling of the Rising, of home rule, and of conscription. These three issues destroyed the moderate Irish Party, drove the All For Ireland League and other dissidents behind Sinn Féin, and gave the latter command of the nationalist electorate. Divided and radicalized along with its flock, the Catholic Church was likewise lost as a counter-revolutionary bulwark. Much of its personnel was in the separatist camp by 1919.

---

[19] Theda Skocpol's is the classic analysis: *States and Social Revolutions* (Cambridge, Mass., 1979). See also the more recent work of Jack Goldstone, esp. *Revolution and Rebellion in the Early Modern World* (Berkeley, 1991), and Timothy Wickham-Crowley, esp. *Guerrillas and Revolution in Latin America* (New York, 1992).

[20] See esp. Townshend, *British Campaign in Ireland* and O'Halpin, *Decline of the Union*.

Finally, the Lloyd George administrations of 1916–22 also faced two important externally imposed political constraints. The first was the Great War and its settlement, which imposed conflicting priorities and bad policy and exhausted nationalist patience. The second was British public opinion, reinforced by that of other nations, especially the United States, which wanted rid of the problem but would not tolerate ruthless repression. Early mistakes could not be 'fixed' by fighting to win the ensuing guerrilla war.

State mismanagement provided the revolutionaries with a unique opportunity but they still needed strong leadership, a powerful organization, and substantial resources to mount their challenge. All were available for mobilization in early twentieth-century Ireland. Untapped cadres were to be found in the activist and articulate cultural and dissident sectors of nationalism populated by well-educated and pre-politicized young patriots. Also important were the swelling tributaries of labour unionism. Women were recruited alongside men for the first time in modern Irish history, providing a huge new source of organizational energy. The Easter Rising itself was crucial for transforming many of its participants into an energetic vanguard, and for inspiring other young people to follow their example. They in turn were able to build a sophisticated political machine based on the familiar model of the Irish Party and its auxiliaries. The guerrilla fringe could tap deep traditional and communal wells of solidarity and resistance. The movement as a whole could bank on the new wartime wealth of farmers and merchants, and on well-established and organized emigrant communities in the United States.

Most of these conditions for republican success disappeared in 1922. The apparent opportunity provided by a governmental vacuum and an initially weak successor regime in the south were offset by the Provisional Government's majority support—including from labour and the Catholic Church—and its lack of constraints or distractions in prosecuting its war. Mobilizing for such a fight was far more problematic for the revolutionaries as their opponents could claim the same nationalist legitimacy in addition to that inherent in an elected government. The I.R.A. was militarily stronger and the forces of the government were much feebler than in 1920, but the Provisional Government was actually in a politically superior position to that of Dublin Castle, and it exploited these advantages ruthlessly to crush the guerrillas very quickly. The Northern Irish government was in much the same position and met with even greater success in 1922–3.

## The Revolutionary Movement

A successful revolution required as broad a movement as possible, accommodated within a variety of specialized organizations: political (Sinn Féin), governmental (the Dáil, its departments, and Sinn Féin-controlled local councils), paramilitary (Irish Volunteers, later the I.R.A.), fraternal/conspiratorial (Irish Republican Brotherhood), boys' (Fianna Éireann), and women's (Cumann na mBan). American and British leagues (the Friends of Irish Freedom; the Irish Self-Determination League) were important. Also, while unions, trades councils, and the Labour Party were not part of the movement proper, the members of the Irish Transport and General Workers' Union in particular were often perceived as fellow-travellers, and many candidates in local elections in 1920 ran under both the Sinn Féin and Labour banners. Mention should also be made of the role of the socialist Irish Citizen's Army in 1916 as an important part of the original revolutionary coalition.

The movement was male-dominated but far from gender exclusive. In a completely unprecedented wave of inclusion and participation in mainstream politics, women became members of parliament (TDs), cabinet ministers, party officers and activists, rioters and hunger strikers (the latter role having been pioneered by suffragists). For the first time outside the local arena they were also a potentially crucial electoral constituency. Female TDs formed a key anti-Treaty bloc, and women formed a similarly vital part of Sinn Féin and its public support in 1922 and 1923. Even in 1918, there is reason to believe that Sinn Féin's massive success was due in part to its enormous advantage in claiming first-time female voters. The I.R.A. and I.R.B. were exclusively male, but the guerrillas required a constant support network of women, organized or informally active in their own homes, to survive. Revolutionary republicanism is likely the most female-dependent major movement in modern Irish history.

The two most important developments—and analytical issues—here are the evolution of Sinn Féin into a hegemonic nationalist popular front with a republican agenda, and the emergence of the I.R.A. as a guerrilla army. How did the small band of defeated and unrepresentative Easter rebels capture their host organizations—Sinn Féin and the Volunteers—and turn them into successful revolutionary institutions?

The rise of republican Sinn Féin after the Easter Rising has never seemed especially mysterious. A clear precedent had been established in the nationalist reformation of 1880–5, which established one great party linking a parliamentary cadre with one or more nationwide leagues and American fund-raisers. The geography of its electoral fortunes and membership in large part follow those of its predecessor: Sinn Féin did not so much kill the Irish Party as reproduce it.[21] In so doing, the new party had numerous advantages, including a dynamic and efficient organization and a multitude of political opportunities afforded by disastrous British policies. The causes of the Irish Party's rapid decline are equally numerous and well rehearsed, ranging from an exhausted leadership to the countervailing success of parliamentary Unionism. There is thus a retrospective air of inevitability or irresistibility about the seemingly extraordinary republican political performance in 1917–18. This achievement required the work and commitment of numerous activists, but the shape and completeness of this political shift, with one monopoly replacing another, suggests it was pre-patterned and even determined by the underlying structure and culture of nationalism and of the whole polarized political system.

Two basic aspects of the phenomenon seem clear. First, Sinn Féin (like the Irish Party) was a coalition; a flag of convenience as well as conviction for a spectrum of groups and tendencies. These included old (non-republican) Sinn Féin, the Volunteers, the I.R.B., agrarian factions and interests, organized labour, feminists, anti-partitionists, former members of the A.F.I.L. and—unofficially—the Gaelic League.[22] It was also a coalition of urban, suburban, and rural interests, landed and landless, propertied and unpropertied, farmers and agricultural labourers, shopkeepers and shop assistants. This omnibus 'Sinn Féin' flew a republican flag but it could also stand for simple self-government, political and social reform, an end to corruption and profiteering, a voice for youth and women, an alternative to the Irish Party, a hard line against partition, a prophylactic against conscription, land for the landless, or Gaelicization.

Secondly, whatever about the diversity within the party, its leadership was dominated (when it counted) by republicans who did manage to build a substantial and enduring republican constituency, as the 1920, 1922, and 1923 elections showed. That is to say, a large, enduring, and geographically coherent bloc of voters was assembled who defined themselves against the alternatives of home rule or Free State and supported the republic

---

[21] See Fitzpatrick, 'Geography of Irish Nationalism'; Garvin, *Evolution of Irish Nationalist Politics*; Ch. 2.

[22] Michael Laffan, *The Resurrection of Ireland: The Sinn Fein Party, 1916–1923* (Cambridge, 1999).

through the Tan and Civil Wars. Thus, while republican cadres built a familiar party monolith on the ruins of the old in 1917–18, they also created within it a new and rigid ideological formation which, by its opposition to the Treaty, would ultimately destroy its structural integrity.

The emergence of the I.R.A. as a mature guerrilla force in 1920 was the product of the piecemeal reorganization and radicalization of the Volunteers.[23] However, these processes do not fully explain the 1920 upheaval any more than they explain that of 1916. In fact, the I.R.A. also grew out of an internal political struggle—beginning before 1916—to transform the Volunteers into a revolutionary institution in the spirit of Patrick Pearse and Tom Clarke.[24] The Rising was intended to involve the non-revolutionary Irish Volunteers in a separatist rebellion. In the event, that aspect of the plan failed and only a fraction of the organization was involved.

The looked-for conversion did come after the fact and was inspired by its failure. From early 1917 on, the same debate and conflict was repeated on a much greater scale within the reborn Volunteers. The rejuvenated Irish Republican Brotherhood was once again in the vanguard and now it could attract a wider radical base. As in 1915–16, this militant tendency had its own agenda—a second round soon—and its own arms, as well as the will to use them. Its aims were twofold: an armed struggle against the state and a final victory over (in Michael Collins's words) 'the forces of moderation'. Both were achieved, and the result was the winter offensive begun in January 1920, the long-awaited second rising. The ensuing guerrilla war was not merely a symptom of state oppression or political stalemate. It was willed into being, a labour of love.

Thus was born the I.R.A. as a distinct entity, no longer the Volunteers as public mass movement but instead a much-reduced fusion of the I.R.B. and the Volunteers.[25] As Adjutant General and Director of Organization and Intelligence, and master of the Supreme Council of the I.R.B., Michael Collins acted as godfather to this new creation. The creature turned against him in the end, however, when once again—in 1922—a militant minority (although possibly a majority of the fighting men) took control of the organization and weeded out the moderate majority, preparatory to round three of patriotic combat.

[23] See Townshend, 'Irish Republican Army' and Augusteijn, *From Public Defiance to Guerrilla Warfare*.

[24] See Ch. 4.

[25] See my *The I.R.A. and Its Enemies* for a reconstruction of this process in Cork.

## The Revolutionary Process

The revolution began and ended with violence, the product of three interwoven struggles. The first of these was the campaign to overthrow the British state, begun with the Rising and resumed in earnest in 1919. In both cases, the rebels were the aggressors. In 1916 the conspirators within the I.R.B. launched a long-planned surprise attack without direct provocation. Between 1917 and 1919 the I.R.A. was responsible for over two-thirds of total casualties, and the 1920 winter offensive pushed this to over three-quarters of shootings.[26] In other words (in terms of armed violence), the rebels started it. However, as in 1916, the 1920 offensive provoked counter-escalation. Government and loyalist forces rose to the challenge, outpacing guerrilla violence over the spring and summer. This in turn stimulated the republicans to yet greater efforts, so that the I.R.A.'s contribution to the casualty lists thereafter held up at slightly over 50 per cent until the July 1921 truce. At each escalatory step, violence intended to suppress an enemy rebounded to produce the opposite effect.

In fact, by 1921 both the I.R.A. and Crown forces were shooting civilians more often than they shot each other. Unorganized or informal violence was flourishing as well, particularly in Belfast. The 'real war' of ambushes and raids was being overtaken by another reality. What the second, sustained, rising of 1920 triggered was not just a countervailing state response but also a new communal conflict in the north: one waged on familiar battlegrounds and according to well-established precedent—loyalist shipyard workers to the fore—but with fatally improved weaponry and organization. The Ulster I.R.A. had weapons and money from the south in 1921–2 and unionist counter-revolutionaries had the powers of the Northern Irish state. Thousands of northern Catholics and southern Protestants—and thousands more political or social undesirables of other sorts (including northern Protestants and southern Catholics) became temporary or permanent refugees.[27]

The third arena of struggle was the revolutionary coalition and nationalist community itself: the site of the Civil War of 1922–3. The splitting of the movement into two combatant 'sides' was not a simple or predictable process. The question of who was on what side over the Treaty was decided at many different levels, for many different reasons, personal as

---

[26] See Ch. 3.    [27] See Chs. 9 and 10.

well as political. Even the number of sides were unclear prior to July 1922, as both pro- and anti-Treaty forces were divided and factionalized.[28] The conflict was not simply the result of decisions made at that time, potentially avoidable if key people had acted differently. Nor do details of personnel matter greatly in structural terms. What was more or less inevitable, given the prior development of republicanism within the I.R.A. and the nationalist polity, was a violent defence of the Republic and of the principles of 1916 by a self-consciously militant minority. Such a response was what had driven the revolutionary process in 1916 and again in 1917. In the ideological terms set by the leaders and circumstances of 1916, the defence of the Four Courts and the anti-Treaty republic was an end in itself, and the radicalization of nationalist politics meant it would be endorsed by a significant section of public opinion.

Revolutionary violence was thus constituted out of three overlapping struggles: anti-British, communal, and intranationalist. All three were built into the structure of events. We cannot and should not separate out the anti-British element as if it was the whole, or the 'real' revolution; the consequences and casualties arising from other dynamics were too great. Nor can we draw convenient chronological or geographical lines around or between them. The fight over the control and direction of the revolutionary movement runs through the whole of the period. It was one of the main forces driving the revolutionary process. The Easter Rising, the sporadic militant violence of 1917–19 and the creation of the I.R.A., the Treaty split and the Civil War: none can be properly explained without taking the inner battles into account. The violent character of the movement was inherent in the republican will to revolution and enabled by the existence of paramilitary forces. The sectarian division in Irish politics and society and the revolution's central organizing principle of nationalist/Catholic ethnicity (along with the role of Protestantism in unionism) inevitably structured the revolution north and south. The violence of 1916 catalyzed a new movement. The rise of republicanism meant more violence; this produced official and loyalist reactions in kind; the resulting escalatory logic was significantly ethnic and sectarian in nature.

---

[28] See John Regan, *The Irish Counter-Revolution, 1921–1936: Treatyite Politics and Settlement in Independent Ireland* (Dublin, 1999).

## What Kind of Revolution?

What did the Irish revolution change? Can we classify it as a social revolution, either realized or attempted? On both counts, the answer is no. Not only did it not bring social transformation, there was no socially revolutionary situation in Ireland even in prospect. The republican movement itself had no serious social agenda and was not class-based. Its activists and membership was drawn from a wide variety of backgrounds, forming a cross-class coalition of groups, in which organized labour had little power.[29] Nor did the new Free State—whose establishment was backed by the Labour Party—offer any adjustment to property or labour relations. If the land question had remained unsettled, events might well have taken another turn, but most farmers owned their land by 1918. Ulster unionism was similarly broad-based and even more conservative.

Ireland did share in the international rise in working-class power driven by wartime inflation and shortages. The numerous strikes and disputes of the period were accompanied by an uncommon level of violence, but organized labour never contemplated an overthrow of the state, except insofar as it supported Sinn Féin in doing so. The few socialists who did think along these lines had neither the numbers nor the influence to do anything about it. There was no split in any Irish elite in this regard, nor was there any attempted factional or rank-and-file insurgency within unions or the Labour Party. No workers' militia was formed to replace James Connolly's Citizen Army. Judging by the social background and geography of anti-Treaty republicanism, the Civil War did not represent an insurgency of the poor or dispossessed, as is sometimes suggested.[30] The social violence that did occur in the revolutionary years, from sabotage to murder, was as much a by-product of the availability of guns and the absence of a normal police force as of class conflict. This is not to say that nothing happened in terms of social unrest, or that nothing important happened, but rather that nothing revolutionary happened.[31]

[29] For the social structure of the movement, see Ch. 5.

[30] See Ch. 2.

[31] This is a much-discussed issue. See Emmet O'Connor, *Syndicalism in Ireland* (Cork, 1988); Michael Laffan, 'Labour Must Wait: Ireland's Conservative Revolution', in Patrick Corish (ed.), *Radicals, Rebels and Establishments* (Belfast, 1985); and Paul Bew, 'Sinn Fein, Agrarian Radicalism and the War of Independence, 1919–1921', in D. G. Boyce (ed.), *The Revolution in Ireland, 1879–1923* (London, 1988).

The revolution did not produce an institutional upheaval either. Parts of the *ancien régime* did crumble or collapse and had to be reconstructed: the police, the judicial system, local government finances. On the other hand, there was no uprooting of elites, or purging or forced politicization of the state on the scale of France after 1789, Russia after 1917, or Algeria after 1962. Much of the civil service remained intact, along with its previous ideals and methods. A new political system was introduced, but its differences from the British model were matters of detail rather than principle. What was revolutionary was that Irish people had fought for and won their sovereignty. From 1922 on, government in the south would be self-determined.

It was a nationalist revolution, of course, but not simply that. Irish revolutionaries were nationalists, just as unionist counter-revolutionaries were anti-nationalist. But many other nationalists were opposed to Sinn Féin and the I.R.A. even before the Treaty split. So while in comparative terms the revolutionary movement was clearly nationalist, in Irish terms it would be more precisely described as republican. Moreover, while the revolutionary movement was a genuinely popular phenomenon, it was not 'national' in a pluralistic sense. Unlike the United Irishmen, the Yugoslav communist resistance, the Palestine Liberation Organization, or the African National Congress, revolutionary republicanism was effectively an ideological and ethnic monoculture drawn overwhelmingly from the Catholic majority and asserting a separatist cultural identity.

Can we then describe the Irish revolution as a whole as 'ethnic' in direction, structure, or outcome? In many ways, yes. Much of its violence (including state violence) was organized along ethnic lines, as were its successor states. The fact of partition, and its frankly sectarian border, is evidence of the importance of ethnic identity to its outcome. Equally significant was the displacement of Catholic and Protestant minorities. Nevertheless, we should still be careful in using ethnic categorizations, as they easily slip from analytical to perjorative labels. It applies to all 'sides' and it is not a fair description of revolutionary ideology or motives. Republican organizations were officially non-sectarian, and this had played an important part in damping down southern ethnic violence, even though the I.R.A. were its main practitioners. Neither republicans nor unionists held the goal of an ethnically purified homeland by exclusion or forced assimilation. Nor did shared ethnicity prevent a civil war between fellow republicans and nationalists, although it probably reduced the number of fatalities.[32]

An interesting test of the role of ethnicity in activist mobilization and identity is in the laboratory of British cities. Why would migrants or their children (or grandchildren) spend their time and money, risk their lives and freedom, for the republican cause? Most didn't, but most did not join any nationalist or self-consciously ethnic organization. They were certainly not encouraged to do so by the central institutions of Irish life in Britain, the Catholic Church and schools. Some activists—Michael Collins for one—graduated from apprenticeships in the Gaelic League, the G.A.A., or Sinn Féin but most did not. The usual networks of family, work, and friendship helped bind them together as in Ireland, but what they had in common was a politicized sense of Irishness and their activism was aimed at helping the movement in Ireland in any way possible.[33] When the Irish Self-Determination League was set up in 1919 to 'support their compatriots in Ireland', it was stipulated that members must be 'of Irish birth and descent'. They were distinguished within the Irish population in Britain as a small radical minority, but their baseline identity was ethnic and their primary motive was national—not factional or ideological—solidarity.

The other region where republicans operated as a minority of a minority was in north-east Ulster, and particularly Belfast. Here was one place in Ireland where Sinn Féin and the Volunteers were unable to outbid their 'moderate' rivals for the allegiance of the nationalist population or even to monopolize nationalist violence. Nowhere was the revolution so clearly drawn along ethnic battle-lines, yet the Catholic minority was unable or unwilling to form a united political front to match that of unionism—loyalists did not tolerate dissent. Part of the explanation for this may lie in the peculiar development of Belfast and northern nationalism (which was more clerical), and part may be found in the genuine communal solidarity exhibited in Catholic communities which did mobilize to defend and help themselves. Parties competed at election time, but partisan differences may have been eliminated at the neighbourhood level under siege conditions. It might also be suggested that the local Irish Party leadership, and especially Joseph Devlin, retained more credibility and resources on their home turf than John Redmond and John Dillon did nationally. Whatever

---

[32] See Ch. 10.    [33] See Ch. 6.

the reasons, it is clear that nationalism was not simply a matter of ethnicity, even in West Belfast.

Was the revolution democratic or anti-democratic? Its constitutional outcome can be said to have been freely ratified by majorities on both sides of the border in elections in 1921, 1922, and 1923. Partition did not reflect the wishes of the nationalist majority in Ireland but it did reflect the priorities of those in the twenty-six Free State counties. When offered the option of continued conflict and attempted coercion of northern unionists, neither nationalist voters nor their representatives supported a continued revolution on either side of the border. Even more to the point perhaps, when voters, interest groups, and politicians in the south had a chance to raise the issue in late 1921 and 1922 they very rarely did so. Beyond simple majoritarianism, however, the Northern Ireland government and the Unionist Party certainly failed the democratic test in their exclusionary sectarianism and drive for one-party rule.

We cannot push this line of argument too far, though. Organized violence is inherently coercive and traumatic, and therefore subversive of rational decision-making and political choice. All sides used force to suppress or eliminate political opponents, whether constituted by allegiance, opinion, or identity. Violence did not gain a hearing for moderation: moderation was for traitors or spies, and those suspected of 'moderation'—nationalist or unionist—were liable to have their windows broken, their doors kicked in, their houses burned down. Neither the republic, the Free State, nor Northern Ireland was defended by moderate men or means.

Were the revolutionaries themselves undemocratic in their attitudes or behaviour? Perhaps the best description is that of Richard English: they had 'a complicated relationship with democracy'.[34] This captures well the ambivalence and tension between the two republican concepts of sovereignty—of 'the people' (expressed politically in elections) and of 'the nation' (revealed historically and spiritually in heroic rebellions). They were willing to act without an electoral mandate, as in 1916 and 1922, but only in order to uphold the rights of the nation. There was no fascist- or communist-style dismissal of electoral democracy, nor was the ideal republic ever envisioned as other than democratic. Republicans never sought to rig or suppress an election, or to seize power without the backing of one. Sinn Féin's electoral trickery and intimidation in 1917–18 and 1922

[34] English, *Ernie O'Malley*, 84.

was no greater than the Irish Party's in its heyday, and was never enough to sway an election result. A republican *coup d'état* was never seriously contemplated in 1922, hostile newspaper reporting and Rory O'Connor's off-the-cuff commentary notwithstanding. Even British politicians were ultimately off-limits for assassination (with the singular case of Henry Wilson excepted[35]). It can also be said that the 'revolutionary moment' of multiple sovereignty was enabled by electoral victory in 1918 and re-inforced by further success in local elections in 1920. Sinn Féin's rhetoric and its official platform before and during the first election made its revolutionary intentions plain, so it cannot reasonably be argued that voters were seriously misled, however mixed their motives may have been.

Nevertheless, leaving more subjective ethical or political issues aside, in structural terms it can still be argued that paramilitary and state violence only succeeded in early twentieth-century Ireland when it was used to achieve goals that received a clear popular mandate: Irish independence and northern exclusion. It was for this reason that Free State repression succeeded where Britain's had failed. Much the same tactics were used as had been employed in 1920–1, but in the earlier period the guerrillas retained strong popular backing; in 1922–3 it was the forces of the state who possessed electoral legitimacy.

The presence of paramilitaries and the prevalence of violence raises another question: did the Irish revolution represent a breakdown of democracy? The survival of democracy in independent Ireland has often been analyzed, with republican insurgency and civil war in 1922 depicted as its first and greatest challenge.[36] From this perspective, democracy is seen as a product of a separate Irish state—or of the revolutionary insti-tutions that preceded it. Thus, the Treaty cleavage, the role of the I.R.A. in Irish politics, and the fate of the Free State are seen as the fundamental problems of analysis. These are important, of course, but I do not think democracy is the same thing as self-government, or that the split within nationalism was in fact the most basic dividing line in Irish political culture. To start from this premiss is to fall prey to the partitionist fallacy—extending the Northern Irish border back in time and excluding the six counties from the definition of 'Irish'—and to thereby ignore the role of ethnicity in nationalism and in the revolution. For it is surely the ethnic/national cleavage between Protestant unionism and Catholic

[35] See Ch. 8.
[36] See Tom Garvin, *1922: The Birth of Irish Democracy* (Dublin, 1996), and Bill Kissane, *Explaining Irish Democracy* (Dublin, 2002).

nationalism, institutionalized in the 1880s as a result of Gladstonian democratization, that is fundamental to modern Irish politics. As part of the United Kingdom, Ireland was then a part of an increasingly democratic political system: one which excluded no competitors, granted considerable freedom of speech, was relatively free of corruption, and allowed new anti-establishment parties to emerge and wield power. A constitutional settlement of nationalist grievances was in prospect thanks to the Irish Party's alliance with the pro-home rule Liberals, in power after 1905. Radical agrarian change had already been achieved, thanks to successive governments' responses to popular pressure and political negotiation.

Therefore the entire period from 1913 to 1923 can plausibly be considered as a case of at least incipient democratic breakdown. All the symptoms were present: violence and paramilitaries, plebiscitary elections, partisan and ethnic polarization, the 'unsolvable problem' of Ulster resistance to home rule and consequent loss of constitutional and governmental legitimacy. The phenomena of revolutions and democratic breakdowns share many features, so it is hardly surprising to find them in Ireland at this time. But the process was arguably underway after 1912, and contributed greatly to the subsequent revolution.

The home rule struggle was suspended after the outbreak of war in 1914, but it marked the beginning of a crisis for Irish and British democracy. The Unionist movement had declared its willingness to use force to block constitutional legislation and, more importantly, one of the two main British parties had backed it. This made it tricky for the Liberal government to suppress the Unionist paramilitary force, and tolerating one meant tolerating all the others that followed it. The Curragh incident made the army unusable in any pre-emptive role. In Ireland, this loss of control left government legitimacy in tatters, driving public opinion on both sides behind the rival militias. Negotiations in 1914 were homing in on the partition of Ulster as a solution, but making a mutually acceptable deal would still have been very difficult, given the arming of extremists, the lack of trust, and the number of competing agendas within the British political elite. The Irish question in 1914 would appear to fall into the category of what Juan Linz called 'unsolvable problems'.[37] Unsolvable, that is, by constitutional and democratic means, at least from the point of view of one or other of the Irish parties. Such a situation typically benefits

---

[37] Juan Linz, *The Breakdown of Democratic Regimes: Crisis, Breakdown, and Reequilibrium* (Baltimore, 1978), 50–5.

extremist parties who can outbid their mainstream rivals and offer a new source of political legitimacy, and so it did in the Irish case, leading to the rise of Sinn Féin and the consolidation of the Irish Volunteers as a powerful guerrilla force. The former was willing to act unconstitutionally, the latter undemocratically.

One possible outcome of these developments would have been the total suspension of Irish democracy by the British government and the imposition of colonial rule and martial law (at least in the twenty-six counties). However, a solution was possible if the Anglo-Irish dimension of the problem could be decoupled from its ethnic and territorial dimensions. Partition in 1920—imposed rather than agreed—satisfied the Unionist and Conservative parties. This allowed the Coalition government to offer the south effective sovereignty, thus satisfying the basic nationalist demand. It also crystallized an internal nationalist cleavage, so the main threat to democracy shifted to the third dimension of the conflict: republican rejection of the new Free State regime. The anti-Treaty republicans rejected a straight electoral contest in early 1922 but were willing to run an agreed slate of candidates with the pro-Treatyites leading to a coalition government. Unfortunately, the republicans themselves were an unstable coalition and the British government was applying countervailing pressure to exclude them from power. The ideological and institutional prerequisites of an all-inclusive nationalist regime were simply not present in 1922. Even if one had been formed, it would not have been in control of the I.R.A., whose radical faction was planning to attack the British army. The Provisional Government struck first, but civil war was probable under any scenario given the impossibility of satisfying both the anti-Treaty republicans and the British partners in the new order. Irish politics were in transition and a new system was emerging, no longer dictated by ethnicity. The main Irish actors were not antidemocratic, but all were somewhat ademocratic in their behaviour. It was the republicans who refused to accept the parliamentary vote on the Treaty, however, and who delayed an electoral contest on the issue, fearing the result. It was the anti-Treaty I.R.A. that insisted on preserving its weapons and freedom of action. And if it managed to provoke Britain into reintervention, the prospect of systemic collapse loomed. The Civil War did reimpose democratic rules on southern Irish politics, re-establishing effective government and eliminating paramilitary competition while—crucially—remaining open to its disloyal opposition. The threat to democracy finally ended when revolution did, with the I.R.A. ceasefire in April 1923.

## Thinking Again

All of these propositions are debatable, and I hope they will be argued with. The Irish revolution needs to be reconceptualized and to have all the myriad assumptions underlying its standard narratives interrogated. Gender, class, community, elites and masses, religion and ethnicity, the nature of violence and power, periodization and geography: all need to be explored without compartmentalization. Violence cannot be satisfactorily understood as a straightforward matter of strategy and tactics. The gender of the revolutionary movement cannot be fully analysed by just adding women to the narrative or by compiling female activist biographies, valuable though these are. Ethnic difference existed beyond the borders of Ulster: it was a constitutive element of nationalism, republicanism, and unionism throughout Ireland. Class was reflected in all mobilizations and coalitions, not just those of land and labour. The I.R.A., the I.R.B., and Sinn Féin were active throughout the United Kingdom, not just in Ireland. Nor were they just political or military organizations. They were communal entities, and responded to local loyalties and drives as much as to ideology or orders from above. And it is questionable to what extent the so-called revolutionary 'elite' actually displaced pre-existing social, institutional, bureaucratic, and media elites (whose place in the narrative has yet to be addressed).

Perhaps most importantly, the revolution needs to be envisioned as a chronological, spatial, and thematic whole. The period is commonly divided into the discrete units of the Easter Rising, the Tan War, the Civil War, and so forth. But what of the months and years lying between these episodes? What of the politics and violence that does not fit this framework? Protestants in Cork and Catholics in Belfast, for example, had a very different sense of when the conflict began and ended. How can the 'wars' be explained without reference to their experiences? Similarly, we should not write partitionist histories whereby events north and south are treated independently even before the boundary was drawn. This convention eliminates ethnic conflict and counter-revolution from the 'Irish' narrative of (normal) national liberation, while reducing the 'northern' narrative to a matter of (abnormal) sectarianism.

A new revolutionary history can be built on two great foundations. The first is that offered by the truly extraordinary volume and range of sources. When nearly every activist and victim can be named, placed, and profiled, both macro- and micro-studies can be carried out with great precision.

Vast slabs of data can be assembled. Hundreds of social and political variables can be mapped, tracked over time, counted, correlated, and regressed. Networks and events can be reconstructed and the progress of the revolution followed townland by townland, street by street, house by house.

The second foundation is comparative and theoretical. Irish events helped to inaugurate an era of mass movements, citizens' revolts, and guerrilla wars of liberation. From Palestine to Nicaragua, these upheavals have been studied and their place in the history and sociology of revolutions argued. Students of the Irish revolution can use these ideas to generate new questions and answers and to engage a broader debate, which would also give Ireland a place in the analytical canon. The intimacy and precision with which we are able to reconstruct these processes and experiences makes Ireland one of the best historical laboratories in which to study revolution.

# 2

# The Geography of Revolution in Ireland

The revolution of 1917–23 represents a marriage of activists and outcomes almost unique in the history of Irish nationalism. Revolutionaries there had been—of one sort or another—for well over a century, political upheavals and crises were frequent, but rarely had one anything to do with the other. In the aftermath of the Easter Rising of 1916, however, radicals did achieve radical change: a Sinn Féin majority in Ireland in the 1918 general election; an avowedly separatist parliament, Dáil Éireann, in 1919; republican local governments, police, and courts in 1920; the Anglo-Irish Treaty in 1921; and ultimately, in 1922, an independent Free State separate from both Great Britain and Northern Ireland.

What made these changes revolutionary was not just their outcomes, but also their violence. Between January 1917 and June 1923 well over 7,500 people were killed or wounded, in a country where murder had been a rarity.[1] If the casualties of the Easter Rising are included, the toll rises to over 10,000.[2] Thousands more lost their homes or livelihoods or were driven from them. Not since 1798 had there been an outbreak of fighting on this scale, and just as unprecedented was the extraordinary role played,

[1] By my count, the minimum figures are 3,269 people killed and 4,318 wounded by bombs or bullets alone. This total excludes several dozen shootings which took place in mainland Britain and one in New York, 118 shootings attributed to agrarian motives, 43 which took place during robberies, 21 during labour disputes, and several hundred self-inflicted, accidental casualties (at least 81 in National Army ranks alone).

[2] See Breandán Mac Giolla Ghoille (ed.), *Intelligence Notes 1913–16* (Dublin, 1966), 240–1.

again, by the insurgent activists. Political violence, like political opportunity, had usually found Ireland's declared rebels on the sidelines or
occasionally even in opposition; when rebellions arrived they were most
often stillborn. By contrast, after 1916 the revolutionary faith in direct
action was finally, triumphantly, justified by the emergence of the Irish
Republican Army, whose guerrillas were responsible for fully 71 per cent
of the revolution's attributable casualties.[3]

While the whole of Ireland was transformed by the efforts of these few
thousand men, the whole of Ireland did not participate equally in this
change. Although most towns and parishes had their I.R.A. (originally
Irish Volunteer) companies or Sinn Féin clubs, revolutionary activity and
violence were heavily concentrated in some areas and nearly non-existent
in others. The single district of Bandon, in County Cork (in this respect
the Gaza strip of the Irish *intifada*), produced eleven times as many
casualties (190) as the whole county of Antrim; it was 128 times as violent
per capita. In this sense, the revolution was not so much a national conflict
as a collection of regional ones. Ernie O'Malley, an organizer for I.R.A.
headquarters, recalled that 'each county was different; the very map
boundaries in many places seemed to make a distinction'.[4] His British
opponents were no less aware of the uneven geography of revolution:
'a very noticeable feature of the rebellion in the South of Ireland is the fact
that the war was waged far more vigorously and far more bitterly in some
parts of the area than in others.'[5] To understand the origins and outcomes
of the revolution, and the sources of its violence, therefore, we must
understand its geography.

Of course, no revolution has ever been waged with equal vigour in all
parts of a country, just as we would not expect uniformity in any society or
economy. And herein lies the approach of this chapter: to compare statistically the distribution of violence and other political activities with those
of a variety of social and economic variables. In so doing I am following in
the footsteps of Erhard Rumpf, David Fitzpatrick, and Tom Garvin, all of
whom have tackled this question along similar lines in their own work.[6]

---

[3] Unattributable victims include those bystanders caught in firefights or ambushes, all civilian
casualties in Belfast, and those where a motive appears political but is unclear. Even if these are
included, the I.R.A. was responsible for at least 45 per cent of total casualties.

[4] Ernie O'Malley, *On Another Man's Wound* (Dublin, 1936), 129.

[5] General Staff 6th Division, *The Irish Rebellion in the 6th Divisional Area From After 1916
Rebellion to December 1921* (Imperial War Museum [IWM], Sir Peter Strickland Papers, P.362), 3.

[6] Rumpf and Hepburn, *Nationalism and Socialism in Twentieth-Century Ireland*; David
Fitzpatrick, 'The Geography of Irish Nationalism, 1910–1921'; Tom Garvin, *The Evolution of*

Thus, while I am presenting my own data, I will also be testing their conclusions.

## Revolutionary Violence

The first problem in such a study is one of definition. What constitutes 'violence' or its 'political' or 'revolutionary' manifestations? How can we define such notoriously slippery categories of analysis? The fields of political science and sociology are littered with theories and typologies, but my aim here is far more modest: to establish a reliable and statistically useful set of figures.

In this respect, no one so far has gone beyond the work of Erhard Rumpf in his pioneering book *Nationalism and Socialism in Twentieth-Century Ireland*. Rumpf used 'significant I.R.A. operations' and British reprisals against property to map guerrilla activity between September 1919 and July 1921 on a county-by-county basis.[7] Both methods are incomplete and inadequate. Reprisals offer only an indirect indication of I.R.A. performance and were governed by different rules in different areas. The more direct measure of 'significant' operations contains very large chronological and territorial gaps (including Dublin city and Northern Ireland) and generally excludes operations other than more or less 'military' engagements. This leaves out the huge number of casualties which did not occur in combat—the majority of the revolution's victims, in fact. Nor does this measure tell us anything about the intensity of the violence, as it does not differentiate between operations which caused many casualties or captured many arms and those that did neither. Finally, Rumpf does not attempt to calculate or compare events before or after this period.

A far better approach, I believe, is to measure the violence of the whole revolution—from 1917 to 1923—in terms of its victims, meaning here those killed or wounded by bullets or bombs. This encompasses all types of violence regardless of motive, but also allows us to categorize the results in many different ways and to compare different areas and periods using a single, comparable scale. This method is also very reliable. While raids on private homes, vandalism, assaults, and robberies are uncountable

*Irish Nationalist Politics.* See also Charles Townshend, 'The Irish Republican Army and the Development of Guerrilla Warfare, 1916–21'.

[7] Rumpf and Hepburn, *Nationalism and Socialism*, 38–50.

because (for most of this period) so rarely reported, death and serious injury from gunshots or explosives were almost always recorded somewhere. Limiting the numbers to these weapons also provides a threshold, below which it is often impossible to tell how badly someone was hurt. One death or serious gunshot wound can be assumed to be essentially the same as any other, and can thus be used as equivalent units of statistical analysis wherever and whenever they occur. A further crucial advantage to using this method is that it eliminates the biases inherent in official figures of 'outrages', 'murders', or 'operations', whether Irish or British.

To assemble these figures I have used the monthly Royal Irish Constabulary County Inspectors' reports for each county for 1917–21, the separate R.I.C. tabulations of agrarian outrages, the daily reports of the *Irish Times*, *Cork Examiner* (which covered all of the province of Munster), and London *Times* for 1917–23, those of the *Freeman's Journal* for 1921–3, I.R.A. and British and Irish military reports and casualty lists, and a variety of supplementary sources.[8] I relied upon republican sources for I.R.A. losses, R.I.C., British army, and National Army reports for their casualties and, where accounts differed, I generally used the lower figure. Shootings or bombings whose motives were unclear were classed as 'unknown' rather than attributed to a particular organization or category. 'Serious' wounds are defined by excluding those described as 'slight', 'light', 'not serious', or those which apparently did not require hospitalization. I believe the results to be well over 90 per cent accurate, erring on the side of conservatism. The only exception is Belfast, where it is frequently impossible to sort out who was doing what to whom. I was able to arrive at quite satisfactory numbers for total victims but, except for police and military casualties, they could not be broken down further. This explains why Belfast is absent from maps other than Map 1.

Several sets of numbers could be chosen to represent I.R.A. activity, but the broadest and most robust is that of total I.R.A. victims, civilians as well as policemen and soldiers.[9] These numbers are broken down by county (and by city in the case of Dublin), and expressed as rates per 10,000 people in order to control for population differences. The county is the primary

---

[8] For a complete discussion of the sources and methodology used, see Hart, *The I.R.A. and Its Enemies*.

[9] Unfortunately, there are no comprehensive and reliable figures for I.R.A. membership to provide an alternate index of the organization's vitality. Police and I.R.A. estimates do exist, but the former offer little more than bad guesses, while the latter were only assembled retrospectively, and do not reflect changes over time.

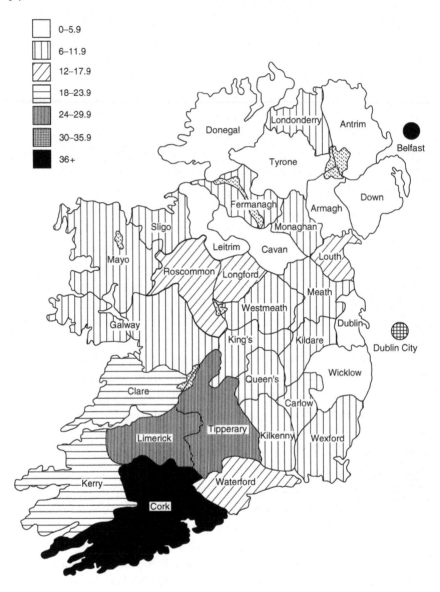

MAP 1.   Total violence per 10,000 people, 1917–1923

unit of analysis in this and previous studies, for a number of reasons. As the county was the standard administrative unit, using it allows easy comparison with census and (some) electoral figures. It was also the basis for Volunteer organization. Each county might have one or more brigades—Cork had up to five—but their assigned territory very rarely crossed county lines and was jealously guarded. As a result, operations within a county were almost always carried out by local men, and we can match their actions with their social characteristics and environment.

The resulting data (Map 2 and Table 1) show I.R.A. violence between 1917 and 1923 to have been overwhelmingly concentrated in the southern

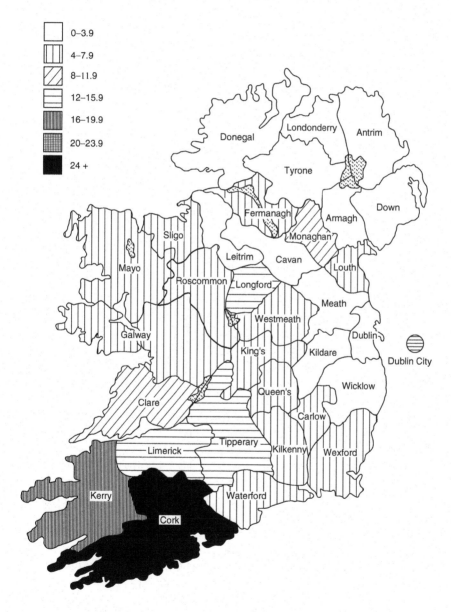

MAP 2.  I.R.A. violence per 10,000 people, 1917–1923

TABLE 1.  *Revolutionary violence, 1917–1923 (per 10,000 people)*

| | I.R.A. violence | | | | | Total violence (1917–23) |
|---|---|---|---|---|---|---|
| | 1917–19 | 1920–1 | 1921–2 | 1922–3 | 1917–23 | |
| *Leinster* | | | | | | |
| Carlow | 0.0 | 3.6 | 0.8 | 0.0 | 4.4 | 6.7 |
| Dublin | 0.0 | 1.3 | 0.1 | 1.0 | 2.4 | 4.6 |
| Kildare | 0.0 | 1.1 | 0.3 | 2.0 | 3.4 | 6.3 |
| Kilkenny | 0.0 | 2.4 | 1.1 | 1.5 | 5.0 | 8.3 |
| King's | 0.0 | 2.6 | 0.0 | 1.6 | 4.2 | 8.1 |
| Longford | 0.0 | 12.3 | 0.0 | 1.4 | 13.7 | 14.6 |
| Louth | 0.0 | 1.4 | 0.2 | 4.2 | 5.8 | 13.1 |
| Meath | 0.5 | 2.6 | 0.2 | 0.5 | 3.8 | 6.3 |
| Queen's | 0.0 | 1.8 | 0.0 | 4.8 | 6.6 | 11.2 |
| Westmeath | 0.0 | 4.0 | 1.0 | 1.5 | 6.5 | 11.4 |
| Wexford | 0.0 | 2.0 | 0.0 | 3.2 | 5.2 | 7.5 |
| Wicklow | 0.0 | 0.3 | 0.0 | 0.5 | 0.8 | 2.3 |
| *Ulster* | | | | | | |
| Antrim | 0.0 | 0.2 | 0.0 | 0.0 | 0.2 | 0.9 |
| Armagh | 0.1 | 2.2 | 1.2 | 0.2 | 3.7 | 5.6 |
| Cavan | 0.0 | 1.4 | 0.2 | 1.0 | 2.6 | 3.7 |
| Donegal | 0.3 | 0.8 | 0.9 | 0.7 | 2.7 | 4.4 |
| Down | 0.0 | 1.0 | 0.6 | 0.0 | 1.6 | 2.9 |
| Fermanagh | 0.0 | 2.9 | 2.1 | 0.0 | 5.0 | 6.2 |
| Londonderry | 0.0 | 1.4 | 0.8 | 0.0 | 2.2 | 8.7 |
| Monaghan | 0.3 | 4.7 | 1.8 | 1.3 | 8.1 | 11.8 |
| Tyrone | 0.0 | 1.4 | 0.6 | 0.0 | 2.0 | 3.7 |
| *Munster* | | | | | | |
| Clare | 1.5 | 8.9 | 0.8 | 0.7 | 11.9 | 21.8 |
| Cork | 0.6 | 15.4 | 1.1 | 6.9 | 24.0 | 39.1 |
| Kerry | 0.2 | 9.8 | 0.4 | 7.2 | 17.6 | 23.4 |
| Limerick | 0.3 | 7.1 | 0.4 | 6.2 | 14.0 | 28.2 |
| Tipperary | 0.6 | 8.8 | 1.0 | 5.1 | 15.5 | 27.5 |
| Waterford | 0.5 | 2.4 | 0.1 | 2.9 | 5.9 | 13.6 |
| *Connaught* | | | | | | |
| Galway | 0.2 | 2.6 | 0.8 | 1.3 | 4.9 | 10.4 |
| Leitrim | 0.0 | 2.4 | 0.0 | 1.1 | 3.5 | 5.7 |
| Mayo | 0.05 | 2.2 | 0.2 | 3.6 | 6.0 | 9.4 |
| Roscommon | 0.2 | 6.1 | 0.3 | 1.2 | 7.8 | 12.4 |
| Sligo | 0.1 | 3.4 | 0.4 | 2.9 | 6.8 | 10.0 |
| Dublin City | 0.4 | 6.5 | 0.5 | 5.7 | 13.1 | 30.7 |
| Belfast | — | — | — | — | — | 44.3 |

*Note*: For the construction of these figures, see text and notes.

province of Munster (with the exception of county Waterford) and in the city of Dublin. The Cork brigades alone were responsible for 28 per cent of all of the I.R.A.'s victims, thereby earning pre-eminent notoriety. They and neighbouring units made Munster the heartland of the revolution, although even here there was considerable variation as the fighting in Cork was almost twice as intense as in Clare, for example. Only the counties of Longford and—to a much lesser extent—Monaghan, stand out beyond this activist region.

Map 2 represents a cumulative accounting of revolution. I have also broken these aggregate figures down chronologically, as shown in Maps 3–6. The years of 1917–19 were dominated by the reorganization and political triumph of Sinn Féin and the Irish Volunteers as a mass movement, and were marked by comparatively little fatal violence. The following period, from January 1920 to 11 July 1921, was one of rapidly escalating guerrilla war (the 'Tan War' or 'War of Independence'), ending in a truce. From then until the end of June 1922 there was almost no actual fighting between British forces and the I.R.A., but a great deal of violence was directed against former and suspected enemies of the republic (ex-policemen, ex-soldiers, accused informers, and loyalists). The rebels also mounted a brief insurrection against the new government of Northern Ireland. The spring of 1922 brought increasing friction between rival factions of the revolutionary army over the Anglo-Irish Treaty concluded in December 1921. On 28 June this erupted into outright confrontation— and then a second guerrilla war—between the anti-Treaty I.R.A. and the new National Army of the Free State (the 'Civil War'), more or less ending with a unilateral I.R.A. ceasefire on 30 April 1923.

As we move from 1917 to 1923, the fairly clear geographical pattern displayed in Map 2 blurs with the passage of time. The leading rebel county changes from Clare to Cork to Fermanagh to Kerry. The Cork I.R.A. emerges as the strongest overall, chiefly by virtue of its consistency. The boys of County Clare, on the other hand, fell further and further behind their comrades as the revolution progressed, and played almost no part in the war of 1922–3. Longford owes its prominence solely to its performance in the Tan War of 1920–1, at the centre of a second activist region in the north midlands. A third key cluster of combative brigades emerged in the south Ulster borderlands as the Northern Irish state was being consolidated in 1921–2, but largely fell silent again thereafter. North Connaught and south Leinster became relatively more important in the Civil War.

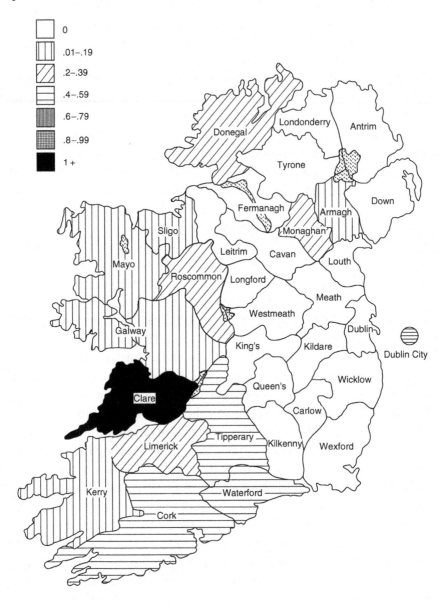

MAP 3.   I.R.A. violence per 10,000 people, 1917–1919

Despite these shifts in revolutionary vigour, the maps also reveal significant continuities. Munster and Dublin bore the brunt of the revolution at its every stage, while north-eastern Ulster and counties Dublin, Wicklow, and Meath remained passive throughout. The map for 1920–1 broadly

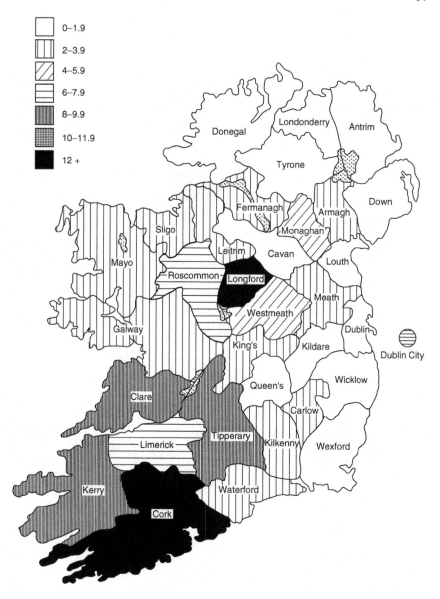

MAP 4.   I.R.A. violence per 10,000 people, January 1920–11 July 1921

confirms those produced by Rumpf and Garvin, although with some important differences. Both ignore the key role played by Dublin city, usually absent from geographical analysis but a crucial arena for I.R.A. campaigns. Garvin (and others after him) described the 'central Munster

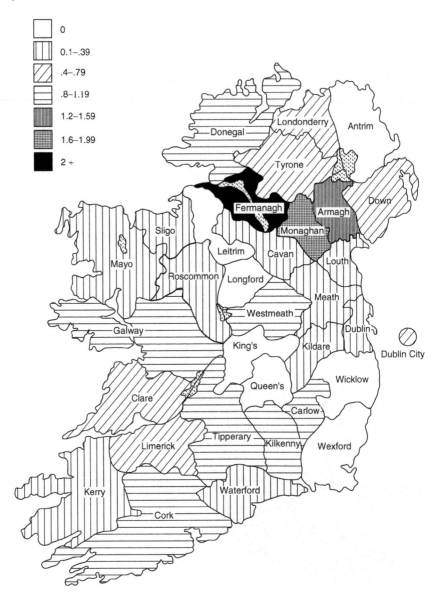

MAP 5.   I.R.A. violence per 10,000 people, 12 July 1921–27 June 1922

area' as being the main theatre, when southern and western areas, notably
Kerry and West Cork, were at least as active as those to the east or north.[10]
Similarly, the description of 'a smaller theatre . . . in the Cavan–Sligo area'

    [10]  Garvin, *The Evolution of Irish Nationalist Politics*, 122.

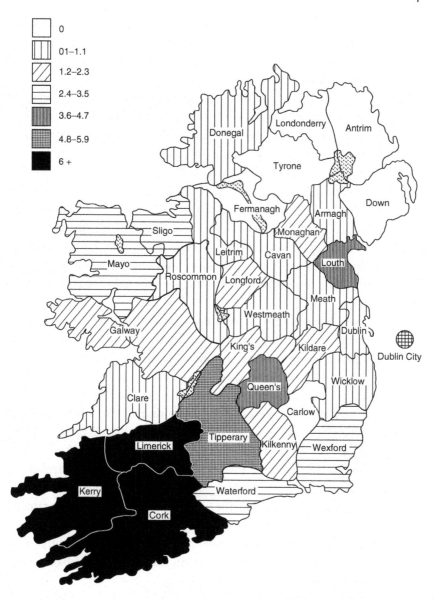

MAP 6. I.R.A. violence per 10,000 people, 28 June 1922–30 April 1923

overstates the level of violence in these counties as compared to their southern neighbours Roscommon, Longford, and Westmeath, and applies only to the 1920–1 period.

One factor missing from the maps presented here which must be acknowledged is that of religion. These maps measure and compare

I.R.A. performance on the basis of each county's total population, when the organization was almost exclusively Roman Catholic. How comparable, then, are these figures, given that Monaghan, which was 75 per cent Catholic in 1911, had a proportionately smaller recruiting base than Clare (98 per cent) or Kilkenny (95 per cent)? In fact, leaving Protestants out of the calculations does very little to alter the pattern of I.R.A. activity. Cork and Dublin city score even higher because of their high rates of violence and comparatively large Protestant populations. Most of the rest of the country stays the same: southern counties because of their overwhelmingly Catholic populations, northern counties because of their negligible levels of violence. The only significant change to come of this adjustment is in the border counties of Monaghan, Fermanagh, and Armagh where confessional and I.R.A. strengths lay at neither extreme. Even here, however, the differences are moderate ones. Thus, while a useful exercise, there is little value in substituting this measure for the global one used in Maps 1–6.

We should also be wary of refining our figures too far as at each successive stage—controlling for population, then for the Catholic population (and perhaps next for the Catholic male population and so on)—we move farther away from how events were perceived at the time. Partly for this reason I have included Map 1, which charts police, military, accidental, and unattributable violence along with that of the I.R.A. (see also Table 1). The distribution of total violence tallied closely with I.R.A. activity except in the case of Belfast, whose civil war of 1920–2 consumed almost as many lives as were lost in the whole of southern Ireland in 1922–3. However, while the similarity of Maps 1 and 2 reflect the reciprocal nature of guerrilla warfare, the near doubling of casualty rates in Map 1 indicates the sheer scope of the British and Free State response to the republican challenge. These total figures give the best picture of the scale of the revolution and of its impact on the country, combatants and non-combatants alike.

## Perceptions

What possible explanations are there for this geography of violence? Before examining what historians have said, let us turn first to opinions within the I.R.A., where the wildly differing performances of its units in their campaign against the British was the subject of a heated dialogue between the Dublin headquarters and the provincial brigades. For the self-appointed experts in G.H.Q. there was only one cause: 'slackers'— volunteers who 'share in the reflected glory of achievements elsewhere, while themselves neglecting to do their own share of work'.[11] *An tOglach*, the army's in-house journal, constantly berated these areas for letting 'the gallant men' of Munster do most of the fighting.[12] Michael Collins in particular, in his role as adjutant-general (and leading hero of the revolution), was notorious for his abuse of 'backward' commanders.[13]

Not surprisingly, things looked very different to the browbeaten men in the field, who placed the blame on factors they felt to be beyond their control. Their most common complaint was of a lack of arms—rifles in particular—for which they in turn blamed their superiors in Dublin. In April 1921, for example, the adjutant of the South Mayo Brigade wrote to Richard Mulcahy, the I.R.A. chief of staff, to say that 'we have material here, from a man-power point of view, good enough to make the place hot as Hell . . . men I believe as good as any in Ireland. But we have absolutely no stuff. Under the circumstances how can G.H.Q. expect big results here?'[14] All staff officers soon became familiar with what one called 'making a poor mouth about rifles . . . a useful argument for . . . areas less contented with their lot'.[15]

Unfortunately, guns are one variable for which numbers are neither available for each county, nor entirely reliable when recorded by unit.[16] Since most of the I.R.A.'s pre-Truce armoury was captured from their opponents, however, we can use arms seizures from Crown forces as an indicator of the distribution of military weapons. And indeed, the capture of arms in the formative years of 1917–19 does correlate moderately well with subsequent guerrilla activity in 1920–1, yielding

---

[11] *An tOglach*, 1 May 1920.

[12] Ibid., 15 Feb. 1921. See also for 15 May, 1 June, 1 Sept., 1 Oct. 1920; 1 Mar., 8 Apr. 1921.

[13] Rex Taylor, *Michael Collins* (London, 1958), 78, 81.

[14] Adj., South Mayo Bde. to Chief of Staff [C/S], 28 Apr. 1921 (University College Dublin Archives [UCD], Richard Mulcahy Papers, P7/A/38).

[15] G.H.Q. organizer's report on 3rd Southern Div., 2–5 Sept. 1921 (Irish Military Archives [MA], A/0670).

[16] We do have divisional and some brigade records from after the Truce and, following David Fitzpatrick, we can break these down into approximate numbers of rifles held in each province. These do indeed show that those areas with the most arms were also more violent, but such broad figures can only be suggestive; Fitzpatrick, 'The Geography of Irish Nationalism', 116–7. For the difficulty of reconciling I.R.A. arms accounts, compare statement of munitions, Oct. 1921 (MA, A/0606), with divisional arms returns, Sept. 1921 (Mulcahy Papers, P7a/17); report on 3rd Southern Div., 31 July 1921 and G.H.Q. report on 3rd Southern Div., 2–5 Sept. 1921 (MA, A/0674); report on 1st Western Div., 28 Sept. 1921 (A/0674).

a coefficient of .54.[17] It correlates even more closely with violence in the same period (.85), thus underlining an argument made by G.H.Q. at the time, and by historians since, that the acquisition of arms was necessarily a result of I.R.A. operations, as well as a precondition for them. In other words, violence was as much a cause as a consequence of the distribution of rifles.

Another test of this conviction would be to compare the geography of the shooting war with that of other types of I.R.A. activity that required less resources and risk and did not require military weapons. Before 1920, for example, most I.R.A. 'operations' took the form of drilling and marching. In late 1917 and early 1918 these were carried out frequently and publicly, to display the strength of the movement and to defy a government ban. These incidents were closely monitored by the R.I.C. and can thus be satisfactorily quantified by the historian. Correlating I.R.A. violence in 1917–19 and drilling in each month between October 1917 and February 1918 produces coefficients from .75 to .82—a uniformly strong result. This confirms that the same units that took the lead in gunplay and arms seizures were also generally the most energetic in other respects. Local initiative and organization was the deciding factor, not guns.

A similar comparison can be made between attacks on people and on property during the 1920–1 period. Every I.R.A. brigade burned 'enemy' buildings (principally police barracks and the houses of supposed loyalists) and robbed post offices and postmen. These activities can be mapped with a high degree of accuracy. Correlations in this case (.42 for arson, .49 for raids on mails) are still positive and significant, although less emphatic than those for drilling in earlier years. Brigades which shot fewer foes also tended to burn fewer houses and rob fewer post offices. There were exceptions to this rule, but there was nevertheless a relationship between shooting, arson, and raiding.

Most shootings did not require rifles in the first place. In county Cork in 1921, for example, only one-third of the I.R.A.'s victims were killed or wounded in actual combat. The rest—suspected informers, lone or unarmed soldiers or policemen—were usually shot with pistols or shotguns, which every unit in Ireland possessed in relative abundance.[18] Many successful ambushes were brought off using nothing else; the pivotal Rathclarin ambush in West Cork in 1919 garnered five Lee-Enfield rifles

---

[17] The correlation coefficients produced by this and the other variables under discussion can be found in Table 3, along with the sources for the figures used.

[18] For further analysis of I.R.A. combat performance, see Hart, *The I.R.A. and Its Enemies*.

using only one revolver and one shotgun.[19] By the same token, the possession of rifles did not guarantee effective action. The Carlow flying column had eleven rifles when it was wiped out in April 1921, yet had not managed to carry out a single ambush.[20]

Furthermore, if more and better arms meant more casualties, the Civil War should have been far bloodier than anything which preceded it. Instead, despite the enormously improved firepower of all its units, the I.R.A. was effectively defeated within a matter of months. The legendary Cork flying columns had twice as many rifles in 1922 as they had in 1920 and many more machine guns, including the much celebrated Thompson guns.[21] In terms of combat performance, however, they inflicted only half as many enemy casualties per ambush as they had previously. Clearly it was something other than means they lacked. Arms limitations did set strict limits on the military conduct of the revolution, but they do not explain its violence. It is determination and activity that we need to measure, not guns.

The second most common complaint put forward by 'slack' brigades was against adverse physical geography. Flat, open terrain, it was often claimed, inhibited guerrilla warfare. In the spring of 1921 Michael Brennan of East Clare wrote of 'the impossibility of campaigning under present circumstances in level country',[22] and the commander of the South Roscommon Brigade attributed his lack of action to the fact that 'the country is almost one vast plain with scarcely a bit of cover'.[23] The natural corollary to this idea was that mountains were the best ground for waging war and that 'mountainy men' made the best guerrillas. As one staff officer of the West Cork Brigade put it, 'all the mountain and poor areas were good'.[24] These assumptions were once again shared by the British army—the 6th Division historian wrote that 'it was indeed noticeable that areas in and around mountains were the most disaffected'.[25]

The idea certainly appears plausible. In wild, remote country guerrillas should be harder to locate, have better cover for their operations, and find

---

[19] Liam Deasy, *Towards Ireland Free* (Cork, 1973), 66–7.

[20] *Irish Times*, 20 Apr. 1921.

[21] Inspector of Org. to O/C 1st Southern Div., 7 Sept. 1922 (MA, A/0991/2); O/C 1st Southern Div. report, 5 Sept. 1922 (MA, IRA/2). For a discussion of the Thompson gun and I.R.A. weaponry, see Ch. 7.

[22] O/C East Clare to C/S, 29 Apr. 1921 (P7/A/38).

[23] O/C South Roscommon Bde. to C/S, 26 Mar. 1921 (P7/A/38). See also report on South Roscommon Bde., n.d. (P7/A/26).

[24] Interview with Ted O'Sullivan (UCD, Ernie O'Malley Papers, P17b/108).

[25] *The Irish Rebellion in the 6th Division Area*, 4.

it easier to hold prisoners and hide bodies. A statistical test, using the percentage of each county's area covered by 'wilderness' ('barren mountains', 'bogs', and 'marshes'), produces a positive but insignificant correlation with I.R.A. violence as a whole (.14), and a negative correlation with violence in 1917–19 (−.05). Even a glance at the map shows that the most rugged parts of Ireland were not necessarily the most active. Longford and Clare are not noticeably mountainous, while Donegal, Mayo, and Galway were not very violent. Terrain may well have made a difference in some areas under specific local circumstances, but it was not an important factor nationwide.

The last frequent local excuse for an absence of I.R.A. activity was the presence of what the commander of the Fermanagh Brigade referred to as 'a hostile element'—namely, Protestants and unionists.[26] This seems an obvious point and, indeed, when we correlate violence with the Catholic population, we do find a moderately significant result of .48 for the whole revolution. This number disguises considerable changes over time, however, as the relationship was far more tenuous in the early years of 1917–19 (.32), and was actually negative (−.20) in the interregnum of 1921–2.[27] These figures seem unexpectedly low when we consider that not only were Protestants usually hostile, but that the I.R.A. was almost exclusively dependent on Catholic members and supporters. A glance at Maps 3–6 shows that, while much of Ulster was quiet, so too were many highly Catholic southern and western counties. County Cork and Dublin city, on the other hand, were intensely active despite having comparatively large Protestant minorities. The Monaghan Brigade seems to have been especially active, partly because it faced loyalist paramilitaries. All in all, this seems less of a national than a regional explanation. Where Protestants made up a powerful majority—as in Antrim or Down—or formed a large minority in conjunction with strong anti-republican nationalists—as in Donegal or counties Dublin and Wicklow—I.R.A. activity might well be smothered. Elsewhere, the presence or absence of Protestants was largely irrelevant, except as 'soft targets'.

[26] O/C Fermanagh to C/S, 22 Feb. 1921 (P7/A/38).

[27] This shift is only partially accounted for by the eruption of fighting in Northern Ireland in this period. Taking the thirty-two counties as a whole, the correlation between the Catholic population and I.R.A. violence shifted from .41 in 1920–1 to −.20 in 1921–2. If we look only at the twenty-six counties of the Free State, the same figures are .35 to −.07. These numbers seem to be related to an upsurge in sectarian violence in the south: see Ch. 9.

## Explanations

Historians thus far have focused on the structure of rural society in trying to explain the geography of the revolution. How rural a county was, how wealthy or poor, and whether or not it had a tradition of agrarian organization or resistance: all these factors have been suggested as determinants of violence. The question of rurality is key to these broader theories. David Fitzpatrick has declared that 'Irish nationalism was above all a rural preoccupation. Its most violent manifestations were concentrated in the countryside.'[28] Tom Garvin advances a similar line of argument in *The Evolution of Irish Nationalist Politics*.[29] As it happens, these conclusions coincide with the views of a great many guerrillas, who firmly believed that 'the country always was ahead of the towns' and that towns and villages were 'the organising centres of evil'.[30]

There are several possible numbers that can be used as an index of rurality—the percentage of a county's population living outside towns of 500 residents or more, the percentage living on agricultural holdings or working in agricultural occupations—and none has any significant relationship with I.R.A. violence. In fact, cities played a crucial part in the revolution. Nearly 20 per cent of British losses occurred in the cities of Cork and Dublin, and 23 per cent of all victims came from Belfast.

These statistics are reinforced by an analysis of the social backgrounds of I.R.A. officers and men throughout provincial Ireland. As can be seen from Table 9 (in Chapter 5), the number of those working on farms was disproportionately low given their share of the working male population, while skilled workers, shop assistants, and other typically urban trades were overrepresented. Moreover, this tendency—which grew stronger as the revolution progressed—was particularly pronounced among officers, who were not only leaders but also often made up a majority of active fighters. These same trends appear in every province, and do not even include the formidable Dublin Brigade.

How do we reconcile these data with I.R.A. perceptions? One possible explanation is provided by North Cork Brigade records (Table 2), which show that urban companies did indeed have fewer 'reliable' members, but that those volunteers deemed as such were far more likely to be on active

---

[28] Fitzpatrick, 'Geography of Irish Nationalism', 423.
[29] Garvin, *Evolution of Irish Nationalist Politics*, 120–4.
[30] Con Leddy (O'Malley papers, P17b/123); *An Phoblacht*, 31 Dec. 1926.

TABLE 2.    *Urban and rural companies in the North Cork Brigade, 1921*

| (%) | Reliable | In Jail | On the Run | Active |
|---|---|---|---|---|
| Urban | 52 | 30 | 12 | 16 |
| Rural | 63 | 11 | 5 | 10 |

*Source*: 2nd Cork Brigade Company returns, Feb.–June 1921 (NLI, Florence O'Donoghue Papers, MS 31,223).

service, on the run, or in jail. Thus, republicans might well have been correct in seeing towns as dangerous places full of untrustworthy people, but these very conditions probably helped produce a hard core of militants.

Following this logic, Joost Augusteijn has theorized that, since urban opposition produced more radical volunteers, urbanization was itself one of the determinants of violence.[31] This fails statistical tests of significance as badly as does rurality, however. The political culture of Irish towns helps to account for who became I.R.A. activists, not the geography of their activity. I.R.A. activities and activists were both rural and urban.

The fact that shop assistants and the practitioners of certain trades were prone to republican militancy suggests a further hypothesis: that I.R.A. activity might vary depending on their presence or absence within a local economy. This idea cannot be sustained very far. Correlating violence with the percentage of occupied males who were shop assistants or clerks, shoemakers, or in building or tailoring trades (all well represented in I.R.A. ranks), produces mostly insignificant numbers. That this would be so is apparent from the maps. If the dearth of skilled or white-collar workers in Connaught helps explain why that region was quiet, why then were Clare, Kerry, and West Cork—also poor and rural—so explosive? And why should Leinster and Ulster be even more apathetic, when they had an abundance of such men? The sole exception to these results is in the case of drapers' assistants. This profession stood out perhaps above all others in producing revolutionaries and, in apparent confirmation of this, the distribution of its membership correlates quite well (.48) with that of guerrilla endeavours. This intriguing relationship does not extend to shop assistants in general, however (.11), so this finding cannot bear too much explanatory weight. We cannot blame the Irish revolution on drapers' assistants alone.

[31] Joost Augusteijn, *From Public Defiance to Guerrilla Warfare*, 342–8.

Within rural society, both Rumpf and Garvin have asserted the importance of a strong rural middle class as a primary source of Volunteer leadership, and as a possible determinant of organizational strength.[32] The guerrillas themselves frequently declared that it was poor farmers who made the best republicans. Using land values as an index of rural wealth, neither poverty (the percentage living on holdings valued under £15) nor relative prosperity (those on holdings between £15 and £50) demonstrate any influence on the shape of the revolution; the correlations are .11 and .08 respectively. That the rate of violence was equally indifferent to the mean rateable value of a county's land (−.11) or to the presence of agricultural labourers (−.09) no doubt also reflects the basic non-relationship between rurality and violence. In addition, these results challenge the perennial claim that the Civil War was one of social as well as political disaffection, as the 1922–3 campaign did not follow the geography of poverty, rurality, or agrarian or labour troubles.

Rumpf further argues that dairy co-operatives, dependent on 'a fair degree of rural wealth, community spirit, and organization',[33] may have encouraged the formation of active I.R.A. units. The British army certainly viewed creameries as nodes of rebellion, and it is also true that a considerable number of creamery managers were I.R.A. officers, at least in Munster. Nevertheless, this hypothesis cannot be substantiated. The correlation coefficients between violence and either the number of co-operative creameries or their members as of 1912 are mostly positive but low (as low as .02 for membership). Nor have more recent historians of the co-operative movement endorsed the 'co-operative ideal'—Rumpf's presumption of 'community spirit'—as the mainspring of its development.[34]

A possibly related factor is the tradition of agrarian organization and violence as embodied in the Land War of the early 1880s and subsequent episodes. Rumpf, Fitzpatrick, and Garvin have all proposed a relationship between the guerrilla war and the geography of agrarian 'outrages' in 1879–82.[35] That there is indeed such a relationship is indicated by a

---

[32] Rumpf and Hepburn, *Nationalism and Socialism*, 55–8; Garvin, *Evolution of Irish Nationalist Politics*, 123–5. Garvin also concludes that the I.R.A. 'was far more than the creation of one rural class' (p. 124).

[33] Rumpf and Hepburn, *Nationalism and Socialism*, 49.

[34] See Cormac O Grada, 'The Beginnings of the Irish Creamery System, 1880–1914', *Economic History Review*, 30 (1977).

[35] Rumpf and Hepburn, *Nationalism and Socialism*, 50–5; Fitzpatrick, 'Geography of Irish Nationalism', 136–7; Garvin, *Evolution of Irish Nationalist Politics*, 123–4. For analysis of the geography of agrarian violence, see Joseph Lee, 'Patterns of Rural Unrest in Nineteenth-Century

correlation of .50 between 'outrages' and revolutionary violence. Moving forward in time, we find an even stronger correlation with 'outrages' during the Plan of Campaign of 1886–91 (.60). There may well be some connection between the campaigns of the 1880s and those of the 1920s. On the other hand, as we move from one generation to another, the link between agrarian and nationalist conflict seems less and less clear. There is no correlation between the revolution and the cattle drives which took place in 1913–16, for example (.02), and very little with the agrarian eruptions which occurred in 1917–18 and 1920 (.16 and .18).[36] Only in 1917–19 did agrarian and I.R.A. violence coincide (.44). We are thus faced with a tradition which appears to have been more influential in memory than in practice.

A parallel contradiction presents itself in the case of another potentially crucial variable: emigration. It was frequently claimed (although never by republicans themselves) that wartime restrictions on travel out of Ireland had provided Sinn Féin and the I.R.A. with a large pool of underemployed and frustrated recruits. This implied that the revolution was generated by the personal, rather than political, grievances of would-be emigrants. According to the lord lieutenant, Lord French: 'the main cause of the trouble is that for the last five years [before 1920] emigration has practically stopped. There are here a hundred thousand or more young men, between eighteen and twenty five years of age, who normally would have expatriated themselves.'[37] Perhaps, then, those counties which had previously experienced high emigration would produce the strongest I.R.A. brigades? This argument, which would help explain the timing of the revolution, has an obvious plausibility but is also problematic on several counts. For one thing, the British armed forces absorbed more Irish men between 1914 and 1918 than would likely have emigrated in those years, so there was no exceptional overall surplus for the republican organizations to draw on. For another, the great majority of emigrants described themselves as 'labourers', whereas (as Table 9 shows) volunteers tended to be drawn from other occupational groups. There does seem to be a very strong relationship between a county's historical emigration rate (1851–1920)

Ireland: A Preliminary Survey', in L. M. Cullen and F. Furet (eds.), *Ireland and France 17th–20th Centuries: Towards a Comparative Study of Rural History* (Paris, 1980); K. Theodore Hoppen, *Elections, Politics, and Society in Ireland 1832–1885* (Oxford, 1984), 362–78.

[36] See also Paul Bew, 'Sinn Féin, Agrarian Radicalism and the War of Independence, 1919–1921' in Boyce (ed.), *The Revolution in Ireland*, esp. 232–4.

[37] *Irish Times*, 24 May 1920.

and its rate of I.R.A. violence (.74), but the correlation grows weaker the closer in time we approach the revolution. If we use only rates of emigration for 1891–1911, the coefficient falls to .56; for 1913–14 it is only .20; for 1920 it is .35. Once again, therefore, a variable seems to exert its influence from before its agents were born, but not through their agency. The lack of any third social or economic variable (or any other sort of evidence) to explain this renders its analytical value highly questionable.

Finally, David Fitzpatrick has suggested police effectiveness as a factor in allowing or curbing I.R.A. activity, using the ratio of arrests to indictable crimes for the year 1919 as an approximate index of R.I.C. and Dublin Metropolitan Police success.[38] Did how well a county was policed help determine the performance of its rebels? Applying this measure to the data does produce a weak but significant negative correlation of −.32. As predicted, there is an inverse relationship between arrest rates and violence. Because the relationship is stronger for the 1917–19 period (−.40) than for the subsequent guerrilla war (−.22 for 1920–1), it might be argued that, as with the possession of rifles, this number is as much a result of I.R.A. operations as a contributing cause. However, if we use the same judicial statistics for the year 1917, at the very beginning of the revolution, the results confirm Fitzpatrick's hypothesis, producing robust correlations of −.47 for violence in 1917–23 and −.56 for 1917–19. From this it seems safe to conclude that the initial geography of 'law and order' helped shape the contours of the ensuing rebellion.

County and district inspectors of the R.I.C., like their opposite numbers in the I.R.A., had standard excuses for a poor record ready to hand. One was that their forces were undermanned, that 'their numbers were too small to deal with the existing state of things'.[39] It is true that each county force was below its established strength by between 10 and 22 per cent in 1917, but if we map police numbers per capita, we actually get the opposite result. In fact, the police often did worst where they were strongest, whether in terms of arrests (−.51 in 1917), agrarian outrages (.69 for 1917–18), or I.R.A. violence (.46 for 1917–19). Which tends to support the second reason commonly given for failure: an uncooperative population. In October 1917 the inspector-general reported that, 'particularly in the Provinces of Connaught and Munster...the defiant attitude of the people towards law and authority has made the duties of

---

[38] Fitzpatrick, 'Geography of Irish Nationalism', 120–2.
[39] County Inspector for West Cork, quoted in 'I.O.' [C. J. C. Street], *The Administration of Ireland* 1920 (London, 1921), 66.

the police extremely difficult'.[40] The following summer one judge remarked that 'one could not but be struck with the statement in nearly every case: "The police have been unable to procure sufficient evidence to bring the perpetrators to justice."'[41] It was the lack of witnesses and informants, not policemen, that made crimes insoluble.

Beyond this, there are also intriguingly strong negative associations between the 1917 arrest rates and agrarian outrages in 1879–82 (−.60) and 1886–91 (−.67). Might this provide further support for the argument linking the 'moonlighters' of the 1880s with those of the 1920s? Agrarian unrest may have reflected or created a tradition of resistance to authority, which resurfaced in 1917 in the form of non-cooperation with the R.I.C. and support for the Volunteers. This supposition is strengthened by the absence of any discernible external factor—such as poverty or rurality—to explain the connection.

## Nationalism

So I.R.A. violence cannot be construed as the sum of the organization's social parts, physical setting, or arsenal. One obvious explanation that remains is that regional differences in guerrilla activity reflect local variations in the strength of republicanism, of popular support for the revolution. It is, of course, a truism that successful guerrilla warfare depends on such support, and it was certainly an article of faith among 'the boys' that they could not have done anything 'without the silence, patience and loyal help of the whole people'.[42] At the same time, however, every activist carried a mental map of 'good' and 'bad' communities, the former secure and hospitable, the latter potentially treacherous. It would seem reasonable to suppose that the 'better' a county was in republican terms, the more support it would give to its I.R.A. units, and the more effective their operations would be. To test this statistically, we can use Sinn Féin party membership, branch numbers, and election results as an indicator of the strength of republican loyalties in each county, and to compare the political and military sides of the revolution.

Republican violence may be stubbornly resistant to social explication: not so republican politics. The rise of Sinn Féin seems to have been

---

[40] R.I.C. Inspector-General's Report, Oct. 1917 (Public Record Office [PRO], CO/904/104).

[41] *Notes From Ireland*, Aug. 1918.

[42] Sean O Faolain, *Vive Moi!* (Boston, 1963), 181.

guided by a whole cluster of social and economic factors. Judged by the distribution of its membership at its peak, in January 1919 (see Table 3), the party flourished in rural (.61) and Catholic (.66) counties with high emigration rates (.40–.63), and among small farmers (.60) rather than shop assistants (−.50), tradesmen, or their employers. This divide between town and country was manifested in the urban and rural local election results in 1920. In each province, Sinn Féin gathered a much greater share of seats on rural district councils than it did in towns: 72 per cent of the former throughout Ireland, compared with only 30 per cent on urban councils.[43] As this well-defined social profile suggests, the geography of Sinn Féin was quite distinct from that of the I.R.A. While the guerrillas were most active in Munster, party organizers were most successful in the midlands and north Connaught—in Longford, Roscommon, Cavan and King's, Sligo, and Leitrim—with the western counties of Galway, Clare, and Kerry comprising a second regional front. That this was nothing new to Irish nationalist politics is demonstrated by the very close statistical association between the republican movement and Land League meetings in 1879–80 (.60), Land War outrages (.73), and its own electoral enemies, the United Irish League (.67).[44] Sinn Féin was harvesting political ground well broken by its predecessors.

This regional pattern remained essentially unchanged even as the number of official members and affiliated clubs declined through 1920. The following year witnessed both complete collapse under British pressure and spectacular rebirth after the Truce. By 1923, in the wake of the Treaty split and Civil War, the battered organization was still recognizably a descendent of the united and triumphant party of earlier years, with its strongholds to be found in the midlands and Clare.[45]

Electoral data are less plentiful, partly because constituency boundaries did not generally follow county boundaries before 1923, and partly because too many seats went uncontested in the general elections of 1918 and 1920 and in the rural and county council elections of 1920. This leaves us with the municipal elections of 1920 and the Free State general

---

[43] H. van der Wusten, *Iers verzet tegen de staatkundige eenheid der Britse eilanden 1800–1921; een politiek-geografische studie van integratie-en desintegratieprocessen* (Amsterdam, 1977), 209–11, quoted in Augusteijn, *From Public Defiance to Guerrilla Warfare*, 264.

[44] Fitzpatrick, 'Geography of Irish Nationalism', 135–7.

[45] For lists of affiliated clubs, see Report on organization of Sinn Féin to 17 Dec. 1917 (NLI, Count Plunkett papers, MS 11,405); Report of Sinn Féin Ard-Fheis 1921 (Art O'Brien papers, MS 8431); Report of Hon. Sec., Ard Comhairle, 12 Jan. 1922 (MS 21,134); Sinn Féin organization report, 27 Nov. 1923: (MS 8786[4]).

election of 1923 as evidence of the county-by-county support for Sinn Féin in contested elections. These results show a significant but surprisingly distant relationship between party membership and electoral success. There is a moderate correlation between members in January 1919 and municipal seats won in January 1920 (.52), although there is none of significance when the distribution of seats and party branches in 1920 are compared. The situation in 1923 was nearly identical, producing a correlation of .50 between Sinn Féin clubs and the percentage of votes received by riding.[46] While there was a connection between joining Sinn Féin and voting for it, the party's electoral geography was still quite different from that of its organization.

Voting for the republican party in 1920 or 1923 was different from joining it, and fighting for the republic was something else again. The only significant correlations that can be found between political and military activity are between I.R.A. activity in 1920–1 and Sinn Féin membership in 1917–19 (.48–.54) or municipal voting in 1920 (.35). No similar relationship exists for earlier or later periods. In the Civil War, for example, correlations between I.R.A. violence and Sinn Féin clubs and votes in 1923 were .23 and .21 respectively. Political mobilization was thus neither a sufficient nor a necessary condition for sustained I.R.A. operations.

If party republicanism is a much poorer predictor of violence than might be expected, this was not the only form of nationalism that might have shaped the I.R.A., or that we can examine statistically. Contemporary observers and historians alike have frequently assigned great importance to the role of cultural nationalism and its organizations in paving the way for a political revolution. Tom Garvin identified the Gaelic League, which campaigned for the revival of the Irish language, as 'in many ways the central institution in the development of the revolutionary elite'.[47] W. F. Mandle wrote of the Gaelic Athletic Association, which sought to do the same for Irish games: 'It is arguable that no organization had done

[46] For election returns, see Brian M. Walker (ed.), *Parliamentary Election Results in Ireland, 1918–92* (Dublin, 1992), 108–15. The 1923 electoral figures are for the twenty-six Free State counties only and in some cases for constituencies smaller than, or larger than, a single county. In the former case, I recalculated the votes for the county as a single unit to compare with other figures. Where two counties formed a single constituency, I similarly amalgamated the statistics for violence or clubs to match. In no case did the counties have very different numbers to begin with, so the resulting distortion was not too great. The result is imperfect, but still useful when combined with other data.

[47] Tom Garvin, *Nationalist Revolutionaries in Ireland* (Oxford, 1987), 78.

more for Irish nationalism than the G.A.A.—not the I.R.B.... not the Gaelic League... not even Sinn Féin.'[48]

Judged by membership figures as of January 1917, however, there was at best a weak geographic association between these two organizations and Sinn Féin and the I.R.A. A significant correlation can be found for G.A.A. and Sinn Féin membership as of July 1917 (.42), but this shrank as the party grew over subsequent months. Comparing the G.A.A. and I.R.A. activity produces only a .06 result. There is little other evidence to suggest a strong link between the two. Indeed, J. J. O'Connell, a leading military organizer, recalled that 'it was a fact that the Volunteers did not receive from the G.A.A. the help they expected'.[49] The Irish War of Independence was not won on the playing fields of Croke Park.

The Gaelic League likewise had no significant relationship with either Sinn Féin or revolutionary violence as a whole. The one significant correlation was with I.R.A. activity in 1917–19 (.41), so it might still be argued that the League had some influence on the early development of the Volunteers. A better index of linguistic patriotism, however, is the extent to which the language was actually being taught and learned. Most children after the turn of the century would have learned their Irish in school.[50] Since the provision of Irish classes in the national school system was dependent on local initiative, the number of schools offering Irish classes—and therefore the proportion of young Irish speakers in a county—indicates the strength of local enthusiasm and activists. As one official observed in 1910:

In many parts of my circuit of counties local committees connected with the Gaelic League take an active interest in the teaching of Irish in the National Schools. They appoint extern teachers to give instruction in the subject where no member of the school staff is competent to do so; they also promote oral and written competitions for school pupils at local *Feiseanna* . . . If these active agents voice local feeling, as no doubt they do, then it must be recognised that much sympathetic interest is manifested in the teaching of Irish.[51]

[48] W. F. Mandle, *The Gaelic Athletic Association and Irish Nationalist Politics 1884–1924* (Dublin, 1987), 221.

[49] J. J. O'Connell, 'A History of the Irish Volunteers', ch. 1, p. 4 (NLI, Bulmer Hobson Papers, MS 13,168). See also C. S. Andrews, *Dublin Made Me* (Dublin, 1979), 113–4.

[50] The correlation coefficient for Irish speakers aged 10–18 and the percentage of schools teaching Irish for fees in 1911 is .83.

[51] General Report on Irish, *Appendix to the 76th Report of the Commissioners of National Education in Ireland, School Year 1909–10*, Parliamentary Papers [hereafter P.P.], 1911 (Cd.5491), xxi, 169.

Did one generation of activists help produce another? Correlating the percentage of Irish-speaking young men aged 10–18 in 1911 with I.R.A. activity does produce a positive and significant result (.38), which improves greatly if we remove from our calculations those *Gaeltacht* counties where native speakers were still numerous (.58).[52] It is the latter, higher figure which is supported by the data for language teaching. In fact, the percentage of national schools in which Irish was taught for fees in 1911 emerges as the best single predictor of republican violence out of over 100 tested variables. Their correlation coefficient is .61. Just as important, this statistical relationship remains consistently high for almost every phase of Volunteer activity, from before the 1916 rising to the end of the Civil War.

We can move several degrees beyond simple inference here by exploring the question of what sort of young men spoke Irish as a second language. A survey of the 1911 census returns from two towns in county Cork, Bandon and Bantry, produced the following result: among the 85 occupied men aged 30 and under who claimed to know Irish, 45 (53 per cent) were shop assistants or clerks, 15 (18 per cent) were tradesmen, and only 8 (9 per cent) were labourers.[53] In other words, those classes which contributed disproportionately to the leadership and ranks of the I.R.A. were also the foot-soldiers of the Irish revival.

For Sinn Féin, the picture looks very different yet again. Party membership only produces a significant correlation with the teaching of Irish after March 1918, rising to .38 as of January 1919. With the municipal poll results in 1920, this rises again to .44, a level maintained through 1923 (.43). Cultural activists may have played a part in the rise of Sinn Féin as a mass movement and may have helped sustain it in defeat. On this evidence, though, their role was far from decisive.

One set of teachers dedicated to the revival of the language and frequently singled out as a key influence on the development of revolutionary nationalism were the Irish Christian Brothers (who operated outside the national system). C. S. Andrews, a Dublin I.R.A. veteran, wrote: 'Without the groundwork of the Christian Brothers' schooling it is improbable that there would ever have been a 1916 Rising, and certain that the subsequent

---

[52] That is, excluding counties Clare, Kerry, Galway, and Mayo.

[53] National Archives [NA], 1911 manuscript census returns. Interestingly, drapers' assistants correlated almost as well with the teaching of Irish (.52) as with I.R.A. activity (.54: see above). See also John Hutchinson, *The Dynamics of Cultural Nationalism: The Gaelic Revival and the Creation of the Irish Nation State* (London, 1987), 179, 287.

fight for independence would not have been successfully carried through. The leadership of the I.R.A. came largely from those who got their education from the Brothers, and got it free.'[54] These conclusions have been echoed by several historians of the revolution, and have been recently and aggressively reiterated by Conor Cruise O'Brien.[55] Barry Coldrey, who has studied the question of the Christian Brothers' nationalism, has detailed its central place in their teaching and has amassed considerable circumstantial evidence concerning the importance of their students to the revolutionary movement.[56] In Coldrey's view, the Brothers created 'the ideal revolutionary group': 'a pool of well-educated lower-middle-class young men', imbued with a strongly nationalist ethos.[57] Irish-speaking drapers' assistants, please step forward.

We can test this notion by comparing the ratio of Christian Brothers' primary-school pupils to each county's (and Dublin's) population with the rates of political activity and violence. The results go some way towards confirmation. Correlating pupils in 1911 with violence in 1917–23 produces a coefficient of .40, although the result is far higher for 1922–3 (.59) than for 1920–1 (.22). Coldrey stresses the importance of intermediate education—that is, for those aged 14 and over—for the Brothers' political influence, and if we look at students in this category, we do indeed find even stronger results: a correlation of .51 for cumulative I.R.A. violence, significant in every period. So perhaps Coldrey and O'Brien are correct. In teaching patriotism, the Christian Brothers created gunmen.

This analysis of the Brothers' possible role must be accompanied by the usual disclaimer with regard to Sinn Féin. The same comparisons produce low or negative results in every period of party membership or support. Also, a final caveat: as the Brothers had no female pupils, this explanation only works for men (of course, armed violence was an exclusively male activity as well). The thousands of militant female revolutionaries received their nationalism, cultural and political, from other sources. Clearly, one did not need to be schooled in patriotism in this way to acquire or practise it.

---

[54] Andrews, *Dublin Made Me*, 74.

[55] Conor Cruise O'Brien, *Ancestral Voices: Religion and Nationalism in Ireland* (Dublin, 1994), 9–10, 24–7.

[56] Seven of the fourteen men executed in Dublin after the 1916 Rising had attended Christian Brothers schools; a majority of both the Sinn Féin and the Irish Volunteer executives elected in 1917 were former students, and so on. See Barry Coldrey, *Faith and Fatherland: The Christian Brothers and the Development of Irish Nationalism 1838–1921* (Dublin, 1988), esp. 248–70.

[57] Ibid. 248.

## Why Violence?

The I.R.A. brought something new to Irish politics: not just guns, but the determination to use them. Was there something equally new about the gunmen that explains why? We can eliminate those explanations for violence based on wealth, class, occupation, or rurality. Nor was there any simple equation between nationalism or republicanism—as expressed through voting or party membership—and activism. However, besides the dead ends revealed by these statistics, there are some promising lines of inquiry. It would seem that, as a generation, I.R.A. activists were clearly influenced by the programmatic patriotism of their teachers and by the cultural revivalists of Edwardian Ireland. As an organization, the I.R.A. tended to be more violent where the police and courts were least effective, which in turn may have been related to a tradition of resistance inherited from the agrarian rebels of Victorian Ireland. The guerrillas were indeed a new political phenomenon: an explosive fusion of ideological conviction and communal solidarity.

This political chemistry can not only be traced in the national outlines of the resulting explosion, but also within the myriad local groups and networks who made up the vanguard of the revolution. If Catholic and Gaelic idealism provided an overriding motive for violence, and popular alienation from the state supplied the opportunity, the means—the gunmen—still had to be mobilized locally; within families, neighbourhoods, and workplaces. It was at this level that I.R.A. units were formed, commitments and decisions made, local 'republics' founded and defended, and that brothers, friends, and neighbours became comrades in a greater cause. Such groups of aggressive young men had functioned as Defenders, Whiteboys, or Ribbonmen in the past, and were not in themselves a novelty. What was new after 1916 was the radicalization of these sub-political bonds and drives by militant republicanism, and the incorporation of 'the boys' into a wider movement which they came to dominate. This seizure of power by formerly marginal young men in itself marked a political revolution.[58]

Finally, the results of this exercise point to the need to understand the nature of violence itself: its dynamics, motives, and victims. How did the process of escalation begin and sustain itself? When it did not, why not? Did it follow the same path in different regions and periods? Who were

[58] See Hart, 'Youth Culture and the Cork I.R.A.', in David Fitzpatrick (ed.), *Revolution? Ireland 1917–1923* (Dublin, 1990).

the killers and who were their targets, and why? At least part of the answer lies in the identities and interactions of the men of violence on all sides. These too must be mapped.

TABLE 3. *Correlation coefficients*

| | | I.R.A. violence | | | | | Sinn Féin members (Jan. 1919) |
|---|---|---|---|---|---|---|---|
| | | 1917–19 | 1920–1 | 1921–2 | 1922–3 | 1917–23 | |
| 1. | I.R.A. violence 1917–19 | — | .52 | .20 | .22 | .52 | .21 |
| 2. | " 1920–1 | — | — | .19 | .57 | .95 | .48 |
| 3. | " 1921–2 | — | — | — | −.12 | .18 | .01 |
| 4. | " 1922–23 | — | — | — | — | .78 | .21 |
| 5. | Arms seizures 1917–19 | .85 | .54 | .13 | .34 | .57 | .09 |
| 6. | I.R.A. drilling Nov. 1917 | .82 | .46 | .08 | .06 | .46 | .22 |
| 7. | Arson, 1920–1 | .27 | .42 | −.08 | .40 | .45 | .54 |
| 8. | Raids on mails, 1920–1 | .49 | .36 | −.16 | .23 | .43 | .67 |
| 9. | 'Wilderness' | −.06 | .15 | −.20 | .15 | .14 | .50 |
| 10. | Catholic population | .32 | .41 | −.20 | .50 | .48 | .66 |
| 11. | Rurality | .08 | .10 | .15 | −.13 | .03 | .61 |
| 12. | Drapers' assistants | .20 | .46 | .19 | .49 | .54 | −.03 |
| 13. | Shop assistants/clerks | −.06 | .12 | .04 | .41 | .24 | −.50 |
| 14. | Small farmers | .08 | .11 | −.03 | .07 | .11 | .60 |
| 15. | Medium farmers | −.04 | .10 | .33 | −.06 | .08 | −.30 |
| 16. | Mean rateable valuation | .01 | −.12 | −.19 | −.03 | −.11 | −.47 |
| 17. | Agricultural labourers | −.06 | −.13 | −.30 | .08 | −.09 | −.40 |
| 18. | Dairy Co-op members | .03 | .16 | .37 | .20 | .23 | .45 |
| 19. | Agrarian outrages, 1879–82 | .25 | .48 | .17 | .45 | .50 | .73 |
| 20. | " " 1886–91 | .67 | .59 | .04 | .39 | .60 | .60 |
| 21. | Land League, 1879–80 | −.02 | .16 | −.17 | .10 | .13 | .60 |
| 22. | Cattle drives, 1913–16 | .08 | .00 | −.06 | .05 | .02 | .06 |
| 23. | Agrarian outrages, Dec. 1917–Mar. 1918 | .44 | .19 | −.06 | .04 | .16 | .43 |
| 24. | " Jan.–June 1920 | .23 | .21 | −.07 | .09 | .18 | .25 |
| 25. | Emigration, 1851–1920 | .53 | .72 | .05 | .50 | .74 | .63 |
| 26. | " 1891–1911 | .38 | .55 | .01 | .41 | .56 | .56 |
| 27. | " 1913–14 | .14 | .25 | −.05 | .06 | .20 | .40 |
| 28. | " 1920 | .29 | .41 | −.06 | .19 | .35 | .46 |
| 29. | Police efficiency, 1917 | −.56 | −.43 | −.05 | −.36 | −.47 | −.55 |
| 30. | Police strength, 1917 | .46 | .26 | .03 | .05 | .23 | .61 |

*(continues)*

TABLE 3.    (*Contd.*)

| | I.R.A. violence | | | | | Sinn Féin members (Jan. 1919) |
|---|---|---|---|---|---|---|
| | 1917–19 | 1920–1 | 1921–2 | 1922–3 | 1917–23 | |
| 31. Sinn Féin members, Dec. 1917 | .09 | .54 | .03 | .20 | .45 | .93 |
| 32.    "   "   "  Mar. 1918 | .22 | .52 | −.02 | .16 | .43 | .94 |
| 33.    "   "   "  Jan. 1919 | .21 | .48 | .01 | .21 | .42 | — |
| 34. Sinn Féin clubs 1920 | .12 | .13 | .03 | −.01 | .08 | .68 |
| 35.    "   "   "  1923 | .26 | .30 | −.24 | .23 | .29 | .55 |
| 36. Sinn Féin votes 1920 | .21 | .35 | −.10 | .41 | .41 | .52 |
| 37. U.I.L. members 1913 | −.07 | .05 | .07 | −.09 | −.01 | .67 |
| 38. G.A.A. members, Jan. 1917 | −.04 | −.03 | −.27 | .29 | .06 | .26 |
| 39. Gaelic League, Jan. 1917 | .41 | .19 | −.25 | .26 | .23 | .05 |
| 40. Irish speakers, aged 10–18 | .38 | .32 | .04 | .36 | .38 | .34 |
| 41. Irish speakers—Gaeltacht | .49 | .47 | .05 | .63 | .58 | .40 |
| 42. Schools Teaching Irish | .57 | .48 | .13 | .50 | .61 | .38 |
| 43. Christian Brothers pupils | .33 | .22 | −.09 | .59 | .40 | −.13 |
| 44.    "    "   aged 14+ | .50 | .35 | −.06 | .62 | .51 | .07 |

*Sources*: Unless otherwise noted, these variables are calculated as rates per 10,000 people, for each county and the city of Dublin.

1. People deliberately killed or wounded in I.R.A. shootings or bombings, 1917–19. For sources, see text.
2. Same as (1), 1920–11 July 1921.
3. Same as (1), 12 July 1921–27 June 1922.
4. Same as (1), 28 June 1922–June 1923.
5. Attacks on Crown forces which resulted in the loss of arms, 1917–19. R.I.C. County Inspectors' (C.I.) monthly reports: CO 904/102–110; *Cork Examiner, Irish Times*.
6. Incidence of drilling or marching: C.I. reports; R.I.C. reports on illegal drilling, 1917–18: CO 904/122.
7. Buildings burned by the I.R.A., 1920–1: C.I. reports, 1920–1: CO 904/111–16; *Irish Times, Cork Examiner*.
8. Incidence of mail theft by the I.R.A., 1920–1: same as (7).
9. Percentage of area defined as bog, marsh, or barren mountain: *Census of Ireland 1911*, General Report, Table 42.
10. Percentage of population who were Roman Catholic: *Irish Historical Statistics: Population 1821–1971*, ed. W. E. Vaughan and A. J. Fitzpatrick (Dublin, 1978).
11. Percentage of population living outside towns of 500 inhabitants or more (1911 census): David Fitzpatrick, 'The Geography of Irish Nationalism 1910–1921'.
12–13. Male drapers' assistants or shop assistants or clerks: *Saorstat Eireann Census of Population 1926*, vol. 2, Table 5.
14. Percentage of population on agricultural holdings living on holdings valued at £15 or under: *Census of Ireland 1911*, General Report, Table 159.

15. Percentage of population on agricultural holdings living on holdings valued between £15 and £50: same as (14).
16. Mean value of agricultural holdings: *Census of Ireland 1911*, General Report, Table 157.
17. Male agricultural labourers: *Census of Ireland 1911*, county reports.
18. Members of dairy co-operative societies: *Report of the Irish Agricultural Organisation Society Ltd.*, 1913, pp. 104–5.
19. R.I.C. returns of agrarian outrages, 1879–82: P.P., 1880 (131), lx; 1881 (12), lxxvii; 1882 (8), lv; 1883 (Cd.12), lvi. Fitzpatrick, 'Geography of Irish Nationalism'.
20. R.I.C. returns of agrarian outrages, 1886–91: Laurence M. Geary, *The Plan of Campaign 1886–91* (Cork, 1986), 184–6.
21. R.I.C. returns of Land League meetings, 1879–80: P.P., 1881 (5), lxxvii.
22. R.I.C. returns of cattle drives: Breandan Mac Giolla Choille, *Intelligence Notes, 1913–16* (Dublin, 1966).
23–4. R.I.C. returns of agrarian outrages, Dec. 1917–June 1920: C.I. reports, 1917–21; R.I.C. agrarian outrage returns, 1920–1: CO 904/121; NA, Chief Secretary's Office, agrarian outrage returns, 1920.
25. *Emigration Statistics of Ireland, 1920*, P.P., 1921 (Cd.1414), xli.
26. *Census of Ireland 1911*, General Report, p. lix.
27. *Emigration Statistics (Ireland), 1913–14*: P.P., 1913 (Cd. 7313), lxix; 1914–16 (Cd.7883), lxxx.
28. *Emigration Statistics of Ireland, 1920*.
29. Ratio of arrests to indictable crimes, 1917: *Judicial Statistics, Ireland, 1917*, P.P., 1919 (Cd.43), lii.
30. R.I.C. strength, 1917: Return of sergeants and constables; NA, CSO, misc. papers.
31. C.I. reports, Dec. 1917: CO 904/104.
32. C.I. reports, Mar. 1918: CO 904/105.
33. C.I. reports, Jan. 1919: CO 904/108.
34. Clubs affiliated with Sinn Féin, 1920: Report of Sinn Féin *Ard-Fheis*, 1921, NLI, Art O'Brien Papers, MS 8431.
35. Clubs affiliated with Sinn Féin, Nov. 1923: Sinn Féin organization report, 27 Nov. 1923, NLI, MS 8786[4].
36. Percentage of first-preference votes in municipal and urban council elections won by Sinn Féin, 1920: *Evening Telegraph*, 19, 20, 21 Jan. 1920; *Watchword of Labour*, 6 Mar. 1920.
37. United Irish League members, 1913: CO 904/20/2; Fitzpatrick, 'Geography of Irish Nationalism'.
38–9. Gaelic Athletic Association and Gaelic League members: C.I. reports, Jan. 1917: CO 904/102.
40. Irish and English speakers aged 10–18: *Census of Ireland 1911*, provincial summaries, Table xxxvii.
41. Irish and English speakers aged 10–18, excluding the counties of Clare, Kerry, Galway, and Mayo: same as (39).
42. Percentage of national schools teaching Irish for fees, 1911: General Report on Irish, *Appendix to the 77th Report of the Commissioners of National Education in Ireland for the Year 1911*, P.P., 1912–13 (Cd. 6042), xxiv, p.136.
43. Christian Brothers' pupils: *Census of Ireland 1911*, provincial summaries, Table xxxviii.
44. Christian Brothers' intermediate students (aged 14 and over): same as (42).

# 3

# The Dynamics of Violence

When did war come to twentieth-century Ireland? The home rule crisis of 1912–14 introduced guns and armies into party politics, but the oncoming confrontation between nationalists, unionists, and the British government was shunted aside by the greater war in Europe. 'Crisis' in 1914 was succeeded by rebellion in 1916. In April of that year revolutionary conspirators did manage to turn Dublin into a battlefield for a week. Nevertheless, the small numbers mustered by the army of the Irish republic and the limited scope of their enterprise only earned the title of 'rising' (albeit *the* Rising).

The term 'war' is traditionally reserved for two periods of violence preceding and subsequent to the Anglo-Irish Treaty of December 1921. The first war, the guerrilla struggle between the I.R.A. and the forces of the old (United Kingdom) regime, is known by a variety of more or less interchangeable titles: the War of Independence, the Anglo-Irish War, and the more colloquial Tan War (after the imported British ex-soldiers-turned-policemen known as Black and Tans). Next came the 'Civil War' between the anti-Treaty section of the Irish Republican Army and the forces of the Irish Provisional Government and Free State, commencing on 28 June 1922 with the new regime's assault on republican strongholds in Dublin, and finishing with the I.R.A.'s official suspension of 'offensive operations' on 30 April 1923.

The different names given to the first republican war suggest the difficulty of exact definition. Its end seems clearly demarcated by the truce between the I.R.A. and Crown forces which came into effect on 11 July

1921 (referred to as *the* Truce), but its beginning is a different matter, as the conflict did not begin with a declaration or *casus belli*. The date most often used as a starting or turning point is that of 21 January 1919, when a group of south Tipperary Volunteers ambushed and killed two policemen at Soloheadbeg. This marked, in Charles Townshend's words, the 'first fatal police casualties in a rebel attack'[1] and coincided with the first meeting of the republican assembly, the Dáil, in Dublin. But this was not the spark that ignited the armed struggle. It was only one of a long series of revolutionary (post-1916) 'firsts'. Men of the Royal Irish Constabulary had been attacked before, shot before, and killed before, as had members of the Volunteers. The coincidence of the killings and the declaration of independence was just that, although it would prove irresistibly convenient for chroniclers of the revolution. It also, explicitly or implicitly, suggests a political coherence for this and subsequent violence, further defining it as a real war.

The start date for guerrilla war proper might be pushed back to January 1920, when the rebels' general headquarters (G.H.Q.) first authorized and encouraged a general offensive against the police. This triggered a military counter-offensive, so that two armies can be said to have been engaged, as opposed to police and militants. But again, neither provincial I.R.A. brigades nor their British opponents were doing anything that had not been done before. Police barracks had been attacked, 'political' police had been assassinated, military parties had been ambushed. The British army had been aiding the civil power off and on for years, using emergency legislation and courts martial to do so.

If the popular term 'Tan War' is preferred, then the Black and Tans did not make much of an impact until the late spring of 1920. If war requires permanent military formations, full-time insurgent flying columns and active service units did not officially emerge until the autumn of that year. Another key marker, martial law, was not declared until December—and then only in some southern counties. The Dáil, supposedly the seat of revolutionary authority, did not take responsibility for its self-appointed army until March 1921.

Of course, it is also possible to see guerrilla war in evolutionary terms— as progressing in stages, each one a necessary precursor to the next. Some historians and many rebel autobiographers describe this as a planned, orderly process in the spirit of the innumerable 'how to' manuals of

---

[1] Townshend, *The British Campaign in Ireland 1919–1921*, 41. See also Liam Kennedy, 'Was There an Irish War of Independence?' in Bruce Stewart (ed.), *Hearts and Minds: Irish Culture and Society Under the Act of Union* (Gerrards Cross, 2002), 188–229.

rural rebellion produced by Polish, Italian, and South American revolutionaries. Others have seen it as a rudderless 'drift to war', a response to political frustration and vacuum and an accumulation of local initiatives and official blunders.[2] These assumptions and arguments lead to a large, and largely unexplored, question: what were the causes of political violence in early twentieth-century Ireland? Was it the product of a rational strategy or decision-making? A breakdown in law and order? A culture of violence and ethnic division? To understand why events happened as they did, we must also ask how. By what process did relatively peaceful politics and protest escalate into war?

If we drop inevitably arbitrary and politicized chronologies and definitions in order to examine the problems of origin and escalation, we should also question the supposed beginning and end points of 21 January 1919, 11 July 1921, 28 June 1922, and 30 April 1923. To what extent did violence follow this schedule? If it did not, is it analytically useful to adhere to the convention that armed violence stopped with the Truce, or that a singular civil war broke out on a particular day in June and ended on a particular day in April?

This chapter sets out to test these conventions of periodization and categorization by establishing a statistical chronology of revolutionary (including counter-revolutionary) violence from January 1917 to September 1923, shorn of any military or partisan definitions that restrict our analysis of its nature or victims. This new and comprehensive data allows the exploration of the crucial problem of escalation and, more generally, the dynamics of violence over the course of the Irish revolution.

## The Shape of Escalation

The nature of Irish violence presents both a problem and an opportunity. It is problematic because military or paramilitary engagements were fairly rare and very small in scale, the Soloheadbeg ambush being a fairly representative example. Most military, police, and I.R.A. casualties did not even occur in combat. Like the many civilians killed or wounded, they were attacked while defenceless, alone, or in small groups. There were almost no conventionally recognizable campaigns, battles, or decisive encounters between substantial forces, very few advances or retreats, and little or no progress measurable in territorial or even attritional terms.

---

[2] The term was first used by P. S. O'Hegarty: see David Fitzpatrick, *Politics and Irish Life*, 215.

On the other hand, because violent incidents were closely observed and usually reported in detail from a variety of perspectives, it is possible to place and date them and weigh them in terms of their results. Shootings, bombings, and deaths can be reliably counted and mapped as well as categorized by victim and attacker. Using newspapers and police, military, and I.R.A. reports between 1917 and 1923, I have enumerated the victims of revolutionary violence by the dates on which they were killed or wounded and the county or city where this occurred.[3] The resulting data is broken down chronologically for the whole of Ireland and displayed in Figure 1 and the last column in Table 4, which charts rebel,

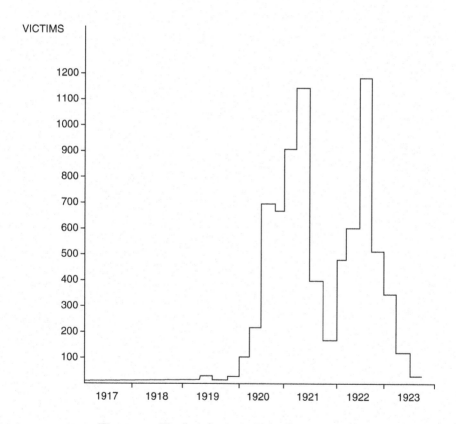

Figure 1.   Total violence in Ireland, 1917–1923

[3] These are the same numbers as used in Ch. 2, with the addition of those victims executed by governments or killed by means other than guns or bombs. The latter is a very small total, while the former only make a noticeable impact on the statistics in 1923, due to the number of Free State executions. This change was made because the focus of this chapter is on timing and escalation, when executions were clearly part of the dynamic of action and reaction. For details of sources and methods, see my *The I.R.A. and Its Enemies*, 319–23.

TABLE 4. *Quarterly violence in Ireland, 1917–1923*

| | Leinster | | Ulster | | Munster | | Connaught | | Dublin | | Belfast | Ireland | | |
|---|---|---|---|---|---|---|---|---|---|---|---|---|---|---|
| | I.R.A. | Govt. | I.R.A. | Govt. | I.R.A. | Govt. | I.R.A. | Govt. | I.R.A. | Govt. | Total | I.R.A. | Govt. | Total |
| **1917** | | | | | | | | | | | | | | |
| 1 | | | | | 1 | | 1 | | | | | 2 | | 2 |
| 2 | | | | | 2 | 10 | 2 | | 1 | | | 5 | 10 | 15 |
| 3 | | | | | 1 | 1 | 1 | | | | | 2 | 1 | 4 |
| 4 | | | | | 2 | 1 | 2 | | | | | 4 | 1 | 5 |
| **1918** | | | | | | | | | | | | | | |
| 1 | | | | | 3 | 8 | | | | | | 3 | 8 | 13 |
| 2 | | | 2 | 1 | | 3 | | | | | | 2 | 4 | 7 |
| 3 | | | | | 4 | 1 | | | | | | 4 | 1 | 5 |
| 4 | | | 2 | | 3 | | 1 | | | | | 6 | | 6 |
| **1919** | | | | | | | | | | | | | | |
| 1 | 1 | | | | 5 | | 1 | 1 | 1 | | | 8 | 1 | 9 |
| 2 | 1 | | | | 14 | 4 | | | 6 | | | 21 | 4 | 27 |
| 3 | | | | | 13 | 2 | | | 3 | | | 16 | 2 | 19 |
| 4 | 2 | | 4 | 1 | 11 | 1 | 1 | 2 | 5 | 2 | | 23 | 6 | 32 |
| **1920** | | | | | | | | | | | | | | |
| 1 | 6 | 1 | 5 | | 43 | 12 | 9 | 1 | 1 | | 3 | 73 | 14 | 96 |
| 2 | 6 | | 15 | | 66 | 21 | 13 | | 4 | | 2 | 104 | 21 | 229 |
| 3 | 28 | 12 | 16 | 13 | 133 | 74 | 22 | 11 | 10 | 2 | 321 | 209 | 112 | 682 |
| 4 | 32 | 18 | 31 | 26 | 225 | 140 | 23 | 28 | 35 | 30 | 27 | 346 | 243 | 658 |

| | | | | | | | | | | | | | | |
|---|---|---|---|---|---|---|---|---|---|---|---|---|---|---|
| **1921** | | | | | | | | | | | | | | |
| 1 | 48 | 24 | 52 | 16 | 273 | 193 | 49 | 21 | 62 | 32 | 12 | 484 | 286 | 907 |
| 2 | 66 | 28 | 72 | 20 | 307 | 166 | 59 | 44 | 84 | 16 | 81 | 588 | 274 | 1,127 |
| 3 | 18 | 4 | 13 | 18 | 66 | 13 | 13 | 1 | 3 | 2 | 247 | 113 | 38 | 402 |
| 4 | 1 | | 4 | 1 | 6 | 3 | 3 | | | | 148 | 14 | 4 | 169 |
| **1922** | | | | | | | | | | | | | | |
| 1 | 3 | | 35 | 9 | 27 | 2 | 9 | | 4 | | 363 | 78 | 11 | 481 |
| 2 | 19 | 8 | 54 | 34 | 41 | | 13 | 1 | 10 | 4 | 357 | 137 | 47 | 590 |
| 3 | 84 | 27 | 14 | 3 | 322 | 91 | 66 | 12 | 109 | 30 | 43 | 595 | 163 | 1,169 |
| 4 | 42 | 16 | 11 | 4 | 148 | 56 | 29 | 18 | 45 | 17 | 7 | 275 | 111 | 508 |
| **1923** | | | | | | | | | | | | | | |
| 1 | 31 | 10 | 5 | 2 | 98 | 71 | 18 | 15 | 20 | 14 | | 172 | 112 | 346 |
| 2 | 4 | 7 | 1 | 1 | 15 | 38 | 21 | 2 | 1 | 4 | | 42 | 52 | 113 |
| 3 | 4 | | 4 | 3 | 3 | 13 | 2 | 2 | | 1 | | 5 | 22 | 34 |

*Note*: Ulster figures do not include Belfast; those for Leinster do not include Dublin.

government (Irish and British), and total violence over these seven years of revolution. It must be noted that the sum of the first two numbers does not always add up to the third, as they do not include those victims whose attackers are unknown or unclear. Each year is divided into three-month quarters (winter, spring, summer, autumn), which provide the most suitable units of time to track change beyond short-term fluctuations. The only serious problem of attribution is in the case of Belfast, where events were often so chaotic that the perpetrators cannot be identified.[4] If we knew their identities, the total figures for victims attributable to the I.R.A. and Crown forces would be somewhat higher in 1920, 1921, and 1922.

Table 4 breaks the single national and aggregate line of Figure 1 into a less simple and more intriguing set of statistics. Here, victims of the I.R.A. and of government forces are also tabulated separately for each province and the two major cities, Dublin and Belfast. Table 5 tracks changes in the rate of violence in percentage terms. Since this is only meaningful if activity is continuous from one quarter to the next, the percentages have only been calculated from the point when each region began such a period of continuous activity. This point is marked with a star, followed by the relative rise or fall in the number of victims in each successive quarter in percentage terms.

As Figure 1 and Table 4 show, these cumulative numbers do broadly follow the standard narrative line for these years, dominated by the twin peaks of the Tan War and the Civil War. Certainly, armed and fatal violence was concentrated in two twelve-month periods between the summers of 1920 and 1921, and in the same portion of 1922–3. Several other features of the statistical chronology should not thereby be overshadowed, however. First, the apparent trough between these great waves of killing still claimed hundreds of lives. The Truce did not bring peace to Ireland, if peace is defined as the absence of violence. Second, fighting—or shooting, at any rate—continued well beyond the I.R.A. ceasefire of April 1923 and remained comparable to 1919 figures for the rest of that year. That is, violence persisted at a level defined as being a state of war by the standard narrative reckoning. In this period, as in early 1922, southern elections and state building coincided with a very uneasy 'peace'. One thing is clear: when assessing the impact and meaning of revolutionary violence, its direction—rising or falling—was as important as the absolute number of casualties. Also crucial were sequence and precedence. Thus,

---

[4] For further discussion of violence in Belfast, see Ch. 10.

TABLE 5. *Percentage rates of change in violence in Ireland, 1917–1923*

| | Leinster | | Ulster | | Munster | | Connaught | | Dublin | | Ireland | |
|---|---|---|---|---|---|---|---|---|---|---|---|---|
| | I.R.A. | Govt. | I.R.A. | Govt. | I.R.A. | Govt. | I.R.A. | Govt. | I.R.A. | Govt. | I.R.A. | Govt. |
| **1917** | | | | | | | | | | | | |
| 1 | | | | | | | | | | | | |
| 2 | | | | | | | | | | | | |
| 3 | | | | | | | | | | | | |
| 4 | | | | | | | | | | | | |
| **1918** | | | | | | | | | | | | |
| 1 | | | | | | | | | | | | |
| 2 | | | | | | | | | | | | |
| 3 | | | * | | * | | | | | | | |
| 4 | | | | | −25 | | | | | | 50 | |
| **1919** | | | | | | | | | | | | |
| 1 | | | | | 67 | | | | * | | 33 | * |
| 2 | * | | | | 180 | * | | | 500 | | 163 | 300 |
| 3 | | | | | −7 | −50 | | | −50 | | −24 | −50 |
| 4 | 100 | | * | | −15 | −50 | * | | 67 | | 44 | 200 |
| **1920** | | | | | | | | | | | | |
| 1 | 200 | | 25 | | 290 | 1100 | 900 | | −80 | | 217 | 133 |
| 2 | 0 | * | 200 | | 53 | 75 | 44 | | 400 | | 42 | 50 |
| 3 | 470 | * | 7 | * | 102 | 252 | 69 | * | 150 | * | 101 | 433 |
| 4 | 14 | 50 | 94 | 100 | 69 | 89 | 05 | 155 | 250 | 1,500 | 137 | 117 |

(*continues*)

TABLE 5. (Contd.)

| | Leinster | | Ulster | | Munster | | Connaught | | Dublin | | Ireland | |
|---|---|---|---|---|---|---|---|---|---|---|---|---|
| | I.R.A. | Govt. | I.R.A. | Govt. | I.R.A. | Govt. | I.R.A. | Govt. | I.R.A. | Govt. | I.R.A. | Govt. |
| **1921** | | | | | | | | | | | | |
| 1 | 50 | 33 | 68 | -38 | 21 | 38 | 113 | -25 | 77 | 07 | 40 | 18 |
| 2 | 38 | 17 | 38 | 25 | 12 | 14 | 20 | 109 | 35 | 50 | 21 | -04 |
| J11 | 142 | 29 | -38 | 570 | 71 | -52 | 97 | -80 | -89 | 13 | 45 | 01 |
| 3 | | | | | | | | | | | | |
| 4 | | | | | | | | | | | | |
| **1922** | | | | | | | | | | | | |
| 1 | 300 | | 775 | 900 | 350 | | 300 | | * | | 457 | 175 |
| 2 | 633 | * | 54 | 377 | 52 | | 44 | * | 150 | * | 76 | 427 |
| 3 | 442 | 338 | -74 | -91 | 685 | * | 408 | 1,200 | 990 | 750 | 334 | 347 |
| 4 | -50 | -41 | -21 | 33 | -54 | -38 | -56 | 50 | -59 | -43 | -54 | -32 |
| **1923** | | | | | | | | | | | | |
| 1 | -26 | -38 | -55 | -50 | -34 | 27 | -38 | -16 | -56 | -17 | -37 | 01 |
| 2 | -87 | -30 | -80 | -50 | -85 | -46 | 17 | -87 | -95 | -71 | -76 | -54 |
| 3 | | -43 | | 200 | -80 | -66 | -91 | 0 | | -75 | -88 | -58 |

*Note*: An * marks the beginning of a continuous period of violence, and the benchmark from which escalation is measured. The figures for 'J11' record the percentage change in the rate of violence for the first 10½ days of July 1921, July 11 marking the start of the Anglo-Irish Truce. These numbers have been pro-rated so as to compare them to those for previous whole quarters. Thus, the changes indicated are those which would have taken place if violence had continued at the same rate for the whole of the summer quarter.

one shooting a week could constitute a crisis in 1919, a truce in 1921–2, and a return to normality in 1923.

Table 5 reveals the shape of escalation in Ireland. For the purposes of this essay, 'escalation' will be defined as a consistent, significant increase in the level of violence. To be more specific, a rise in violence is considered escalatory if casualties rise by 100 per cent or more from one quarter to the next, and if that new level is maintained or increased again in the following quarter. In national terms this process began unmistakably, not in January 1919, but rather a year later. Before 1920 violence rose and fell but remained essentially stuck at a low rate for three years. The year 1919 was worse than 1918 and 1917, but not by much. These years are comparable to those of the Land War of 1880–2, which ended in de-escalation and a peaceful political reconstruction. This pattern changed suddenly and decisively from the beginning of 1920. Revolutionary casualties between January and March of that year were three times those of the preceding three months. They doubled, then tripled again over the next six months, stabilized briefly in the autumn, then climbed again in 1921 and continued climbing until 11 July.

Escalation, then, was not gradual. It was marked by sharp discontinuities and proceeded in a series of rapid shifts or jumps. To put it another way, what has often been described as a 'drift' into guerrilla war in 1919–20 might be better understood as a sudden lurch from low to high gear, accelerating all the way to the end.

A parallel process occurred from January 1922 onwards, when the rate of violence climbed nearly 200 per cent by March, continued to rise through June, and then redoubled in the summer to inaugurate the republican Civil War. The difference between these two periods is that the violence was not sustained in 1922 as in 1920–1, instead falling immediately and precipitously from its summertime high.

As Tables 4 and 5 show, violence escalated everywhere in 1920–1 and followed roughly the same pattern in nearly every region. January 1920 was the take-off point for the I.R.A. in every area except Ulster, where it was delayed until the following quarter. From this point on, rebel activity rose continuously nationwide right up to the 11 July truce. Only the Dublin guerrillas took a brief backward step in the spring of 1920. And in each case this upward trend took a cyclical form, with major shifts being punctuated by lesser ones. This began to change in 1921, which saw still-rising numbers of murders, but at a slower rate. The first eleven days in July did bring a last-minute upsurge in provincial activity (again, except in

Ulster), but this was partly a product of the impending truce, allowing I.R.A. units outside Dublin to wreak maximum havoc in the knowledge that they would soon be immune from retaliation. In general, though, I.R.A. (and total) violence had reached a plateau by the spring of 1921— albeit one which was still sloping upwards. It is worth noting, neverthe- less, that smaller relative increases at this stage meant large absolute increases in the number of victims, now running at over a hundred a month.

The aftermath of the Treaty saw massive republican re-escalation in early 1922, with the Dublin I.R.A. being the only laggard on this occasion. And again, Munster and Connaught followed a cyclical pattern, alternat- ing between rapid and slow increases in activity. It is here, however, that Ulster broke decisively with the other areas, as violence in that province dwindled just when it exploded everywhere else. As has been well docu- mented, the southern civil war drained the northern brigades of man- power and support at this crucial point. It could also be said that the northern guerrillas were simply ahead of their time, as an almost equally severe decline in I.R.A. armed violence set in everywhere else from October onwards.

If we turn to government shootings, we again see increases throughout the island in 1920, with a lessening of the pace in 1921. In each area, though, official escalation *followed* the I.R.A.'s lead, lagging by months in a kind of echo effect. In Dublin and Leinster it was a year or more before the guerrillas provoked a sustained armed response. Still, a fair degree of synchronization can be observed among the Crown forces as well. July 1920 marked the beginning of official escalation in four of the five regions. Not coincidentally, these months also saw the arrival of large numbers of British ex-soldiers to join the police counter-insurgency effort. On the other hand, the army and police did not simply follow in the rebels' footsteps, as 1921 saw the number of government victims fall even while I.R.A. shootings continued to mount.

Table 4 also reveals a third distinct pattern of violence in Belfast. Its beginning and end points were not so chronologically deviant, with the first shootings occurring in winter 1920 and the last in the autumn of 1922. What is unusual is the repeated fluctuation. The explosion of violence in the summer of 1920—a delayed reaction to the national trend of escalation—was followed by six months of comparative quiet. The second wave of destruction did not take shape until spring 1921, cresting in the summer just as the Truce took hold elsewhere. Although it did not maintain its momentum through the following quarter, violence in the northern capital still ran at a high level and grew worse than ever in the first half of 1922 before subsiding—a drop which coincided (as in the rest of Ulster) with the onset of open war in the south. So revolutionary violence in Belfast—while clearly linked to escalatory shifts elsewhere—followed its own course, driven by its own logic.

## Why Was Munster So Violent?

The province of Munster dominates these statistics from the outset. As Table 6 shows, with just over a quarter of Ireland's population the Munster combatants accounted for well over half of the revolution's attributable casualties in every year up to 1922, when its share fell to just under 50 per cent. This was as true for official shootings as for those carried out by the I.R.A. The autumn of 1919 did see a decline in activity, in both absolute and relative terms, as the southern province accounted for only two-fifths of that quarter's casualties. But the surge at the beginning of 1920 brought its share back up to 63 per cent, and then to 70 per cent in the spring. The southern counties—Cork, Tipperary, Kerry, and Limerick in particular—were therefore the engine of the revolutionary war. It was here that most of the great ambushes and spy hunts took place. What made Munster different?

One set of answers, or clues at least, can be found in the geography of violence. In Chapter 2 the same data are broken down by county and city

TABLE 6.  *Percentage of annual I.R.A. and government violence by area*

|  | Leinster | Ulster | Munster | Connaught | Dublin |
|---|---|---|---|---|---|
| % Irish population | 21 | 30 | 26 | 15 | 8 |
| 1917 | 0 | 0 | 72 | 24 | 4 |
| 1918 | 0 | 18 | 79 | 4 | 0 |
| 1919 | 6 | 6 | 62 | 6 | 21 |
| 1920 | 9 | 10 | 63 | 10 | 8 |
| 1921 | 10 | 11 | 57 | 11 | 11 |
| 1922 | 14 | 12 | 48 | 10 | 15 |
| 1923 | 14 | 2 | 59 | 15 | 10 |

so as to compare them statistically with a wide variety of social, economic, political, and cultural variables. In this way the question can be asked: why were Cork and its neighbours so much more violent than Antrim or Leitrim? This chapter reverses this analysis by looking at larger geographical units over much shorter periods of time, and by taking into account the relationship between the I.R.A. and its opponents. In this way we can not only ask 'why Munster?', but also: 'why 1920?'

Several aspects of Munster's experience set it apart. The first is timing. As Tables 4 and 5 demonstrate, the Munster brigades began their unbroken run of armed activity in the summer of 1918, six months ahead of Dublin and a year or more ahead of the rest of Ireland (and well before Soloheadbeg). Just as important, these pioneer guerrillas went through their initial cycle of escalation—their first 'jump' forward—in the spring of 1919, again well ahead of their provincial comrades. In Dublin, Michael Collins's 'squad' launched a simultaneous mini-campaign against the hapless detectives of the Metropolitan Police, but it was not sustained in the same way. Nor were they building upon earlier activity, like the men of the south. So when the winter offensive was launched in 1920 the Munster guerrillas took off from a much higher level of activity, the possessors of an early start and with one major escalatory step already taken.

The second, somewhat paradoxical, difference between Munster and other areas was that its rebels had nearly the slowest rate of escalation *after* the spring of 1920. Only the Connaught I.R.A. were slower. By 1921 even the tardy westerners were rising much faster. This allowed the men of the north, east, and west to catch up somewhat and reduce Munster's share of I.R.A. violence from 64 per cent in 1920 to 54 per cent over the first six months of 1921. It was not the speed of Munster's escalation at any given point that gave its units their leading role; it was their early start.

Nor is it likely that other regions—apart from Dublin—would ever have caught up, either in absolute or per capita terms. Even though I.R.A. violence was rising faster outside Munster, its rate of growth was still slowing down everywhere and might have been approaching an effective ceiling by the time of the Truce. Arms limitations and losses, the arrest or death of activists, the shrinking number of reliable company volunteers, the vigorous and improving British security effort—all set an effective limit on guerrilla capabilities. Escalation was not infinite. The police and military may have started up their learning curve well after the rebels climbed theirs, but once both had peaked, so had the rate of violence. The decline in government victims in 1921 may indeed be attributable to the fact that better intelligence and tactics were replacing blind reprisals—although this in turn helped intensify the I.R.A.'s war on civilian informers.[5] Civilian targets, in fact, offered the only remaining untapped market for I.R.A. operations in early 1921, which the guerrillas were already beginning to exploit when the Truce mercifully intervened. Shootings of suspected collaborators were rising fast and, in Munster, Protestant men were being kidnapped *en masse* as hostages for the lives of I.R.A. prisoners on death row. This style of outright terrorism offered a potential new escalatory path, but otherwise no further 'jumps' forward were likely.

The final, immediately observable, difference between Munster and other areas arises from the uniquely close relationship there between insurgency and counter-insurgency. There was a striking synchronization between the two rates of violence from mid-1919, after which the two sides matched each other rise for rise and fall for fall in their escalatory moves until July 1921. Official violence was much more volatile—rising and falling at a greater rate—but that is at least partly accounted for by the fact that the numbers of victims involved were smaller, making changes proportionately greater.

We can test the depth of this apparent harmonization of government and resistance by breaking the Munster figures down into weekly rather than quarterly totals, and measuring the statistical relationship between I.R.A. and government violence from January 1920 to July 1921. What emerges are positive and significant correlations between the two: .36 for 1920, and .50 for the whole of 1920–1. The higher figure for the whole period is probably partly due to the fact that both series of numbers trend upwards (although the correlation for 1921 alone is only .12). However, if we compare I.R.A. activity with that of the Crown forces in subsequent weeks—that is, compare action with reaction—the result is even better: .51 for the first week following, and .62 for the week after that. If we compare I.R.A. activity with that of the Crown forces in following weeks—Crown forces actions with I.R.A. reactions—the correlations remain significant but move slightly in the opposite direction: .48 for the first week after; .45 for the second.

Munster thus seems to demonstrate what I have argued, in *The I.R.A. and Its Enemies*, was the case in county Cork.[6] Revolutionary violence tended to be cyclical or reciprocal in structure, a tendency typically

---

[5] See my *British Intelligence in Ireland: The Final Reports* (Cork, 2002).

[6] See *The I.R.A. and Its Enemies*, 72–108.

most pronounced where there was the most persistent violence. From the spring of 1920 onwards, both sides operated increasingly on the reprisal principle, quite apart from any purely tactical or strategic rationale. These tit-for-tat cycles can be traced at the local level, killing by killing, ambush by ambush, massacre by massacre. Both sides pursued vendettas for weeks, months, and even years, pushing each other to higher levels of violence in an interlocking spiral.

The Munster data further show that these cycles most often followed a pattern of I.R.A. action and British response. This trend can also be tracked at quarterly intervals on a national level (Table 4). Between 1917 and 1919 the I.R.A. was responsible for over two-thirds (67 per cent) of total casualties, and the winter 1920 uprising pushed this to over three-quarters (76 per cent) of shooting and bombing victims attributable to republican gunmen. Once critical velocity had been reached, escalation provoked counter-escalation as government and loyalist forces rose to the challenge, dropping the guerrillas' market share of murder to 45 per cent in the spring of 1920 and a mere 30 per cent in the summer. This in turn stimulated the republicans to yet greater efforts, so that the I.R.A.'s contribution thereafter held up at slightly over 50 per cent until the Truce.

The question of reciprocity also raises the relationship between different forms of violence.[7] Before 1920, clashes between republicans and security forces usually took the form of riots, with shooting an occasional accompaniment. Table 7 charts partisan or ethnic crowd violence—that is, riotous confrontations between republicans and either policemen or anti-republican nationalists, or between Protestants and Catholics. These figures are not as precise as those for deaths and injuries, particularly with regard to Belfast after mid-1920. Nevertheless, the data is useful and highly suggestive. It reveals, once again, an early and substantial Munster lead in popular violence. Fifty-nine per cent of Irish riots took place in the southern province in 1917, 33 per cent in 1918, 52 per cent in 1919, and 30 per cent in 1920. Overall, Cork and company accounted for 41 per cent of all non-agrarian riots before 1921 (when rioting outside Belfast became very rare) and 60 per cent of all those outside Ulster.

These figures suggest an early and violent familiarity between the Munster rebels and their enemies and a correspondingly (and consequently) early local escalation from sticks and stones to guns in 1919.

---

[7] See further discussion of this in Ch. 2.

TABLE 7. *Crowd violence in Ireland, 1917–1920*

|  | Leinster | Ulster | Munster | Connaught | Dublin | Belfast | Ireland |
|---|---|---|---|---|---|---|---|
| **1917** | | | | | | | |
| 1 |  | 2 | 8 |  |  |  | 10 |
| 2 | 3 |  | 18 | 1 | 6 |  | 28 |
| 3 | 4 | 4 | 13 | 5 |  |  | 26 |
| 4 | 3 | 3 | 9 | 2 |  |  | 17 |
| TOTAL | 10 | 9 | 48 | 8 | 6 |  | 81 |
| **1918** | | | | | | | |
| 1 | 7 | 8 | 15 | 10 |  | 5 | 45 |
| 2 | 3 | 7 | 9 | 2 | 1 |  | 22 |
| 3 | 5 | 4 | 11 | 4 | 1 | 1 | 26 |
| 4 | 5 | 8 | 11 | 13 | 6 | 2 | 45 |
| TOTAL | 20 | 27 | 46 | 29 | 8 | 8 | 138 |
| **1919** | | | | | | | |
| 1 | 2 | 5 | 8 | 2 |  |  | 17 |
| 2 | 2 | 1 | 7 |  | 3 |  | 13 |
| 3 | 6 | 6 | 12 |  |  | 3 | 27 |
| 4 | 1 | 5 | 12 |  |  |  | 18 |
| TOTAL | 11 | 17 | 39 | 2 | 3 | 3 | 75 |
| **1920** | | | | | | | |
| 1 | 1 | 4 | 6 | 1 |  | 1 | 13 |
| 2 | 1 | 8 | 11 | 1 | 1 | 1 | 23 |
| 3 | 4 | 17 | 9 | 1 | 1 | 14 | 46 |
| 4 | 1 | 3 | 5 |  | 2 | 9 | 20 |
| TOTAL | 7 | 32 | 31 | 3 | 4 | 25 | 102 |

*Source*: These data were collected from newspapers (especially the *Irish Times*) and monthly county police reports. They do not include police riots in which policemen attacked property or helpless civilians, or agrarian events. I define a riot as the violent action of an unorganized group of at least ten people. Where numbers were unclear, I used my best judgement, excluding doubtful cases.

One example of this connection was the relationship between Tomas MacCurtain, the commandant of the 1st Cork Brigade, and District Inspector Swanzy of the Cork city R.I.C. These two men had faced each other at many public events through 1917, 1918, and 1919, and Swanzy had arrested many Sinn Féiners over the years: both were well known to the other side. MacCurtain was murdered in March 1920 in revenge for the shooting of a policeman. Swanzy was blamed and, in August, was shot in retaliation in Lisburn. Both killings were locally pivotal events and arose out of the shared experiences of the previous years.[8]

On the other hand, there was not a clear departure from one form of violence to another. Riots continued in Munster in 1920 when they had just about stopped everywhere else outside Ulster. Obviously there was a third independent variable at work: popular or movement militancy. What Table 7 does show is the long-term decline in republican riots (almost all of which occurred in the south) even before the guerrilla war was properly under way. Seventy-two riots took place in Munster, Leinster, and Connaught in 1917; forty-five in 1920. The higher total for 1918—111—was a product of election excitement and anti-conscription anger, and reflects the most intense period of mass mobilization by Sinn Féin. Rioting grew riskier after that, as did the parades and meetings that occasioned it. The 1918 general election pretty much ended the political war with the Irish Party. Sinn Féin was itself displaced in importance by Dáil Éireann and lost most of its paying membership after 1919. Part of the escalatory process, then, was the replacement of popular violence by paramilitary operations.

By 1921 the armed struggle had become thoroughly militarized while, paradoxically perhaps, its reprisal dynamic had acquired an autonomous logic and drive, often divorced from the military context of the moment. Proof of this can be found in the I.R.A.'s return to violence in the first six months of 1922, particularly in the southern provinces. While the chronology of the new outbreak might suggest that this represented an escalation arising from the Treaty split and leading to the outbreak of the Civil War, in fact the great majority of its victims had nothing to do with the establishment of a Free State. They were the same targets the rebels had been pursuing the previous year: policemen and soldiers, ex-soldiers and ex-policemen, suspected informers and collaborators, and Protestants in general. Often their alleged crimes had occurred a year or more earlier. Very rarely did the I.R.A. shoot its nationalist political enemies, even after the outbreak of civil war.

## The Structure of Escalation

These patterns of violence and victimization suggest that beneath the tit-for-tat dynamic lay more than a competitive game—more than a series of matching moves leading to stalemate and truce. As in the first half of 1922,

---

[8] See *The I.R.A. and Its Enemies*, 77–9.

so for the whole revolution, it is necessary to ask: who were the victims? Table 8 provides one answer: they were mostly civilians belonging to no fighting organization. Non-combatant casualties rose from 40 per cent of total casualties in 1917–19 to 48 per cent in 1920, 64 per cent in 1921, and 82 per cent in the first half of 1922, before returning to earlier levels for the remainder of the revolution. By 1921 both the I.R.A. and Crown forces were shooting civilians more often than they shot each other, despite the disappearance (except in Belfast) of rioting crowds to shoot at, as in earlier years. The 'real war' of patrols and ambushes was being overtaken by another reality. We can also see from the number of casualties generated by forces other than government or guerrillas that there was a great deal of unorganized or informal violence as well, particularly in the north.

Attacks on civilians and the involvement of civilian vigilantes began to rise on the heels of the I.R.A.'s big push. From March 1920 onwards an unofficial (but officially tolerated or encouraged) reprisal movement grew within the R.I.C., often acting under cover names such as the 'Anti-Sinn Féin Society'. This intensified with the arrival of the Black and Tans in large numbers. The subsequent republican 'war on informers' was provoked by the alarming rise in I.R.A. and Sinn Féin deaths. The rebels faced their first armed civilian opposition in the Derry riots of July 1920, followed by a massive wave of attacks on Catholics by similar groups of loyalists in Belfast and other Ulster towns. As in Munster, violence in Ulster (and especially Belfast) marched to a drumbeat of retaliation.

What the second rising of early 1920 triggered was not just a counter-vailing state response but also a new dynamic of ethnic and communal conflict: in effect, a spin-off civil war. Two lines of ethnic division are important here, helping to channel violence towards particular target groups. The first was between the Catholic nationalist population and

TABLE 8. *Civilians (non-combatants) as a percentage of total victims*

| Period | (%) age |
|---|---|
| 1917–19 | 40 |
| 1920 | 48 |
| 1921 | 64 |
| Jan.–June 1922 | 82 |
| July–Dec. 1922 | 39 |

the non-Irish forces sent in to combat the insurrection: the ex-soldiers of the Black and Tans, the ex-officers of the R.I.C.'s new Auxiliary Division, and the men of the British regiments on counter-insurgency duty. Tans, Auxies, and soldiers tended to see most or all Catholics as racial stereotypes and natural or automatic enemies, and were in turn viewed as alien invaders, their actions as brutal and illegitimate. These mutually reinforcing and dehumanizing images lowered the threshold of violence considerably, making killing much easier. For a member of the Crown forces seeking a target, almost any young Catholic man might do. For guerrillas, the same was true of anyone in uniform—or anyone identified with them.

This latter category included above all southern Protestants—instinctively identified by many republicans as 'loyalists' in the manner of their northern co-religionists, and targeted with rising vigour by the I.R.A. from the summer of 1920 onwards.[9] Ulster Protestants saw the republican guerrilla campaign as an invasion of 'their' territory where they formed the majority. Loyalist activists responded by forming vigilante groups, which soon acquired official status as the Ulster Special Constabulary. These men spearheaded the waves of indiscriminate anti-Catholic violence (immediately dubbed 'pogroms') which began in July 1920 and continued for two years. This could itself be described as a rising—or perhaps anti-rising—given its scale.[10]

The revolution thus became a power struggle, not just between revolutionaries and states, but also between and within communities. Both north and south, this violence was primarily directed at minority groups with the aim of uprooting, expelling, or suppressing perceived enemies within. In the six counties which became Northern Ireland in 1921, this meant that Catholics bore the brunt of the conflict, although Protestants suffered as well and socialists were also frequent targets. In the remaining twenty-six counties that became the Free State in 1922, the main target group was the Protestant minority, followed by ex-soldiers, tinkers and tramps, and others seen as social or political deviants. Throughout Ireland, political mobilization, guerrilla warfare, and state repression radicalized all kinds of communal boundaries, leaving those outside the local majority vulnerable to victimization. Despite the aggression it unleashed, the mentality that lay behind this process was essentially defensive, whether the actors were nationalist, republican, or loyalist. Everywhere, the desire was to impose unity and uniformity on one's own 'people' and to establish or

---

[9] See Ch. 9.        [10] See Ch. 10.

maintain control of territory seen as 'ours'. It was this dynamic that framed the drive for revenge. Nor did this violence stop with the Truce. In fact, both north and south, it peaked in the first six months of 1922: the climax of what might be thought of as a third 'war', hidden beneath and between the two conventional 'wars' of received history.

The Civil War, then, saw a double de-escalation. The outbreak of fighting between pro- and anti-Treaty forces first short-circuited the communal conflicts on both sides of the new border. As the I.R.A. became embroiled in the struggle to defend the republic, it ceased to threaten unionist hegemony in the north. The southern Provisional Government likewise halted its attempts to destabilize its sibling regime. This in turn led to a rapid scaling down of official and unofficial repression of nationalists in the north. The I.R.A. was not only preoccupied militarily, but also on the run, losing most of the territory it controlled by the end of August. The persecution of Protestants and other former 'enemies' continued, but at a much lower—and diminishing—level.

The winding down of communal conflict and the fact that the I.R.A. was now facing nationalist Irish opponents—often former comrades— also helped break the ethnicized cycles of reprisals and counter-reprisals. These still took place (most notoriously in Kerry), but were much more localized and sporadic. Thus, the third republican insurrection of 1922–3 imploded at least partly because of the absence of some of the key communal ingredients of escalation and polarization. The impact of their absence shows their centrality to the revolutionary process.

## Narratives of Violence

On 28 November 1920 the West Cork Brigade flying column attacked an Auxiliary police patrol, killing seventeen and leaving the sole survivor for dead. Three guerrillas also died. This, the Kilmichael ambush, is easily the most famous republican victory of the revolution. The victors' story of what happened there has been written, sung, told, and commemorated many times. On 27, 28, and 29 April 1922, in and around the nearby towns of Dunmanway, Bandon, and Clonakilty, thirteen Protestant men were shot dead and another wounded after an I.R.A. officer had been killed during a raid on a Protestant household. The anonymous killers were also members of the republican army, some of whom may well have been veterans of Kilmichael. Yet this episode, equally violent and with similarly far-reaching local consequences, carried out by the same organization—perhaps even the same individuals—is rarely mentioned in histories or memoirs of the I.R.A. or their revolution, is not preserved in song or stone, and is not even recalled—except privately, by local Protestants.[11]

The differences in public meaning given to these events demonstrate the chronological and categorical problems with the standard narrative of violence-as-war. Kilmichael came at the climax of the first war. The second war did not begin until 28 June 1922. The April massacre (and a large number of other shootings) fell in between, in a year which has no title.

The West Cork massacre fails doubly to fit the reigning paradigm in that it does not fall into the category of acceptably 'military' events. Revolutionary violence is generally narrated and analysed in the terms set by the revolutionaries themselves. Their stories usually begin in 1916, end in 1921, and focus on the war with Britain: a format institutionalized by the official Irish Bureau of Military History. They typically take the form of local, mostly autobiographical chronicles of a selective succession of 'operations', that is, skirmishes, assassinations, or escapes. In my conversations with I.R.A. veterans, many made a strong distinction between the 'real war' in which they had fought and other sorts of violence which, while often regrettable, were essentially marginal and had nothing to do with them. By these conventions, the conduct of the revolutionary war can be reduced to what might be termed ambushography: the cataloguing of 'fighting stories', Kilmichael's being a prime example. Yet, as the figures presented here demonstrate, such fights account for only a small proportion of revolutionary violence, most of which was directed at non-combatants. So the martial paradigm neither describes nor periodizes violence adequately for the revolution as a whole.

We can use the statistics presented here to test other explanations for the origins and escalation of violence. Joost Augusteijn's comparative study of five brigades (one from each province and another from Dublin) is the most extensive investigation of the problem to date, and has produced a multidimensional model of guerrilla violence. The key causal variable, according to Augusteijn, was not the presence of radical nationalists, as they could be found everywhere. What really mattered was the ability of these men to cross the very high social and psychological barriers against violence. This required two things: the alienation of most of the

---

[11] See *The I.R.A. and Its Enemies*, 21–38, 273–92.

community from the state—and particularly the police—and a parallel separation between the proto-guerrillas and their neighbours. Both were needed to overcome the normal restraints against shooting men in uniform, and this meant that there had to be a politically creative balance between support (enough to ostracize the local constables) and opposition (enough to force the Volunteers go on the run, thus freeing them from parental and communal disapproval). Where this combination existed, as in south Tipperary, the I.R.A. campaign got off to an early start whereupon violence became a self-perpetuating mechanism. Relatively inactive areas remained stalled below the martial threshold unless direct experience of state violence, G.H.Q. prodding, and the sheer force of inspiration and outrage over events elsewhere, combined to force men on the run and on the column.[12]

Augusteijn's theory is subtle and convincing in many respects, and his brigade-level and communal analysis stands on its own research and is not really commensurate with the figures presented here. He does locate and date nearly the same starting-point, however—Munster, late 1919, and then more generally in early 1920—and he places equal emphasis on the importance of an early start. He also suggests a similarly reciprocal mechanism for continuing escalation. On the other hand, his depiction of other areas falling behind until later in 1920, when catalysed by the Black and Tans in particular, may miss the mark somewhat. Many Connaught, Leinster, and Ulster units had got themselves on the same track as those in the deep south (and were even moving at higher speeds) by the spring of 1920. Also possibly problematic is the evidence that Crown forces violence was typically an (often delayed) reaction to that of the I.R.A., and not vice versa. Of course, the guerrillas did offer their own response in turn—including, as Augusteijn says, the formation of flying columns. And different localities had different experiences. Still, on a regional or national level, I.R.A. initiative seems paramount and the key to the initial spread of the guerrilla campaign.[13]

One of the most popular theories for the rise in violence is that it grew to fill a political vacuum, a by-product of governmental intransigence and nationalist frustration. Our figures can only provide part of an answer to this complex issue, but what we can say is that there is not a sequential

[12] Augusteijn, *From Public Defiance to Guerrilla Warfare*, 87–123, 335–52.
[13] A point also emphasized by Desmond Hogan in 'The Dynamics of Insurrection: The War of Independence Revisited', in *Mizen Journal*, 6 (1998), 134–53, although he connects the impact of such a grass-roots force to the structural instability of the Irish political system.

relationship between electoral politics, state repression, and violence. The key repressive moments would seem to be the 'German plot' arrests of May 1918 and the outlawing of Sinn Féin and Dáil Éireann in September 1919. On the other hand, 1919 brought a more lenient prison regime and many early releases of convicts and internees, as had happened in 1916 and 1917. The government cracked down again in early 1920, but this only lasted until April when hunger strikes forced yet another mass release of prisoners—mostly active guerrillas. A consistent counter-insurgency regime was not imposed until the Restoration of Order in Ireland Act was implemented in August.

The main sources of nationalist frustration were the non-implementation of home rule between 1916 and 1918 and, for republicans, their failure to achieve international recognition from the United States or the Peace Conference in the first half of 1919. On the other hand, constitutional and largely peaceful outlets for political energy abounded. In 1917 and 1918 there were numerous campaigns and elections to engage in, as there were again on the local level in 1920. The new Dáil administration was given a surprisingly untroubled run from early 1919 to summer 1920 before being systematically suppressed.

None of this coincides obviously with the timing of escalation. The coercion–conciliation two-step of 1917–19 provoked no matching rise and fall in armed activity in Ireland as a whole. The Munster I.R.A.'s first leap forward came after electoral success and the foundation of the revolutionary parliament, and during a phase of light policing. It might be argued that the ban on the Dáil and Sinn Féin led to the second rising of 1920, but this does not explain the earlier and later escalatory jumps, respectively, of Munster and Dublin. Nor does it explain Michael Collins's assassination campaign of 1919. Nor is there any evidence to connect I.R.A. decisions to political events—or to their supposed political masters in the Dáil.

It has also been argued that the 1918 general election gave the revolutionaries a mandate to go to war, and that they acted on this basis. This does not hold up well either. The guerrillas simply did not justify their actions in this way—in fact, quite the opposite. Sinn Féin's political success and the revolution's new administrative thrust made many radicals fear the onset of compromise. The early shootings in Munster and Dublin in 1919 did not receive the backing of either Sinn Féin or 'the people', and were not intended as an armed protest against the denial of recognition and negotiation. They were meant to prevent just such a turn to politics.

The gunmen's revolutionary vision was not predicated on having a demo-cratic mandate. The Dáil itself did not take responsibility for the I.R.A. until well into 1921.

If politicians did not launch the guerrilla war, can we at least locate the decision within the I.R.A.'s General Headquarters? The 1920 offensive suggests a centrally directed or co-ordinated military campaign, a point also emphasized by Joost Augusteijn. The earlier three years of unauthor-ized activity suggest otherwise, as does the late start of the campaign in G.H.Q.'s own backyard in Dublin. The reality seems to have been that Headquarters played a significant role but not a decisive one. It could not make its subordinates stop if they wanted to attack, and it could not make them attack if they could not or would not do so. Local initiative was both a sufficient and a necessary condition for escalation.

Which brings us to the question: where did this initiative come from? The answer lies in radical republican ideology and its carriers, the activists of the I.R.B. and their fellow travellers in the Volunteers. Their will to act was the first main escalatory mechanism, and it is this minority commit-ment to an armed republican revolution that explains the three outbreaks of 1916, 1920, and 1922. And it was the persistent internal struggle within the separatist movement that provided the first dynamic of violence. Prior to the Easter Rising of 1916, and after the re-formation of these organiza-tions in 1917, a militant tendency existed within the Volunteers, often working through the I.R.B., which was ideologically committed to open rebellion. The success of the 1916 conspirators in achieving their goal inspired the next cadre of guerrillas-to-be, particularly in Munster, to seek a second rising. They, like their heroes, faced considerable opposition from moderates within I.R.B. and Volunteer ranks—and from Sinn Féin as well. Ultimately, as in 1916, this was a struggle they won by purging or outmanoeuvring their enemies and by taking direct action on their own. They were ultimately able to launch a new, improved, 'official' rebellion in January 1920, a shift to militancy symbolized by the popular adoption of the 'Irish Republican Army' as their new title.

As the war of liberation escalated in 1920, it mutated and multiplied, unleashing state anarchy and communal repression of minorities: the second and third mechanisms of escalation. Both fed into the reprisal dynamic, which took on a life of its own. Guerrilla war and civil war became inextricably linked in the explosion of fear and destruction that followed, north and south, from the summer of 1920 until the summer of 1922, regardless of Truce or Treaty. It was at this point that the internal struggle within the separatist movement was renewed, with the militants once again upholding the aims, values, and methods of 1916. Only this time the I.R.A. faced a force drawn from its own communities and ethnic and political background—and lost.

The revolt against the British state cannot be understood without reference to the conflicts within republicanism. The guerrilla struggle did not occur in splendid martial isolation; it created and became part of a wider civil conflict. There was more than one dynamic at work in the revolution, creating more than one narrative. 'Anglo-Irish War' and 'Civil War' describe aspects of the revolution, but they were parts of a larger whole. It is time to shift to a wider and more comprehensive paradigm and to a better explanatory package.

# PART II
# Guerrillas At Home

# 4

## Paramilitary Politics in Ireland

Two of the biggest questions facing historians of twentieth-century Ireland are: why revolution, and why violence? That is, why did Ireland's long-standing political conflict metamorphose into a direct challenge to the British state after 1912, and why did this confrontation take the form of armed rebellion after 1915? After all, the Land War of 1879–82 presented many of the same features of mass mobilization, popular violence and official repression, a crisis of state legitimacy and radical political realignment—without descending into mass homicide. On the other hand, moving forward into the twentieth century we quickly encounter numerous civil conflicts in Europe and elsewhere based on the same premises of ethnicity, nationalism, and state breakdown that dwarf the Irish experience in the scale of their suffering. Seen from this perspective, the events of the Irish revolution can appear not only typical but minor.

One of the factors—the key factor in my opinion—that separates 1912–22 from the 1880s, and which unites Ireland with other troubled countries, is the presence of paramilitary organizations: in particular, the Irish Volunteers (later the Irish Republican Army). As far as I know this general phenomenon has received little comparative attention, but it does merit some systematic attention in the Irish case as it was here that paramilitarism was introduced to European politics, underpinning much of what took place in the fatal decade following the introduction of the third Home Rule Bill.

By 'paramilitary' I mean unofficial armed and public militias organized along military lines for the ostensible purpose of fighting one another, the police, or the army of the state. These features distinguish them from clandestine groups such as the Irish Republican Brotherhood or the Defenders, and from unmilitary but occasionally violent organizations like the Orange Order or Land League. Such militias proliferated in interwar Europe, most notoriously in Germany and Italy, and have also appeared in Lebanon and elsewhere. In each of these cases their appearance was symptomatic of political polarization and the decline of governmental legitimacy in the eyes of much of the population. And in each case, the end result was the breakdown of democracy and the imposition of a new state.[1] Thus, the emergence of the Ulster Volunteer Force and the Irish Volunteers says something not just about violence, but also about the structure of politics in Ireland in 1913.

## Political Structures and Decisions

By 1912 Ireland had become a full participant in the United Kingdom political system, but without being fully integrated in the manner of Wales and Scotland. Instead, Ireland had developed its own parties, cleavages, and power dynamics. Victorian democratization produced two great parties, divided by mutually exclusive ideologies (nationalist home rulers versus unionist defenders of the status quo), ethnicity (the former overwhelmingly Catholic, the latter Protestant), and territory (the Unionist Party was concentrated in the northern province of Ulster). Both had allies in the British system (nationalist–Liberal; unionist–Conservative), but Irish parties did not generally seek seats in Britain, and British parties returned the favour after 1886. Moreover, the Irish and Unionist Parties themselves did not seriously compete with each other for votes—and rarely competed for seats—seeking rather to monopolize politics within their own ethnic constituency. Finally, neither party sought power in Westminster: their goals were almost purely Irish.[2]

The nationalist Irish Party emerged out of the agrarian Land War of the 1880s, with its organization and much of its identity based on the semi-revolutionary and ultimately outlawed Land League. Many of its original cadre of activists were drawn from the secret and separatist Irish Repub-

---

[1] See Juan Linz, *The Breakdown of Democratic Regimes: Crisis, Breakdown, and Reequilibrium*, 56–61.

[2] For a discussion of ethnic party systems, see Donald Horowitz, *Ethnic Groups in Conflict* (Berkeley, 1985), 291–364.

lican Brotherhood. Although it gained electoral dominance by building a coalition representing many shades of opinion, and rapidly evolved into a fully (and avowedly) democratic party under Charles Stewart Parnell, the Irish Party's roots ensured it maintained a semiloyal position towards the British state, refusing to accord it full legitimacy.[3] That is, the party accepted the political regime as it was—was willing to achieve its goals through negotiation and legislation—but defined its role as one of permanent opposition until it could change the regime to put itself in power. Ireland was governed by a separate administration headed by a viceroy and a chief secretary—a British minister for Ireland responsible to Whitehall and Downing Street rather than to Irish representatives as such. Nationalists believed this to be an illegal and illegitimate imposition on the Irish nation, and attacked it and its personnel with sustained ferocity.[4] Participation in British politics could only be justified by the Party's ability to fight successfully for nationalist objectives, and in particular for home rule so that Ireland could one day govern itself. Only then would democracy be properly established and the state legitimized. So commitment to the system was explicitly conditional and limited according to nationalist ideology: Irish Party MPs could not accept government office, for example. Compounding this denial of complete regime legitimacy and authority was the counter-legitimation of past nationalist violence as heroic, principled, and aimed at laudable ends. Rebellion might be foolish and useless, but it was understandable and its practitioners should not be harshly punished—nor should fellow nationalists ever co-operate with the authorities in defeating the rebels. As Juan Linz defined it, 'ultimately, semiloyalty can be defined by a basically system-oriented party's greater affinity for extremists on its side of the political spectrum than for system parties closer to the opposite side': in this case, unionism.[5]

The opposing Unionist Party naturally took a loyal stance, but only towards the state as it was then constituted. A home rule parliament and executive in Dublin would represent not just a change in governance but also a total victory by their ethnic rivals and an ethnocratic threat to their own status and identity. When a Liberal government backed in parliament by the Irish Party introduced the third Home Rule Bill in 1912, after removing the previous safeguard of a House of Lords veto, the loyalists

[3] For the distinction between loyal, semiloyal, and disloyal oppositions, see Linz, *Breakdown*, 27–38.
[4] See Patrick Maume, *The Long Gestation: Irish Nationalist Life 1891–1918* (Dublin, 1999).
[5] Linz, *Breakdown*, 33.

moved rapidly to a corresponding semiloyal position, openly challenging
the government's right to legislate on behalf of their enemies. In an
attempt to further deter the legislation, a paramilitary Ulster Volunteer
Force was formed in January 1913 with the stated aim of resisting home
rule by force, at least in the northern province. Numbering in the tens
of thousands, staffed by ex-British army officers, and eventually armed
with thousands of rifles, the U.V.F. was potentially a formidable force:
more than a match for the Royal Irish Constabulary.[6] This was a logical
move in a political system polarized between two segregated constituencies and parties, in which the main prize was not patronage or a turn in
government but rather victory over the rival. If the nationalists won, they
threatened to gain permanent control over Irish politics by virtue of their
numerical advantage. Ulster (and some British) Unionists saw the government's actions as an unconstitutional betrayal with no democratic remedy.
If the system no longer protected them from their enemies, they would do
it for themselves: a common scenario for armed mobilization by parties
and communities in other parts of the world.

The Irish Party eschewed a paramilitary counter-move in anticipation
of achieving self-government by parliamentary means. In a double irony,
however, while the nationalist establishment loyally relied on the British
government to uphold the rule of law, the government refused to do so—
refused, at least, to answer the U.V.F. challenge except by negotiating
away nationalist demands. This did not mean that there would be no
nationalist response, however—it only meant that it would not be led by
the Party. Nationalist politics was not confined to the electoral arena. As
in most ethnically divided party systems, the real threat to Party power
came not from across the divide but from its own left flank, where it was
vulnerable to being outbid by more extreme nationalists. For a generation,
Party leaders had prevented this by anti-landlord activism and by main-
taining their semiloyal 'national' position towards the British state. The
Liberal alliance may have been a sentimental one for some politicians and
voters, but most probably saw it in purely instrumental terms: as a tactic
rather than a principle. Much of the Party's ideological legitimacy, and

---

[6] See Timothy Bowman, 'The Ulster Volunteers 1913–14: Force or Farce?', *History Ireland*,
10: 1 (Spring 2002) 43–7; 'The Ulster Volunteer Force and the Formation of the 36TH (Ulster)
Division', *Irish Historical Studies*, 32: 128 (Nov. 2001), 498–518, for a convincingly critical
assessment of the U.V.F.'s conventional military capabilities. See also Alvin Jackson, 'British
Ireland: What if Home Rule had been Enacted in 1912?', in Ferguson (ed.) *Virtual History*.
Charles Townshend, *Political Violence in Ireland: Government and Resistance Since 1848* (Oxford,
1983), 245–55, provides an alternate view.

hold over voters, was based on this careful balancing act.[7] It could afford to temporarily lose some floating voters to the right-wing conciliationist All for Ireland League in 1910, because they had nowhere to go but back into the fold. Nationalists would never defect to Unionism—but they might answer the siren song of separatism if the Party appeared not to be defending the national interest. Yet, as the home rule crisis deepened, and again after war was declared in Europe, John Redmond and the party leadership stuck to their passive strategy of supporting the Liberal and Coalition governments. The loss of traditional militancy was illustrated by the flaccid slogan of the Party's own paramilitary force, the National Volunteers (founded in October 1914): 'Duty, not Defiance.'

However, an alternative leadership did exist within the cultural and dissident nationalist sector led by Sinn Féin, the Gaelic League, and the I.R.B., with its own newspapers, activists, and leaders. Opinion among these people ranged from apolitical semiloyalty to outright republican disloyalty, and they shared a general contempt for party politicians as well as Dublin Castle. Here was a set of nationalist actors normally shut off from mainstream politics by the Irish Party's electoral hegemony and by their own ideological alienation. The creation of the U.V.F., the Liberal government's tolerance of it, and the Irish Party's passivity in the face of both, provided an opportunity for them to enter politics in a paramilitary guise: as the Irish Volunteers, founded in November 1913. If it had been nationalists who had initiated the process of political militarization, the British elite would have stood united against it and it would likely have been suppressed. Because paramilitarism began with Ulster Unionism, backed by the Conservative Party and much British press and public opinion, it survived and created the space and grudging official tolerance for nationalist imitators.

Thus, Ireland's political structure began to change and destabilize: the Unionist Party moved one way, the Irish Party moved another, and a new player was introduced into the game. Correctly perceiving which militia posed the real threat to their position, the nationalist establishment sought to seize control of the Irish Volunteers once the movement began to gain popularity in the spring of 1914. Redmondite appointees were imposed upon the leading committees, but they failed to control the dissidents once Redmond himself declared that Volunteers should join the

---

[7] See Paul Bew, *Conflict and Conciliation in Ireland, 1890–1910* (Oxford, 1987) and *Ideology and the Irish Question: Ulster Unionism and Irish Nationalism, 1912–1916* (Oxford, 1994).

British army in September 1914. The organization split, producing a new
party militia—the National Volunteers—while leaving the original separatist leadership in charge of an independent anti-war minority (often
dubbed the Sinn Féin Volunteers, but not in fact connected to Arthur
Griffith's organization). Including the even smaller (socialist) Irish Citizen
Army, this gave Ireland four paramilitary bodies.


## Volunteer Ideology

In structural terms, the proliferation and persistence of armed militias
made some sort of violent crisis increasingly likely. It did not mean that a
republican revolution was inevitable though, which raises the question of
ideology. Paramilitaries brought guns into politics; the British government allowed them to stay; the military council of the I.R.B. brought them
into action in 1916. To leave the question there, however, and simply
equate republican conspiracy with revolution would be misleading. The
Irish Volunteers were a coalition of separatists. The most important group
of activists did belong to the Brotherhood, but non-republicans—led by
Chief of Staff Eoin MacNeill—retained a great deal of power and majority
support. The 'secret history' of the Easter Rising, with its plots and
manoeuvres, is a familiar story,[8] but it was not the case that the organization was divided simply into rebels and non-rebels or that it provided an
otherwise empty vehicle for the revolutionaries' secret plans. In fact, the
Volunteers shared a strong collective identity and ethos, forged before the
war broke out, before the split, and before the Easter Rising was planned.

For its founders and activists, the Irish Volunteers represented and
embodied the nation and national honour: 'From the people the National
army has sprung'; 'Ireland called the Volunteers into being'.[9] This national status entailed notions of manhood, virility, virtue, and destiny.
Volunteers saw themselves as the vanguard of a new, idealistic generation
who gave the organization its moral force. Their function was not merely
political or military, but also consciousness-raising: their existence would
demonstrate Ireland's true status as a nation with its own army, not least to
its own citizens. According to the founding manifesto, Irishmen had an
inherent right to bear arms and to defend that right 'in the name of

---

[8] For the latest reconstruction , see Michael Foy and Brian Barton, *The Easter Rising* (Stroud,
1999), 1–51.
[9] *Irish Volunteer*, 15 Aug., 17 Oct. 1914.

National Unity, of National Dignity, of national and Individual Liberty, of manly Citizenship'. Doing so would restore a flagging spirit of nationality. Otherwise: 'If we fail to take such measures ... we become politically the most degraded population in Europe, and no longer worthy of the name of Nation.'[10] Joseph Plunkett—later one of the ringleaders of the rebellion—wrote in February 1914 that: 'With the launching of the Volunteer movement we the Irish people not only reassume our manhood, but once again voice our claim to stand among the nations of the world.'[11] In August a writer in *Irish Freedom* (an I.R.B. journal) declared: 'a National army is the one perfect medium of national endeavour.'[12] For this reason, many Volunteer advocates projected a permanent role for the organization, even beyond a home rule settlement.

Such language was far from novel in the Europe of 1914, and drew also on the self-image and rhetoric of cultural nationalism. As such it carried with it the corollary that the Volunteers were to be non-partisan: 'The Volunteers are the people's army and the People's Army they must remain'; 'they may owe allegiance only to the Irish Nation'.[13] In 1914 the *Irish Volunteer* admonished its readers that 'Irish Volunteers have no concern in election contests. They have their own work to attend to, and it is more important than wrangling about whether this or that gentleman will have the privilege of sitting as a cypher at Westminster until the next General Election.'[14] Even after Sinn Féin was reorganized and republicanized in 1917, the army's political virtue remained intact. When the subject of the relationship between the two was even mildly broached at that year's party convention, it met with angry rebuke from Michael Lennon: 'The Volunteers have so far been able to get along very well without much help from Sinn Féin ... We are not going to take our orders from Sinn Féin and we don't want politicians meddling with a military organization.'[15] When the Volunteer executive advocated 'immediate forward action' on behalf of political prisoners in December 1918—after Sinn Féin's election victory—the party executive left the decision with them, and added that 'in no case should there be interference with the

---

[10] The manifesto is reprinted in F. X. Martin (ed.), *The Irish Volunteers 1913–1915: Recollections and Documents* (Dublin, 1963), 98–104.

[11] *Irish Volunteer*, 7 Feb. 1914.

[12] *Irish Freedom*, Aug. 1914.

[13] *Irish Volunteer*, 15 Aug., 10 Oct. 1914.

[14] Ibid., 12 Dec. 1914.

[15] *Report of the Proceedings of the Sinn Féin Convention, 25ᵀᴴ and 26ᵀᴴ October, 1917* (PRO, CO 904/23), 16.

freedom of action of the Irish Volunteers'.[16] They would be neither a party militia nor a militia party. This differentiates the Volunteers/I.R.A. not only from the other major Irish paramilitaries of its day, but also from those in other countries, such as the Nazi SA or the fascist *squadristi*.

Being antipolitical did not make the Volunteers antidemocratic, however. Internally, an elected hierarchy of unit officers and national executive coexisted with a more conventional chain of command headed by a headquarters staff, and the principles of election and debate survived to become key issues leading up to the Civil War in 1922. Individual members were encouraged to work for Sinn Féin in elections, and units often acted as guards for speakers and polling booths. Many Volunteers traded on their patriotic credentials to become candidates themselves, a trend that peaked in the second Dáil elected in 1921. But the relationship with the Dáil itself was a tricky one. The I.R.A. technically gave its allegiance to the separatist assembly via a new oath administered in 1919, but it still guarded its autonomy and went to war with no requirement for a responsible civil authority or an explicit mandate. As presented *in An tOglach* (the successor to the *Volunteer*) in January 1919, just after the establishment of the Dáil, the Volunteers' task was: 'to safeguard the Irish Republic to which the overwhelming majority of the Irish people give allegiance; it is theirs to interpret the national will, now rendered vocal and authoritative in Dáil Éireann. In 1916 the elected leaders of the Irish Volunteers [felt] that they were truly interpreting the wishes and ideas of the people of Ireland ... it has now been proved that they had truly interpreted the heart of Ireland.'[17] This is a fascinating formulation, ostensibly recognizing the democratic authority of the Dáil while reserving the army's sovereign right to act in the name of the republic and the nation—as in 1916. The only election referred to is that of the Volunteer leadership itself by its own members. In April 1919 newly elected President de Valera said only that his ministry was 'of course, in close association with the voluntary military forces which are the foundation of the National Army'.[18] Tom Barry recalled of Sinn Féin and the Dáil that: 'these things seemed to be of little matter then ... in the main, the young Volunteers were satisfied that they were following in the footsteps of the greatest men in all our history—the men of 1916.'[19]

---

[16] Minutes of Sinn Féin standing committee, 31 Dec. 1918 (UCD, Richard Mulcahy Papers, P7/D/39).

[17] *An tOglach*, 31 Jan. 1919.

[18] *Dáil Proceedings*, 10 Apr. 1919.

[19] *Irish Independent*, 8 Dec. 1970.

As *An tOglach* asserted repeatedly in 1918, the Volunteers were 'the agents of the national will'.[20]

We must immediately make a key distinction in this regard. The Volunteers were ademocratic, not antidemocratic. They typically felt themselves to be above the political process, but they never sought to change or end it in the name of a fascist, communist, or militarist alternative, even in the name of national emergency. They did not frame their struggle in terms of democracy, but they never denied its validity either except insofar as it constrained their own actions. In any case, these were cast as a form of direct democracy: 'A few thousand Irishmen, who took the precaution of providing themselves with lethal weapons of one kind or another, have, without contesting a constituency and without sending a single man to Westminster, compelled the Westminster Parliament to admit publicly that it dares not pass any legislation which they, the armed men, did not choose to permit.'[21] When the mighty 1st Southern Division declared its opposition to the Treaty in December 1921, Sean Moylan (Cork brigadier and TD) defended the action by saying: 'We didn't think it was our business as military men but we thought we had a duty as citizens of the Irish Republic...not with a view to dictating to politicians.'[22] No *coup d'état* was ever seriously contemplated—even in 1922, despite the accusations of the pro-Treaty camp. The guerrillas wanted to fight for Ireland, perhaps even die for Ireland, but they did not want to run Ireland—as demonstrated by the reluctance to govern areas under their control in 1922. The Volunteers saw themselves as martyrs, not gauleiters or commisars.[23]

Absenting themselves as an organization from politics did not mean an absence of political identity, of course. The Volunteers were ostensibly founded as a counter to the U.V.F. and to safeguard home rule, but right from the start eager activists were suggesting that its status as a truly national army required a grander purpose: 'Ireland called the Volunteers into being, and they must follow the inevitable path that every movement springing from the heart of the people has followed—the path of freedom.'[24] At the first convention in October 1914 (following the first split), one of the organization's new policies was 'to secure the abolition of the

---

[20] *An tOglach*, 15 Aug., 14 Sept. 1918; 31 Jan. 1919.        [21] *The Spark*, 2 Apr. 1916.

[22] *Private Sessions of Second Dáil*, 14 Dec. 1921.

[23] Tom Garvin's *1922: The Birth of Irish Democracy* (Dublin, 1996) discusses the relationship between revolutionary thinking and democracy in Ireland.

[24] *Irish Volunteer*, 17 Oct. 1914.

system of governing Ireland through Dublin Castle and the British military power, and the establishment of a National Government in its place'.[25] In July 1915 a manifesto entitled 'The Present Crisis' was issued, which offered the following reinterpretation:

On behalf of the Irish Volunteers, we reaffirm the original pledge 'to secure and maintain the rights and liberties common to all of the people of Ireland.' This pledge implies the attainment of a National Government, free from external political interference. It implies resistance to any partition or dismemberment of Ireland which would exclude a part of the people of Ireland from the benefits of national autonomy. It implies resistance to any scheme of compulsory military service under any authority except a free National Government. It implies resistance to any scheme of taxation which may be imposed without the consent of the people of Ireland, and which may defeat all their hopes of national prosperity and complete the economic ruin consequent on the Legislative Union.[26]

At the second national convention, in November 1915, Eoin MacNeill added that the 'real issue is the old issue between Ireland and English domination'.[27] This implicit separatism was officially confirmed at the third convention in 1917, which declared for a republic: a position defiantly reiterated at the fourth assembly in 1922.

So the Volunteers were beholden to the higher national interest alone—or, to put it another way, to themselves alone—and this was generally accepted to mean something more than Liberal home rule. The principle of military autonomy widened easily to include the choice of action, its timing and goal. Action, like consciousness and honour, depended above all on guns. The rifle, in particular, was almost fetishistically central to the Volunteers' purpose and identity. Without arms, organization was pointless and nationalists would be emasculated. With them, ordinary politics could be disregarded: 'at the moment [1914] the rifle is the only argument of patriotism.'[28] Therefore what Volunteer organizers feared most was being disarmed. Arms were their reason for being, and hanging on to them was their primary aim. *Irish Volunteer* editorials harped on this point: 'Irish Volunteers without arms, and without the firm purpose to get arms and have arms, are a manifest humbug.'[29] Just weeks before the Rising, MacNeill told a meeting that 'There was one thing they were determined

[25] *Irish Volunteer*, 31 Oct. 1914.     [26] Ibid., 24 July 1915.
[27] *Nationality*, 13 Nov. 1915.     [28] *Irish Volunteer*, 12 Sept. 1914.
[29] Ibid., 1 Apr. 1916.

on, that Irish Volunteers meant armed Irish Volunteers. They were bound in honour, for the sake of their country, in order to protect her against an intolerable tyranny, to preserve their arms.'[30]

Self-defence against the government, therefore, headed the list of reasons to use their precious guns. In April 1916, with portents of war all about them, the Volunteer Council announced that government harassment could, 'in the natural course of things, only be met by resistance and bloodshed. None of the Irish Volunteers recognize or will ever recognize the right of the Government to disarm them or to imprison their officers and men in any arbitrary fashion.'[31] MacNeill himself raised the prospect of fighting the British army, and challenged them: 'Whether it is on equal terms, or two or five or twenty or forty to one, let them come against us and we will not shirk it.'[32] When the rebel conspirators forged the 'castle document' purporting to reveal an impending round-up, they knew it would galvanize their more cautious comrades. Other scenarios calling for action followed from the 1915 manifesto and from the circumstances of the war: partition, conscription, and the imposition of new imperial taxes.

Interestingly (and prophetically), Arthur Griffith had cautioned against this whole mindset from the start. The Volunteers were welcomed for their 'backbone', but they were not a panacea, he warned in December 1913. Instead, he urged that 'we must work through public opinion in the circumstances of Ireland rather than through force of arms'.[33] He would be making the same arguments again in 1917 and 1918, and in 1921 and 1922.

Nevertheless, all of these attitudes were shared by nearly all of the Volunteer leadership, republican, revolutionary, or otherwise. So was a growing sense of embattlement and danger through 1915 and the early months of 1916. Organizers were arrested, jailed, and exiled to England. The government looked ever more hostile, as anti-nationalist Conservatives joined the Asquith administration in 1915 and conscription was introduced in Britain in 1916. Volunteer opinions were becoming more and more militant, and expectations were rising that open confrontation was just a matter of time. The Redmondites were dismissed as irrelevant or as traitors. It was the Volunteers who stood alone in defence of a nation abandoned by party and menaced by state.

---

[30] Ibid., 8 Apr. 1916.  
[31] *Nationality*, 1 Apr. 1916.  
[32] *Irish Volunteer*, 8 Apr. 1916.  
[33] *Sinn Féin*, 6, 20 Dec. 1913.

## Paramilitary Strategies

To restate the question: did this Volunteer ideology lead inevitably to a Rising? The answer is no. General propositions may have been shared, but specific conclusions were not. When it came to strategy all paramilitary commanders, unionist, nationalist, or republican, had essentially three options to choose from:

(1) Loyalty to party and/or state. The independent or aggressive use of violence is forgone even as a threat or deterrent. This was the road taken by the National Volunteers, who followed the Redmondite party line and backed the British war effort until 1917. The same could be said of the revived Ulster Volunteers in 1920–1, when they were largely absorbed into the Ulster Special Constabulary.

(2) Deterrence. The group adopts a defensive posture coupled with the threat of action in certain circumstances. The key to this strategy is to maintain an army-in-being, willing to defend itself and its goals in a crisis. This was the official policy of both the U.V.F. in 1913–14 and the Irish Volunteers before and after the 1916 Rising.

(3) Insurrection. Direct action is taken in order to achieve some political goal, to gain an advantage over opponents, or to pre-empt an enemy attack. Where the defensive strategy protects the 'rights and liberties' at issue, an offensive strategy offers positive liberation in their name. The Easter Rising cabalists were model insurrectionists.

Once Irish Party loyalists chose the first option and set up the National Volunteers in 1914, the fate of the residual Irish Volunteers would be determined by the choice between aggression and deterrence, attack or defence. The ensuing debate was partly surreptitious and unrecorded, but was also carried on publicly in the separatist press. On the insurrectionist side, a writer in *Nationality* (owned by the I.R.B. but edited by Arthur Griffith) urged in November 1915 that: 'we have the material, the men and stuff of war, the faith and purpose and cause for revolution.'[34] In March 1916 Sean MacDermott told an audience commemorating Robert Emmet's stillborn rebellion:

His plans were well laid, his prominent supporters well advised, and the fact that his attempt at insurrection was a failure was due to circumstances which could

[34] *Nationality*, 27 Nov. 1915.

not have been foreseen. They would admit that it was better that Emmet should have made the attempt and failed than that he should not have attempted at all ... the present time was opportune for preparation [to succeed where he had failed]. They had the means, and the young men of Ireland would be unworthy of their country if they did not avail of them.[35]

But deterrence was the default position. Several weeks later *The Spark* (a separatist weekly) published a contrary anonymous piece calling for prudence, that concluded: 'let us see that whatever crime the Volunteers may commit, they will never be guilty of the superlative imbecility of suicide, spectacular or otherwise.'[36] It was agreed by all Volunteers—including insurrectionists—that, merely by existing, they had prevented partition and conscription and preserved the future of self-government—not to mention national honour. Another common claim was that they had effected a revolution in Anglo-Irish relations, and 'put an end to the old system of ruling Ireland through police (whom we outarm)'.[37] Those advocating deterrence argued that premature action would destroy these gains by giving the government an excuse to destroy them. And, militarily, they had no hope of winning. 'Defensive warfare', as Bulmer Hobson called the official policy of irregular skirmishing, not only offered the best tactical option, it also guaranteed organizational unity and the widest mobilization of support.[38] If the Volunteers were attacked, all would flock to the banner of self-defence. Insurrection would divide rather than unite. Eoin MacNeill synthesized these and other arguments in two powerful memoranda written in 1916, but they were never circulated or published, a possibly crucial decision in the closely matched battle for control.[39]

While all this made eminent common sense, insurrectionist arguments had their own logic which followed Volunteer ideology to its final conclusion. As MacDermott had stressed in his Dundalk speech, this was an unprecedented opportunity, and the very existence of the option of rebellion (recognized by opponents as well as themselves) called forth its advocates. Use it or lose it. After all, what if the government did act first? They risked losing their weapons and freedom without having the chance to act. And if the idea of 'hedge-fighting' could work as well as the pragmatists suggested, and be combined with German aid, the Volunteers

---

[35] Ibid., 18 Mar. 1916.     [36] *The Spark*, 2 Apr. 1916.
[37] F. X. Martin (ed.), 'Eoin MacNeill on the 1916 Rising', *Irish Historical Studies*, 12 (1961).
[38] *Irish Volunteer*, 15 Apr. 1916.     [39] See Townshend, *Political Violence*, 285–98.

might not only survive but prevail against a distracted Britain. MacNeill himself accepted this line of reasoning when first told of the impending German arms landing. Indeed, this very scenario was sketched in *The Spark* in March 1916 in a series of mock newspaper stories detailing the victory of 'the Provisional Government of the Irish Republic'. After a German landing in the west, 'the Sinn Féin Volunteers mysteriously disappeared from the city [Dublin], marching ostensibly in the direction of Naas', only to return again in triumph in November after a victorious summer campaign.[40] Beyond logic, the Volunteer sense of identity also favoured the bold, as commitment and self-sacrifice easily trumped practical concerns as a demonstration of corporate righteousness and national status.

These arguments took place not just between republicans and more moderate separatists but within republicanism as well, so there was no clear correlation between beliefs in means and ends. The I.R.B. was itself split between offensive and defensive factions. Nor could the insurrectionists claim to have been winning over the Volunteers. They did gain a few converts, but remained a distinct and necessarily duplicitous minority within the organization as a whole. Nevertheless, the logic of the situation always favoured them in the long run. Presuming no government first strike, the insurrectionists were able to plan, prepare, organize, and strike when it suited them. This ability depended on a marked degree of official tolerance, but this was what was on offer between 1914 and 1916. Time was on their side.

## Volunteer Politics

The Easter Rising amply confirmed the warnings of the defensive wing of the Volunteers. Only a small fraction of the total membership took part, many units stayed out of the fight altogether, and the result was a crushing defeat. Despite the military failure and the death of so many leaders, however, the Rising actually strengthened the insurrectionists. Most survived, gained retrospective approbation and political credibility, and were released within a year, astonishingly free to resume and recruit. Official tolerance of paramilitarism was very much reduced—wearing uniforms and drilling became crimes to be prosecuted—but the result was mere harassment rather than thoroughgoing repression. Paramilitarism got a

[40] *The Spark*, 19 Mar. 1916.

second chance because the government again provided it, unwilling either to grant nationalist demands or keep the gunmen in jail. The Volunteers were reorganized in 1917 and 1918 (reabsorbing many members of the National Volunteers and Citizen Army along the way), and soon rivalled in scope the mass mobilization of 1914. At the clandestine third convention—held a year late in October 1917—it declared itself to be the army of the republic in line with the 1916 proclamation, the new touchstone of Volunteer identity. A new journal was launched (*An tOglach*) and a new headquarters staff was appointed, consisting largely of I.R.B.-linked veterans of the Rising.

In many ways, the developments of 1917–18 repeated those of 1914–15. The same strategic debate as existed before 1916 was rehashed, although the revolutionists now had much more organizational power. The same choices had to be made—and the same choices were made. Once again, the default and majoritarian policy was one of deterrence, now focused primarily on the threat of conscription. The Volunteers would make their move if the government acted first, but even then their plans called for an active defence of local communities, not an overthrow of the state: a MacNeillite rather than a MacDermottite strategy, in other words. In this period the main argument lay with the advocates of Sinn Féin's traditional policy of 'passive resistance', which was denounced as worthless and dishonourable, most notoriously in Ernest Blythe's article and pamphlet *Ruthless Warfare*.[41] Once the war ended in November 1918, *An tOglach* editorials began to hint of a coming change of policy: 'The Army of Ireland was not established to resist conscription. Its function is to fight for the rights and liberties of the people of Ireland whenever and however opportunity arises. That fighting might be in the nature of an offensive as in Easter Week, 1916, or it might be of a defensive nature ... but the Irish Volunteers should be ready whenever they are called on to stand to arms.'[42] Revolutionary activists began an underground campaign against the police in 1919, and the organization was once again divided and depleted as the less militant fell away, opposed to an unprovoked and unconventional shooting war.[43] The issue was not just the principle of direct action, but rather the new tactics and targets of guerrilla war. Some rebels were willing to take part in a second rising only if it was modelled on the first. Even with a much firmer command of the leadership, the

[41] *An tOglach*, 14 Oct. 1918.   [42] Ibid., 15 Nov. 1918.
[43] Hart, *The I.R.A. and Its Enemies*, 226–70.

insurrectionists still took over a year and much internal upheaval to get rid of the dissenters. As in 1915–16, time (and British policy) was ultimately on their side. The now clandestine republican army was able to officially renew its offensive in January 1920 with a series of raids on police barracks. The subsequent struggle apparently justified the insurrectionist case, leading to negotiations over the 'full national demand' in 1921.

Which brings me to my final comparison: between the events of 1916 and 1922. The actions of the anti-Treaty I.R.A. in the latter year have often been equated with those of the Easter rebels, not least by themselves. Thus, the occupation and defence of the Four Courts against the Provisional Government has been seen as a kind of self-conscious replay of the last stand in the General Post Office. Can we equate these two events? The same constraints and drives, the same ideology, the same internal conflicts were present in both the run-up to the Rising and the Civil War. In both cases, the lines of division followed the three options that defined para-military strategy. And, just as 1916 was preceded and enabled by the 1914 split, so too was the Civil War by division over the Treaty. In each case, the movement had recently absorbed a huge number of new fair-weather recruits (Redmondites and Trucileers respectively) who overwhelmingly backed the loyal faction: in 1921–2 this meant loyalty to the pro-Treaty majority in the Dáil and G.H.Q. As with the National Volunteers and the U.V.F. before them, the pro-Treaty I.R.A. was rapidly absorbed by the state. This left an unpopular and militant minority, who retained the lion's share of activists and arms but were themselves divided over the remaining choice of direction: insurrection or deterrence. There followed the same sort of internal tug of war as took place in 1915–16. Liam Lynch, and most of the pre-eminent 1st Southern Division, wanted above all to maintain army autonomy and its role as defender of the republic against British tyranny—thereby resurrecting the idea that the Volunteers should remain as the permanent national guardian of national freedom. So long as the army kept its guns, authority, and nerve, the Treaty could not be imposed and the nation could be reunited around the old cause. Civil war, or even precipitous renewal of war with Britain, would destroy everything. In other words, Liam Lynch and his allies were the new MacNeillites, with the Free Staters taking the place of the Irish Party as pro-British collaborators. This semiloyal and defensive option was backed by a slim majority of the fourth (anti-Treaty) Army Convention and newly elected executive.

As before, a belligerent minority lay within the anti-Treaty minority, led by Rory O'Connor and Tom Barry. Not that they wanted to attack their former comrades: that would run against the grain of Volunteer thinking, which always focused on Britain as the enemy. Rather, the offensive options considered were against Northern Ireland and the remaining British garrison in Dublin, with the aim of reuniting the army by renewing the old war (unity also being an aim of the 1916 planners). When these proposals were brought to a vote in the I.R.A. executive and convention in the spring of 1922, however, they were narrowly defeated. The strategic disagreement could not be reconciled, and split the army again in June 1922, leaving the insurrectionists free to act.[44] And then, for the first time, they ran out of time. On 28 June it was the army of the Provisional Government which acted first, by laying siege to the Four Courts.

It is at this point that the 1916–22 analogy breaks down. The rebels in Dublin had not seized buildings as part of a 1916-style military plan, as a site of sacrifice, or in order to seize power. The whole anti-Treaty I.R.A. had done the same thing all over Ireland to maintain their position as a standing army and to keep the Free State at bay. Theirs was a deterrent posture, not an aggressive one: they saw the pro-Treatyites as the aggressors even before the outbreak of open war. If the latter-day insurrectionists had managed to provoke a British attack (as they almost did), then a genuine replay of the first rising might have taken place. But the vital fact was that it was the Irish government that struck first.

We can also turn the comparison around and re-evaluate the more familiar events of 1916. Much has been made of the role of republican spiritualism in framing and driving the Rising. Was it intended by its planners to be an inspirational 'blood sacrifice' to save Ireland's soul, with little consideration for conventional military success? First of all, even though most of the Volunteers chose not to participate come Easter Monday, a thousand or so people were willing to fight that week, most of whom did not seek martyrdom. Patrick Pearse was not Charles Manson and the rebels were not members of a mystical republican cult. As much as anything, they fought for each other, their brothers, cousins, neighbours, workmates, and friends. Nor should we see the conspirators as puppet-masters, stringing along the gullible (a common depiction in the aftermath of the Rising). They were intelligent and dedicated people, who had chosen the separatist and Volunteer world-view as their own. In fact, most of the conspirators' ideas were widely shared within the Volunteers and

---

[44] The most recent account of these events is in Bill Kissane, *Explaining Irish Democracy*, 115–39. See also Michael Hopkinson, *Green Against Green: The Irish Civil War* (Dublin, 1988), 58–76.

I.R.B.: the contempt for the Irish Party and compromise; the concomitant self-identification as the true representatives of the nation; the vanguardist will to act, regardless of public opinion or elected politicians; the framing of the political situation as a Manichaean struggle with Britain; the belief that Dublin Castle was secretly planning their destruction; and their role as the upholders of national honour. Pro- and anti-insurrectionists alike also visualized a campaign in much the same way: as a series of Boer War-style encounters, with themselves in the role of the native militia confounding a larger imperial army. Such a war was expected to last months, not days: Kathleen Clarke reported that the rebels thought they would be six months in the field, allowing time for German intervention and a popular uprising.[45] The possibility of a German landing was much discussed, and was felt by MacNeill and others to be a reasonable justification for action. The failure of this to come off in 1916 was, of course, the key to the last-minute withdrawal of many units and members, not just for MacNeill, but for the commanders in Cork and Limerick as well. No one could accuse Terence and Mary MacSwiney of lacking an ideological commitment to self-sacrifice, but they accepted MacNeill's countermanding order and the logic behind it.[46]

Finally, Pearse's and Connolly's oft-quoted language of blood and martyrdom was not only—as has often been pointed out—part of the European patriotic *Zeitgeist*, it was also part of the shared Volunteer lexicon. The same phrases were used of the people killed by British soldiers in the Bachelor's Walk massacre in July 1914. *Irish Freedom*, in August of that year, declared that 'the Volunteer movement was formally and effectively baptized, baptized in the blood of the Volunteers... The thought of arms and touch of arms have made Ireland into the thing we dreamed of. And the dawn is very near now.'[47] In October, Liam de Roiste, an armchair militant at best, wrote that it was their duty 'to carry on the old fight for Irish freedom, sanctified by the blood of the men who fought under Hugh O'Neill, Owen Roe, and Sarsfield, who struggled in '98, in 1803, in '48, in '67 for sovereign Irish independence':[48] much the same succession claimed in the Easter Proclamation. In November 1915 another writer ('C.') evoked the same lineage, and

[45] 'Conversation with Mrs Tom Clarke, 8 July 1963' (Mulcahy Papers, P7/D/2).

[46] Francis Costello, *Enduring the Most: The Life and Death of Terence MacSwiney* (Dingle, 1995), 62–72.

[47] *Irish Freedom*, Aug. 1914.

[48] *Irish Volunteer*, 10 Oct. 1914.

proclaimed that 'Today again is devotion to Ireland crowned with sacrifice and imprisonment. Today again has Ireland's soul been tortured with anxiety and longing, and her soil sanctified with the blood of her children.'[49] Such language was powerful, especially in a crisis, but it would not have been if it had only made sense to an inner circle of plotters. In the end, the Rising was the creation of public Volunteer ideology as much as of a secret conspiracy.

## Paramilitary Politics and Democracy

It is difficult to imagine the birth and survival of the Irish Volunteers and the I.R.A. without the unique progression of events starting with the parliamentary struggles over the House of Lords and home rule, leading to the creation of the U.V.F. and its backing by the Conservative Party, the passive response of the Liberal government and their Irish Party allies, and then the sudden eruption—and equally surprising longevity—of the Great War. Without an independent nationalist militia, there would have been no rising and no subsequent 'wars'. Sinn Féin might have succeeded the Irish Party as the nationalist front, accompanied by the same arrests and riots. Anger, frustration, mass mobilization, and new leadership might still have produced a revolutionary situation, threatening the authority of the British state. But without rifles and the catalyzing impact of the Easter rebellion, guerrilla and civil war might well have been averted—as in the 1880s. Thus, the decisions made by British and Irish political elites in 1912–14 were absolutely crucial in determining the pattern of politics for the following decade.

Much of what occurred was contingent upon the calculations of leaders, caucuses, and cabinets, and on the sheer unpredictable sequence of events. Nevertheless, the consequences were largely preset by the structure of party politics. The fundamental sectarian cleavage generated the same polarizing effect on either side, squeezing out class-based or other multi-ethnic parties. Popular nationalism and unionism were so constructed that each perceived the other as a permanent threat or obstacle, antithetical not only to collective goals but also to the maintenance of ethnic identity. Rival parties of ethnic or national unity had appeared simultaneously on

---

[49] *Nationality*, 27 Nov. 1915. Presumably the author was again referring to the Bachelor's Walk massacre.

this basis, similarly vulnerable to extremist insurgencies, able to play on the sense of threat. After 1912 the Unionist Party managed this threat, in part by building up a disciplined militia to absorb any loyalist challenge. The Irish Party chose a purely parliamentary strategy, relying on British institutions and elites to solve their problem. Unlike unionism, national-ism was institutionally divided between Irish Party organizations and a separate cluster of non- or anti-Party groups. A group of these alternative activists decided to meet the threat of the U.V.F. and the perceived anti-home rule conspiracy behind it, as the logic of the struggle—and soon public opinion—demanded. One side could not sit by while the other gained a clear advantage in power by acquiring arms. The same logic would work in reverse in 1920–1, when the U.V.F. was revived in 1920 in response to the rise of the I.R.A.

The Volunteers were the creature of sheer opportunity seized by ideo-logical entrepreneurs, and they too were bound by a clear set of rational choices. In strategic terms, the possibility of insurrection was not an irrational fantasy: it was built into the basic structure of events once Irish politics were (para)militarized in 1913. Even the U.V.F. leadership contemplated a pre-emptive operation, and threatened to act independ-ently. The joint failure of the Liberal government and the Irish Party to monopolize armed force provided the means. The presence of republican revolutionaries provided the motive, although attempted conscription or suppression would probably have had much the same result. But beyond ideology or circumstance, the very logic of the situation dictated the availability of an offensive option as a possible strategy. The same was and is true for paramilitaries everywhere who declare their role to be defensive, but harbour an aspirational political agenda. In a version of the prisoner's dilemma, the actors have essentially two choices: act and risk defeat, or wait and risk suppression before having the chance to act. Everything depends on the calculation of the opponent's strategy.

The resulting tension between offensive and defensive strategies, along with the cyclical struggle between loyal, semiloyal, and disloyal factions, defined (and perhaps still defines) the history of the Irish Volunteers/I.R.A. and was one of the crucial dynamics of the revolution. Another was the relationship between democracy and violence. Paramilitaries were a symptom of state and democratic failure: the fate of community and nation were at stake and the government was not trusted to defend their rights of self-government or self-preservation. Only when the new post-partition regimes were established did the majority of both ethnic groups transfer their trust and allegiance back to the state and its armed forces. Full democracy was restored once ethnic sovereignty or security was achieved. The introduction of paramilitary politics illustrates the difficulty—or even impossibility—of a fully democratic outcome to the Irish question in the early twentieth century.

# 5

# The Social Structure of the Irish Republican Army

W. B. Yeats 'met them at close of day | Coming with vivid faces | From counter or desk'.[1] Edith Somerville dismissed them variously as 'tom fools' and 'half-educated cads and upstarts'.[2] Erskine Childers praised them as 'the soul of a new Ireland, taken as a whole the finest young men in the country'.[3] To their neighbours and supporters, they were most often simply 'the boys'. 'They' were the Irish Volunteers—after 1919 the Irish Republican Army—and the question of what sort of people they were is a crucial one for our understanding of the organization, and of the Irish revolution as a whole.

The I.R.A. was part of a much wider phenomenon of martial voluntarism sweeping Ireland between 1912 and 1922. Republican men joined the Volunteers, republican women formed Cumann na mBan, and republican boys had Fianna Éireann. For republican socialists there was the independent Irish Citizen Army.[4] The republican 'army' and its auxiliaries were preceded by the unionist Ulster Volunteer Force and the Irish Party's rival National Volunteers. Both of these bodies in turn delivered recruits to the Irish (10th and 16th) Divisions of the New Army. The Ulster

[1] W.B. Yeats, 'Easter 1916'.
[2] Edith Somerville to Col. John Somerville, 24 Nov. 1917; Somerville to Ethel Smyth, 22 Apr. 1922 (Queen's University Special Collections, Somerville and Ross Papers, Lots 877 and 878).
[3] Erskine Childers, 'The Irish Revolution', p. 8 (Trinity College, Dublin Library, Childers Papers, MS 7808/29).
[4] Although this was largely confined to Dublin and effectively defunct after 1916.

Special Constabulary and the Irish Free State's National Army put yet more men into new uniforms in 1921 and 1922.

Nevertheless, it is the partisans of the republic who stand out as the leading actors in the revolutionary drama. Theirs was by far the most aggressive and violent organization of the 'troubles'. It was they who launched the Easter Rising of 1916 and precipitated the subsequent guerrilla wars, thereby claiming the lion's share of victims.[5] What set these men apart from their school- and workmates and neighbours? How did they become warriors, killers, and martyrs?

At the time, these questions were usually answered in terms of moral or national character. The rebels were—depending on one's point of view—selfless patriots, nihilist fanatics, or depraved thugs. The revolution was represented as either a national awakening or criminal anarchy. Historians since have rarely addressed the rebels' social identity, and those who have done so have generally confined themselves to local studies covering only a portion of the revolutionary period. Many assumptions— about the Volunteers' youth, gender, class, religion, ethnicity, politics, and motives, and how these may have changed over time—therefore remain untested.

Surprisingly, however, useful data for this task are plentiful rather than scarce. For a 'secret army', the guerrillas left an extraordinary paper trail through their own and their opponents' records, as well as in the daily and weekly press. This continued long after the wars were over, as gunmen claimed pensions, wrote memoirs, and commemorated themselves and their comrades. Once identified, their personal and family histories can be tracked back even further through census and land records. The same or analogous sources supply a similar range of information on the members of allied or opposed organizations. Using this material, what follows is a social profile of the I.R.A. and associated groups, encompassing the whole of Ireland (and Britain) from 1916 to 1923.


## Joining and Belonging

Psychological analysis and the 'terrorist personality'[6] aside, there are many different ways to ask who joined the I.R.A. How old were they?

---

[5] See Chs. 2 and 3.

[6] For a variety of psychological perspectives, see Walter Reich (ed.), *Origins of Terrorism* (Cambridge, 1990).

Were they married? What sort of work did they do? How much property did they or their families own? Where did they live? How did members of the I.R.A. compare with those of other organizations?

Answering these questions also requires a definition of what it meant to belong. Membership and commitment ebbed and flowed as the levels of risk and political popularity rose and fell. On paper, the army's strength peaked at over 100,000 during the 1918 conscription crisis, and at over 70,000 after the July 1921 Truce.[7] In early 1921, at the height of the guerrilla war against Britain, and again in early 1922, after the I.R.A. split over the Anglo-Irish Treaty, a third or more of these men dropped off unit rolls.[8] By October of the latter year, the Volunteers—now fighting a second war against the Irish Free State—had lost around 90 per cent of their pre-Treaty strength.[9] Well over 100,000 men were Volunteers at some point during the revolution, but many were involved for only a few months, and only a small fraction belonged from beginning to end.

Joining was not the same as participation, however. The I.R.A. was divided territorially into fifty-odd brigades (the number changed nearly every year), and further subdivided into battalions and companies. Every unit distinguished between members who were reliable and unreliable; between those who were active and those who were not. Broadly speaking, 'reliable' men could be called upon to perform occasional tasks, while 'active' men were regularly engaged in actual operations. Between 1919 and 1921 only one- to two-thirds of even the most aggressive companies were deemed reliable by their officers: less than half of the Mid-Clare and Sligo Brigades, around 60 per cent of the Dublin Brigade.[10] Activists represented an even smaller fraction of the total membership—usually less than 20 per cent—except in the later stages of the Civil War, when the rest of the army simply melted away.

It is this active and reliable core of committed guerrillas—'the men who count', in the words of Cathal Brugha[11]—who are the primary subjects of

[7] Dorothy Macardle, *The Irish Republic* (London, 1937), 241; Army strength tables, Oct. and Nov. 1921 (University College Dublin Archives [UCD], Richard Mulcahy Papers, P17a/18).

[8] For the situation in 1921, see North Cork Bde. company rolls, Feb.–June 1921 (National Library of Ireland [NLI], Florence O'Donoghue Papers, MS 31,223). For 1922, see North Cork Bde. report, 29 Feb. 1922 (UCD, Ernie O'Malley Papers, P17a/87); Carlow Bde. reports (O'Malley Papers, P17a/73, 74).

[9] See 1st Southern Div. strength report, c.Oct. 1922 (O'Malley Papers, P17a/89); O/C 1st Southern Div. to Deputy C/S., 2 Mar. 1923 (P17a/90).

[10] Fitzpatrick, *Politics and Irish Life*, 219; Sligo Bde. returns, June 1921 (Mulcahy Papers, P7/A/22); 'Figures for Companies Working', 2nd Bn., Dublin Bde. (NLI, MS 901).

[11] *Official Report: Debate on the Treaty between Great Britain and Ireland* (Dublin, 1922), 329.

this study and who largely populate its statistical samples, numbering approximately 5,000 Volunteers. This focus is partly a reflection of the main available sources. Newspapers, Royal Irish Constabulary, British, and National Army records, prison registers, and I.R.A. rolls provide the ranks, addresses, occupations, and ages of those men who were under police surveillance, or were arrested, imprisoned, or killed.[12] Since most of these men came to public or official attention by virtue of their activity, it was the activists' vital statistics that got recorded.

The resulting membership sample (see Tables 9, 11, 17) is divided between officers and other ranks, and between three periods of time, corresponding roughly to different stages of the revolution: those of mass movement (1917–19), open insurrection against the British government (1920–1), and civil war against its northern and southern successor states (1922–3). Figures for the Easter Rising of 1916 are presented separately. Many individuals appear in the figures for more than one period. The sample has also been divided geographically, first between Dublin and provincial Ireland, and then between the four provinces of Munster, Leinster, Connaught, and Ulster. Again because of its sources, the sample favours the more active units in Dublin and Munster.

## Status and Class

The I.R.A. drew members from every walk of life and from every sector of the Irish economy. The appeal of militant republicanism crossed all occupational boundaries. Nevertheless, certain professions stand out as contributing more than their share of rebels, among them the building trades (carpenters, plasterers, bricklayers, painters), drapers' assistants, creamery workers, hairdressers, and teachers. As in other countries and revolutions, medical students and shoe- and bootmakers were in the vanguard. Other groups, such as fishermen and dock labourers, were almost completely unrepresented.

Table 9 groups I.R.A. members into broad categories of employment. The comparative census figures from 1911 and 1926 describe all occupied adult men. The former include all of Ireland; the latter only the twenty-six counties which made up the Irish Free State. Since Northern Ireland was

---

[12] Many of these sources by themselves provide only partial information: addresses and ages only, in the case of General Prisons Board files (National Archives), for example. For the derivation of particular samples, see the notes to tables.

TABLE 9.  *Occupations of Volunteers in provincial Ireland, 1917–1923*
(% ages)

| | Officers | | | Men | | | Census | |
|---|---|---|---|---|---|---|---|---|
| | 1917–19 | 1920–1 | 1922–3 | 1917–19 | 1920–1 | 1922–3 | 1911 | 1926 |
| Sample | 682 | 461 | 150 | 1,439 | 1,985 | 1,089 | | |
| Farmer/son | 27 | 22 | 21 | 40 | 29 | 13 | 36 | 49 |
| Farm labourer | 5 | 4 | 8 | 11 | 12 | 19 | 22 | 17 |
| Un/semi-skilled | 4 | 5 | 9 | 9 | 15 | 27 | 10 | |
| Skilled | 23 | 26 | 28 | 16 | 19 | 23 | 9 | |
| Shop asst./clerk | 19 | 22 | 19 | 12 | 14 | 11 | 4 | |
| Professional | 9 | 7 | 7 | 1 | 4 | 2 | 2 | |
| Merchant/son | 10 | 12 | 4 | 7 | 5 | 2 | 4 | |
| Student | 1 | 0.3 | — | 1 | 1 | 1 | 1 | |
| Other | 3 | 4 | 3 | 2 | 2 | 3 | 4 | |

*Source*: This table covers the whole of Ireland except for the Dublin urban area. Men described simply as 'labourers' were categorized as 'farm labourers' (70%) or as 'unskilled' (30%). 'Shop assistants' include clerks; 'professionals' include teachers. These figures were assembled from a large number of sources, primarily: *Irish Times* and *Cork Examiner*, 1917–23; R.I.C. County Inspectors' monthly reports, 1917–21: PRO, CO 904/102–16 and reports of illegal drilling, 1917–18: CO 904/122; Irish Command Dublin District raid and search reports, 1920–1: PRO, WO 35/70–9, reports of military courts of inquiry, 1920–2: WO 35/146A–160 and register of prisoners in military prisons: WO 35/143; National Army prisoners' location books, charge records and prison ledgers, 1922–4: MA, P/1–6 and miscellaneous; I.R.A. prison rolls, 1923: MA, A/1135; A/1137; A/1138; A/1185. The division of occupations into categories follows Guy Routh, *Occupations and Pay in Great Britain 1906–79* (London, 1980).

more urban and industrialized, the differences are considerable. Nevertheless, because the majority of the northern population was hostile to the I.R.A. by virtue of their political and religious loyalties, and because the great bulk of the active membership (and the sample) lived in southern Ireland, the 1926 numbers are a better reflection of the organization's pool of potential recruits.

If we compare provincial Volunteers with employed adult men as a whole, some clear patterns emerge. Those who worked behind counters or desks—shop assistants and clerks—made up only 4 per cent of the workforce outside Dublin but accounted for one-tenth to one-fifth of the active I.R.A. membership. Skilled tradesmen and artisans were also twice or three times as likely to be found in the I.R.A. as in the general population. Those who fell into the un- or semi-skilled category tended not to be casual labourers but rather porters, drivers, factory workers, or the like. These were men with steady jobs for the most part, few of whom were unemployed until the recession of 1921.[13]

Agriculture absorbed most of Ireland's male labour, so its consistent under-representation in the ranks of the I.R.A. is the most notable aspect of these statistics. It is also the one we can explore furthest, as we can contrast the 1911 and 1926 census figures and break down the former by age and religion. This allows us to compare I.R.A. members solely with members of their own generation, roughly identifiable in the 1911 census as occupied men aged 15 to 44 (for volunteers' ages, see below). Farmers and their sons made up only 32 per cent of this age group (as opposed to 38 per cent of adult men), while the percentage who were labourers rose to 24 per cent (from 22 per cent). Younger people were thus slightly less likely to work on farms, so the gap between volunteers and their age cohort was less than with the general population. This probably remained true in 1926, but that year's census also shows a much larger proportion of farmers and a lower proportion of farm labourers than in 1911. As already noted, the later figures are a better description of the I.R.A.'s recruitment pool in ethnic and geographic terms, and they also reflect social change over the intervening sixteen-year period. The pre-war numbers must be judged accordingly.

In addition, since Volunteers were overwhelmingly Catholic (see below), perhaps this should also be taken into account in defining the guerrillas' peer group. In this case, the rurality gap between organization and population widens, as Catholic men were more likely to be 'persons engaged in agriculture' (42 per cent were farmers and sons, 24 per cent were labourers in 1911). Thus, the guerrillas' ethnic reference group was more rural than the general population, while their age group was less so. Ultimately, all of these statistics still point to the same conclusion. Except for rank-and-file members between 1917 and 1919, considerably less than half the Volunteers worked on farms, whether as sons or employees: a significant deficit in a predominantly agricultural economy.

Throughout the revolution, then, the guerrillas were disproportionately skilled, trained, and urban. As Table 17 demonstrates, this was a genuinely national characteristic, shared by units in every part of the

[13] Exact employment figures are unavailable, but there is a large body of more impressionistic evidence to support this statement, including many newspaper and other reports that name volunteers' employers.

country. The boys of Connaught may have been more likely to be working on a farm than the boys of Leinster, but both were less likely to be doing so than their provincial peers. The same was not true of their parents. A study of over a thousand fathers of Volunteers in county Cork shows that the majority were farmers and almost none had white-collar jobs.[14] Most Volunteers had grown up on farms but, unlike their fathers, only half or fewer had stayed. Again, this set them somewhat apart from their peers as well as their parents. According to Michael Hout's study of social mobility in Ireland, 58 per cent of farmer's sons born between 1908 and 1925 were still working on family farms at age 20.[15]

As the revolution progressed, it accentuated some of these tendencies. Rural volunteers became even less prominent after 1919, while tradesmen became more so. In the Civil War, though, we can also detect a shift towards a more proletarian army, as farmers' and merchants' sons were replaced by un- or semi-skilled workers. However, as new members were scarce in the republican 'legion of the rearguard', these represent shifts in commitment rather than in recruitment. After 1921, the question was not so much who was joining as who was leaving.

The urban orientation of the I.R.A. is all the more striking when compared to what republicans themselves thought. In this regard, one G.H.Q. inspector's opinion could stand for many: 'the population of all towns is bad. A little terrorism might have a good effect.'[16] Florence O'Donoghue was thus reflecting a strong consensus among I.R.A. men when he wrote that urban nationalism was 'shallow and rootless', the Volunteers being 'predominantly a product of the country, having deeper roots in old traditions'.[17] This view of the rebellion as an expression of an ancient, 'hidden Ireland' was endorsed by Daniel Corkery, the influential nationalist writer, who added that the town–country 'antithesis' was 'one of those inevitable, deeply-based differences that not every historian takes notice of'.[18]

Corkery was correct in his view of historians, if not in his theory of history. For many years, the only social descriptions of the rebels were

[14] Fathers' occupations were derived from the manuscript returns for the 1911 census in the National Archives [NA]. Tom Garvin found a similar pattern in his study of the 'IRB/Sinn Féin/I.R.A. elite' between 1913 and 1922: 'The Anatomy of a Nationalist Revolution: Ireland, 1858–1928', *Comparative Studies in Society and History*, 28 (1986), 485.

[15] Out of a survey sample of 561 farmers' sons: Michael Hout, *Following in Father's Footsteps: Social Mobility in Ireland* (Cambridge, 1989), 127.

[16] G.H.Q. inspector's report on Roscommon and Leitrim, 17 Oct. 1921 (MA, A/0747).

[17] Florence O'Donoghue, *Tomas MacCurtain: Soldier and Patriot* (Tralee, 1955), 59.

[18] Daniel Corkery, Foreword to ibid. 11.

provided by the 'instant histories' of W. Alison Phillips and Sir James O'Connor. Phillips's *The Revolution in Ireland*, which made use of confidential R.I.C. files, categorized the Volunteers (or 'Sinn Féiners', a blanket term) as 'shop assistants and town labourers'.[19] In O'Connor's equally unfriendly view (*A History of Ireland 1798–1924*), 'the "war" was the work of two thousand men and boys, nearly all of them of a low grade of society—farm hands, shop hands and the like'.[20] A contemporary but less scholarly 'study', *The Real Ireland*, was the work of C. H. Bretherton, the *Morning Post*'s Hibernophobic and libellous reporter in Ireland. By his account, the guerrillas were 'a horde of proletarians, grocers' curates, farm labourers, porters, stable boys, car-conductors and what not'.[21] The variously dismissive tones used indicate both disdain and the perceived obviousness of the question, but it is interesting to note the mention of shop assistants and the absence of farmers in each case.

The pioneering analysis of the social composition of the Volunteers came with David Fitzpatrick's path-breaking study of the revolution in county Clare, *Politics and Irish Life*. His findings do reveal an overwhelmingly farm-based rank and file in 1917–19, led by a somewhat less agricultural officer corps. Clare itself was intensely rural and quite poor, so this is not surprising. Fitzpatrick does not provide occupational figures for the years after 1919, so we do not know if Clare matched the nationwide decline in farming Volunteers. However, he does describe the emergence of a town–country divide in 1921, with the guerrillas favouring the countryside.[22]

More recently, Joost Augusteijn has examined the general membership of ten companies in four brigades as of July 1921, and concludes that 'although active members...had a predominantly urban background, the larger part of the rank and file in the provinces was rural'.[23] This is an interesting hypothesis, but an unproven one because, as Augusteijn's careful presentation shows, none of his chosen companies are in urban areas, and he assumes that sons automatically shared their fathers' occupations (as recorded in the 1911 census). As detailed above, such was not the case.

[19] W. Alison Phillips, *The Revolution in Ireland* (London, 1923), 176–7.
[20] Sir James O'Connor, *A History of Ireland 1798–1924*, vol. 2 (London, 1925), 296.
[21] C. H. Bretherton, *The Real Ireland* (London, 1925), 80. This book was withdrawn soon after publication because of threatened lawsuits. For further social and frankly racial analysis, see Bretherton, 'Irish Backgrounds', *Atlantic Monthly* (Dec. 1922), 692–3.
[22] Fitzpatrick, *Politics and Irish Life*, 202–4, 220–4.
[23] Augusteijn, *From Public Defiance to Guerrilla Warfare*, 353.

For those Volunteers who were farmers or farmers' sons, social status was defined not by occupation alone, but also by the value and size of their land. The former is the best guide to a farmer's worth, as an acre of land might be meadow or bog, entirely productive or wholly useless. Unfortunately, sufficient data on property can only properly be collected on a local basis, so my sample in Table 10 is confined to county Cork. From these numbers we can see that I.R.A. family farms (mostly still owned by their parents) were well above the county average in rateable value. At any point during the revolution, the typical volunteer would have been significantly better off than many of his neighbours. The same pattern emerges if we substitute acreage as the unit of comparison. I.R.A. farms tended to be substantially larger than average as well. As with occupations, the I.R.A. tended to draw its members not from the highest or lowest in society, but from the middling ranks in between.[24]

The Dublin city I.R.A. had no farmers, of course, but did it otherwise conform to provincial patterns? Dublin's data are presented in Table 11. Like their country comrades, the Dublin brigades drew heavily on the skilled trades, shops, and offices. Unlike other areas, however, they depended to a greater degree on unskilled members at the outset (again, usually not casual or general labourers) but became less working-class and more white-collar as time went on. Other cities followed a different course, however. The Cork city battalions moved in the opposite direction, being much more likely to have unskilled workers in 1922–3 than in earlier years.[25]

Were officers very different from their men? Outside Dublin, they were much more likely to live in towns or cities, and to be employed in skilled

TABLE 10. *Median value of Volunteers' family farms in county Cork*

| | Officers | | | Men | | | Census |
|---|---|---|---|---|---|---|---|
| | 1917–19 | 1920–1 | 1922–3 | 1917–19 | 1920–1 | 1922–3 | 1911 |
| Sample | 44 | 78 | 17 | 210 | 356 | 72 | |
| Value (£) | 31 | 24 | 23 | 22 | 20 | 25 | 14 |

*Sources*: This table was assembled from manuscript census returns (NA) and land valuation records (Irish Valuation Office). Official valuations often underestimated the real productivity or saleable price of land, but they do provide a reasonable measure of the relative value of different farms.

[24] Joost Augusteijn reaches a broadly similar conclusion for Volunteers as of July 1921: ibid. 360–2.

[25] See *The I.R.A. and Its Enemies*.

TABLE 11.  *Occupations of Volunteers in Dublin, 1917–1923*

| | Officers | | | Men | | | Census | |
|---|---|---|---|---|---|---|---|---|
| | 1917–19 | 1920–1 | 1922–3 | 1917–19 | 1920–1 | 1922–3 | 1911 | 1926 |
| Sample | 49 | 86 | 19 | 201 | 507 | 122 | | |
| Un/semi-skilled | 31 | 27 | 26 | 43 | 46 | 37 | 35 | 44 |
| Skilled | 24 | 23 | 21 | 33 | 23 | 23 | | 23 |
| Shop Asst./clerk | 22 | 32 | 32 | 17 | 18 | 35 | | 15 |
| Professional | 12 | 9 | 11 | 0.5 | 2 | 1 | 2 | 4 |
| Merchant/son | 4 | 6 | 5 | 1 | 3 | — | 5 | 5 |
| Student | 2 | 1 | — | 3 | 3 | 2 | 2 | 2 |
| Other | 4 | 2 | 5 | 1 | 4 | 1 | 3 | 6 |

*Note*: This area includes the suburban towns of Rathmines, Blackrock, etc., and is roughly coterminus with the Dublin Metropolitan Police District. The census figures for 1911 do not include much of this suburban area, and so are not strictly comparable with the 1926 data.

and middle-class jobs. The same gap in occupational status can be found in the capital, albeit to a lesser degree. Far more officers were professionals or were involved in shopkeeping, and fewer were unskilled working men, but tradesmen were spread equally among the ranks. Provincial officers did become more working-class and less mercantile after the Treaty split, and the gap closed somewhat where farm values and sizes were concerned, but a noticeable difference remained. Perhaps most noteworthy was the scarcity of farm labourers among the lieutenants, captains, and commandants who ran the movement in the parishes. Farmers did far better than their servants in this respect. It was not impossible for employees to command their employers, but the reality was usually the other way around.

Another noteworthy difference between the ranks is that there was much less change over time in officers' backgrounds than there was among ordinary Volunteers. If we add up the percentage differences in each occupational category as we move from period to period, we find that officers' numbers shifted by a total of 33 per cent between 1917 and 1923, while the total for their men was 57 per cent. Officers were significantly more stable as a group. Of course, this could at least partly be attributed to variations in samples, but it is probably also related to the fact that officers were much more likely to be activists—which was usually how they acquired their rank in the first place. This heightened sense of commitment meant they were also far less likely to drop out or abandon the republican cause. As evidence of this, the difference between officers and men was greatest between 1921 and 1922. The guerrillas who fought the Free State were, by and large, the same men who had led the struggle against the Black and Tans.

Did occupation or social status determine who joined a particular unit? Companies were often formed around a particular workplace, but any kind of stratification—let alone segregation—between units seems to have been very rare. One apparent exception was the Limerick city I.R.A. Here the Volunteers fell out after the Easter Rising, when the local 'boys' failed to rise alongside Dublin. This was not unusual, but the consequences were. The rival factions split and each formed its own battalion, which stayed apart until 1921. The division was not merely political or personal, but also social. The old guard of the 1st Battalion, criticized for their inactivity, 'was nearly confined to the rugby clubs', while the combative 2nd Battalion 'were more working men'.[26] 'The 2nd Battalion were a different type of people—decent fellows but they were all working people. The 1st Battalion were all white collar workers...I think that was one of the reasons the 1st Battalion didn't like them—the fact that they were all working men.'[27] This division along class lines was, as far as I know, unique.[28]

## Age and Marriage

The Volunteers were much more homogenous when it came to age and marital status. According to the sample presented in Table 12, at least three-quarters were in their late teens or twenties in any given year, and less than 5 per cent were 40 or older. Officers were much less likely to be adolescents, especially after 1921, and were consistently—if only slightly—older as a group. The membership as a whole matured by one year over the six years between 1917 and 1923. This suggests that, while hundreds of activists remained in the struggle for the whole period—and raised the average age as a consequence—turnover in the membership kept the median age fairly constant. Some new recruits continued to

---

[26] Interviews with Sean Hynes and George Embrush (O'Malley Papers, P17b/129, 130).

[27] Richard Mulcahy interview with Lt.-Gen. Peadar McMahon (Mulcahy Papers, P7D/43). See also Deputy C/S report on Mid-Limerick Bde., 7 Nov. 1921 (MA, A/0739).

[28] Although the rugby republicans of Limerick do bear a certain resemblance to the Irish Rugby Football Union 'Pals' Company of the 7th Royal Dublin Fusiliers, formed in 1914. See David Fitzpatrick, 'The Logic of Collective Sacrifice: Ireland and the British Army, 1914–1918', *Historical Journal*, 38 (1995), 1029–30.

TABLE 12.   *Ages of Volunteers in Ireland*

|  | Officers | | | Men | | |
|---|---|---|---|---|---|---|
|  | 1917–19 | 1920–1 | 1922–3 | 1917–19 | 1920–1 | 1922–3 |
| Sample | 675 | 561 | 335 | 2,052 | 2,722 | 1,409 |
| % age-under 20 | 14 | 11 | 3 | 23 | 20 | 17 |
| 20–9 | 65 | 68 | 73 | 59 | 68 | 75 |
| 30–9 | 20 | 19 | 20 | 14 | 9 | 7 |
| 40–9 | 2 | 2 | 3 | 3 | 2 | 1 |
| 50–9 | 1 | 1 | — | 1 | 0.1 | 0.1 |
| Median age | 25 | 25 | 26 | 23 | 24 | 24 |

*Sources*: In addition to the sources listed for the occupational sample, the ages of jailed Volunteers can be found in the Defence of the Realm Act (DORA) Prisoner Records, Cartons 3–6 (NA, General Prison Board records) and in the Art O'Brien Papers (NLI, MS 8443–5). Ages were calculated as of 1918, 1920, and 1922.

trickle in (at least until 1922), and other members faded out as they got older.

The typical Volunteer was not only youthful but also unmarried. The two go together, of course, but I.R.A. members were unusually unwed even by Irish standards. Four per cent of men aged 20–4 in the Irish Free State were married in 1926, rising to 20 per cent among those aged 25–9.[29] Out of a sample of 572 I.R.A. prisoners in 1923 whose marital status is known—and whose median age was 25—less than 5 per cent (27) were married.[30] And, since a higher proportion of the population was married in urban areas (32 per cent of those aged 25–9), where most active Volunteers lived, the marital gap between them and their peers was probably even greater.

Being young and single meant that Irish guerrillas had less to risk (although, of course, celibacy might have been a consequence of activism as well as a contributing factor). It could also mean that they had more to rebel against. A man's position in his community depended as much upon age as upon income, land, or occupation. For most I.R.A. men, this put them in a very subordinate position. 'The boys' were farmers' or shop-keepers' sons rather than owners; apprentices or journeymen rather than

[29] Robert E. Kennedy, *The Irish: Emigration, Marriage, and Fertility* (Berkeley, 1973), 169.
[30] I.R.A. prison and internment camp rolls, 1923 (MA, A/1135, 1137, 1138).

tradesmen or masters; junior clerks and assistant teachers. Property, money, and security, like marriage, lay in the future.[31]


## Gender and Religion

To report that I.R.A. membership was exclusively male may state the obvious, but the first thing that needs to be said about the gender exclusivity of the Volunteers is that it was not representative of the revolution as a whole. There was nothing inherently masculine about militant republicanism. Thousands of women believed as fervently and participated as enthusiastically, either as members of Sinn Féin or Cumann na mBan (a women's paramilitary organization allied to the Volunteers) or as individuals outside any formal body.

Nevertheless, it is one of the interesting features of the revolution that women were often equal—and equally violent—participants in its early stages, but were increasingly confined to an auxiliary role as the movement drifted into guerrilla war. As the front lines of the campaign moved from marching, canvassing, and street fighting in 1917 and 1918 to ambush and assassination in 1919 and 1920, women found themselves left in the rear echelons. They were active still, but largely left out of the action. The Volunteers—and armed struggle—remained a boys' club throughout.[32] The guerrillas' rise to power within the movement was only complete in 1920, however, and was still contested thereafter. It took time for the I.R.A. to emerge as a distinctive entity within the republican movement, and masculinization was an integral part of this militarization. This changed again after the 1921 Truce, when politics came up from underground, and in 1922 and 1923, when most male activists were interned or on the run. Elections and prisoners' rights became key battlegrounds again, as in 1917 and 1918, and women returned to the fray. Gender was an active, transitive element in the movement, not a fixed point.[33]

Politics was not shared as easily across religious lines. Republican women were numerous; Protestant republicans of either sex were extremely rare.

---

[31] For further discussion of the social dimensions of the Volunteers' youth, see Peter Hart, 'Youth Culture and the Cork I.R.A.', in Fitzpatrick (ed.), *Revolution? Ireland, 1917–1923*.

[32] Several women had carried arms in the 1916 Rising, as members of the Irish Citizen Army.

[33] See Sarah Benton, 'Women Disarmed: The Militarization of Politics in Ireland 1913–23', *Feminist Review*, 50 (1995), 148–72.

Non-Catholic guerrillas were almost non-existent. It is perhaps enough to say that, in this most religious of countries, there were far more 'pagans'—as atheists or non-practising Catholics were often known—than Protestants in the I.R.A.[34] A survey of 917 prisoners convicted under the Defence of the Realm Act in 1917–19, for example, produced one declared 'agnostic' and no Protestants.[35] This did not make the army merely or mainly a religious or ethnic militia. It was officially a secular organization open to all Irishmen, and this aspect of its formal constitution, with its implication of even-handedness, was taken seriously by a great many of its officers and men. Nor did its members, however pious, feel obliged to submit to the will of their priests or bishops, even under threat of excommunication, as in the Civil War. Some early Volunteers did listen to their priests and dropped out of the organization when it became violent and illegal but, almost by definition, these had not been activists.

In fact, Irish republicanism had a long history of political anticlericalism, going back to its roots in the 1790s. This must not be confused with any lack of faith. The overwhelming majority were believing and—except where clerical opposition kept them temporarily out of church—practising Catholics. And Catholicism was certainly part of republican politics and of the Volunteers' self-image. The symbolism and rhetoric of hunger strikes, or of I.R.A. obituaries and funerals, are proof enough of that. The existence of a few acknowledged atheists among the guerrillas is interesting, but on an individual level only. I do not think they even formed a self-conscious subculture within the movement. It must also be emphasized that, while nearly all republicans were Catholics, and nearly all Irish Catholics were nationalists, only a minority of Catholics were revolutionaries or supporters of an armed struggle. The *ethnos* did not collectively acknowledge the army as 'theirs', any more than the army wholly or officially acknowledged its identity as ethnic, at least in any sectarian sense.

On the other hand, the Volunteers' corporate and essentially singular religious identity did inevitably shape their attitudes and behaviour, especially toward Protestants. Revolutionary violence in both northern and southern Ireland grew increasingly sectarian as it escalated, leading ultimately to massacres and expulsions in 1921 and 1922.[36] Volunteers did

---

[34] There were at least half-a-dozen I.R.A. activists in county Cork alone who had left the Catholic Church. I know of only three Protestant guerrillas—and only a few more inactive members—in the whole of Ireland in this period.

[35] GPB DORA Prisoner Records, Cartons 3–6.

[36] See Ch. 9.

not generally see themselves as tribal vigilantes, and neither should historians, but the fact that their victims often did should not surprise us
either.


# 1916

Before 1917 the Irish Volunteers were neither a mass movement nor a
revolutionary underground. After splitting from the Irish Party and its
followers in 1914 over service in the British army, the organization—
recovering and growing slowly—was largely ignored until the rising of
1916. This event changed everything. Many old members dropped out,
and a wave of new recruits flooded into the old units and established
hundreds of new ones of their own. The movement that emerged was not
only much larger but also vastly more energetic and ambitious. This
transformation was symbolized by the gradual—albeit unofficial—
adoption of a new title: the Irish Republican Army.

No such transformation occurred in the organization's social profile,
however. Table 13 shows the occupations of men interned in Britain in
May and June 1916. Here we see the revolution in prototype: the same
urban bias, concentrated in the same white-collar and skilled trades.


TABLE 13.  *Occupations of 1916 internees (% ages)*

|  | Provincial 1911 Census | | Dublin 1911 Census | |
| --- | --- | --- | --- | --- |
| Sample | 497 | | 872 | |
| Farmer/son | 29 | 38 | | |
| Farm Labourer | 9 | 22 | | |
| Un/semi-skilled | 16 | | 36 | 35 |
| Skilled | 19 | | 40 | |
| Shop Asst./clerk | 15 | | 18 | |
| Professional | 3 | | 1 | 2 |
| Merchant/son | 6 | | 1 | 5 |
| Student | 0.4 | | 1 | 2 |
| Other | 4 | | 3 | 3 |

*Source*: The names, addresses, and in some cases the occupations of internees were reported in
newspapers at the time, and reprinted in total in the *Weekly Irish Times Sinn Féin Rebellion
Handbook* (Dublin, 1917). The Dublin numbers include members of the Irish Citizen Army,
which was subsequently absorbed by the Volunteers.

In fact, when seen in this context, the 40 per cent of members in 1917–19 who were farmers' sons appears as a blip in the history of the movement, a product perhaps of the mass resistance to conscription in 1917 and 1918. Once this threat to rural homesteads passed and armed conflict began, the I.R.A. returned to its more urban, working-class roots.

If we compare the statistics for Dublin in 1916 and after, one feature that stands out is the very high proportion of skilled workers among the rebels. Their subsequent decline in importance can thus be seen as a long-term trend that began in 1917: the opposite of what was happening in the country units. This apparent difference might simply be due to the drop in the number of farmers' sons in the country brigades, however, rather than to the behaviour of the tradesmen themselves. Fewer of the former meant that a greater proportion of rebels were the latter.

The broad continuity between the pre- and post-Rising Volunteers probably also extended to age. Unfortunately, internees' ages were not published. In county Cork, the median age of Volunteers in 1916 was 27, two to four years older than the national average in 1917. This suggests that the flood of new members and the departure of others after 1916 did add youth—and adolescence. But this represented a moderate shift rather than a real break with the past.

These data do have a few shortcomings, which should be noted. First of all, there is no way to separate officers from men. This is less important in 1916, however, as the distinction did not matter nearly as much then. One group of 'leaders' who can be analysed are those convicted by court-martial in Dublin in 1916. Out of this sample of 101 people, 27 per cent were skilled workers, 16 per cent were clerks or shop assistants, 7 per cent were merchants, 19 per cent were professionals, and another 19 per cent were labourers.[37] Although more firmly middle class, this group does resemble the I.R.A. officers who followed in their wake.

Secondly, an indeterminate but small number of internees were not Volunteers. The effect of this possible distortion can be checked by comparing the backgrounds of 63 internees from county Cork who are part of the sample in Table 13 with a control study of 212 Cork Volunteers who paraded at Easter.[38] As this reveals little difference between the two results, and as it can be confirmed that most of the internees were indeed

---

[37] Brendan MacGiolla Choille (ed.), *Intelligence Notes 1913–16* (Dublin, 1966), 257–70.

[38] A complete list of the Corkmen who paraded at Easter can be found in Florence O'Donoghue, 'History of the Irish Volunteers' (NLI, O'Donoghue Papers, MS 31,437). For further detail, see *The I.R.A. and Its Enemies*.

Volunteers, the numbers seem acceptable. Also, since provincial internment orders were based on police recommendation, the sample does tend
to capture activists rather than the passive majority. Thus, the 1916 results
are at least roughly comparable to the figures for later years.

## Sinn Féin, the British I.R.A., and the National Army

How did the membership of the I.R.A. compare with that of Sinn Féin?
Both organizations acquired a massive membership in a single burst of
political and ideological energy following the Rising, and both numbered
their branches in the hundreds. Unfortunately, much less data is available
on party activists, and almost none for Dublin or for the rest of the
country after 1919. The figures presented in Table 14 are therefore
more suggestive than conclusive.

Nevertheless, this sample does suggest that the parallels ran even
deeper, and that political and military republicanism appealed most
strongly to the same social groups. Many of these individuals were officers
of their local clubs, and as a group they closely resemble I.R.A. officers of
the same period in being generally urban, broadly middle class or aspiring
to it, and in not being farmers or unskilled labourers. Such a resemblance

TABLE 14.    *Provincial Sinn Féin activists, 1917–1919*

(a) *Occupation* (%: sample = 131)

| Farmer/ son | Farm labourer | Un/ semi-skilled | Skilled | Shop assistant/ Clerk | Professional | Merchant/ son | Other |
|---|---|---|---|---|---|---|---|
| 27 | 2 | 7 | 19 | 18 | 11 | 9 | 6 |

(b) *Age* (%: sample = 195)

| Under 20 | 20–9 | 30–9 | 40–9 | 50–9 | 60–9 | Median age |
|---|---|---|---|---|---|---|
| 1 | 48 | 39 | 8 | 2 | 1 | 29 |

*Note:* 'Activists' were defined by their activity. This sample is largely made up of men who were
arrested for giving speeches, canvassing, or collecting money on behalf of Sinn Féin.

*Sources:* The main sources for this sample were: *Cork Examiner* and *Irish Times*, 1917–19; General
Prisons Board records (NA); R.I.C. reports on Sinn Féin meetings, Aug. 1918 (WO/35/64) and
County Inspectors' monthly reports. To keep the figures strictly comparable with those in other
tables, and because of the scarcity of data for female activists, this sample is entirely male.

was not entirely coincidental. In some cases Sinn Féin clubs and Volunteer companies were led by the same people.

The main difference between the organizations lay in age. The average Sinn Féin militant was four or five years older than his counterpart in the Volunteers in 1917–19. There was a much larger contingent of men over 30, and almost none were under 20. In part, this reflects a natural division of labour whereby older and married men stayed out of the firing line. The same point is illustrated by the fact that female Sinn Féin activists tended to be much younger (with a median age of 23[39]). For women, electoral or street politics were almost their only avenues of direct participation in the revolution. Whatever the reason, this age gap between party and army reinforced the increasing tension between Sinn Féin and the I.R.A. When guerrillas spoke sneeringly of the 'Sinn Féin type', this often reflected their mistrust of anyone over 30.[40]

The social character of armed republicanism can be further tested by examining the I.R.A. outside Ireland. Despite the popularity of the cause of independence among the Irish in Britain, there were probably no more than a thousand Volunteers in England and Scotland, and no more than a few hundred who took part in operations. Most companies were not even formed until 1919 or 1920, and only became engaged in gun-running, arson, vandalism, and assassination from late 1920 onwards. It is from this period that the sample described in Table 15 is taken.

TABLE 15.   *Volunteers in Britain, 1920–1922*

|  | Officers | Men |
|---|---|---|
| Sample | 26 | 105 |
| %age un/semi-skilled | 20 | 27 |
| Skilled | 27 | 32 |
| Shop Assist/clerk | 35 | 19 |
| Professional | 8 | 7 |
| Merchant/son | 8 | 9 |
| Student | 4 | 2 |
| Other | 4 |  |
| Median Age | 25 | 23 |

*Source*: The main source for this table is *The Times*, 1920–3.

[39] From a sample of twenty-six women imprisoned for political activity in 1917–19: GPB DORA Prisoner records, Cartons 3–6.

[40] See e.g. the interviews with Sean Breen and Sean Daly (O'Malley Papers, P17b/83, 112).

As in Ireland, these figures are largely made up of men who were arrested or imprisoned, and who can be identified as activists. The relatively small size of the sample reflects the small number of such men. Some were born in Britain. Some were more recent arrivals. It is impossible to say exactly in what proportion, but second-generation immigrants accounted for at least a large minority of the members. British-born guerrillas did sometimes feel a sense of inferiority on this account, but if anything, this made them even more vehemently 'Irish'.[41] What can be said with some confidence is that almost all were permanent residents, not travellers, seasonal migrants, or men sent over *as* guerrillas.[42] This sets them apart from participants in more recent bombing campaigns.

In Britain, the organization was wholly urban and, like the rest of the Irish population, was heavily concentrated in the great cities of London, Liverpool, Manchester, and Glasgow.[43] As with the Dublin sample in Table 11 (with which it can best be compared), its membership was drawn fairly widely from the working and lower middle classes.

The only comparative general figures we have to put this sample into context come from the 1911 Scottish census. This shows Irish-born men to have been most commonly employed as manual labourers, and rarely found in offices or shops.[44] It is probably fair to conclude that, here as well, the I.R.A. had more than its fair share of clerks and teachers. Unlike the Dublin brigades, however (but like the provincial brigades), the mainland units also had what appears to be a disproportionate number of tradesmen. Again, officers can be distinguished by their slightly more advanced age and occupational status. The I.R.A. thus attracted youth, education, and skill on both sides of the Irish Sea.

Another way to place the rebels of 1917–23 in context is to compare them to their organizational ancestors, the Irish Republican Brotherhood (I.R.B.). The Fenians, as they were popularly known, were founded in 1858 as a secular fraternity dedicated to fighting for a republic. 'The organization' (so-called by initiates) still existed in the early 1920s as a secret society within the larger revolutionary movement. In the 1860s it was much larger, more paramilitary, and more open. It is this earlier

---

[41] See Ch. 8.

[42] Almost all of those arrested or otherwise identified as Volunteers had addresses and full-time jobs in Britain.

[43] See David Fitzpatrick, 'The Irish in Britain', in W. E. Vaughan (ed.), *A New History of Ireland*, vol. VI (Oxford, 1996).

[44] Census of Scotland, 1911, P.P., 1914, xliv (Cd.7163), Tables A, III.

incarnation as an autonomous military organization—somewhat analogous to the Volunteers of 1917–18—that is significant for our purposes.

Who became rebels in Victorian Ireland? To answer this question, R. V. Comerford has assembled a list of over a thousand Fenian 'suspects' (according to the Irish constabulary) at the height of I.R.B. strength, between 1865 and 1870.[45] According to Comerford's figures, 48 per cent of the suspects were tradesmen, 8 per cent were shopkeepers or publicans, 9 per cent were clerks, 6 per cent were farmers or their sons, 6 per cent were general labourers, 5 per cent were agricultural labourers, 4 per cent were professionals, and 13 per cent were 'other' than the above. Maura Murphy's figures for Fenian leaders and activists in Cork city in the 1860s and 1870s show similar results, with shop assistants and clerks being even more prominent.[46]

Granted the differences with Irish society in the twentieth century (more urban, educated, and commercial, less artisanal), the similarities with the Volunteers are noteworthy. Tradesmen and shopmen became bold Fenian men; farmers' sons and labourers did not. This sample does include a large number of Dubliners, but even if we calculated provincial suspects alone, the percentage engaged in agriculture would be much lower than among the next generation of Volunteers. This contrast is heightened by the fact that mid-Victorian Ireland was an even more rural society. Continuities also exist at the level of individual trades, as carpenters, masons, shoemakers, and drapers' assistants were prominent in both periods. These men were also close in average age to I.R.A. members: the mean age of another sample of 746 I.R.B. suspects collected by Comerford was 27.

Finally, it is useful to compare the Volunteers to their enemies in the Civil War: the men of the National Army. Joining this force in 1922 was an entirely different undertaking from joining the I.R.A. It was an army with a functioning state behind it. It was disciplined, full-time, and paid wages. Its soldiers lived in barracks or billets, often far from home. This new army drew new recruits, most of whom had not previously been Volunteers.

The first noteworthy feature of of Free State forces—as sampled in Table 16—is the near-complete absence of farmers' sons. In this respect, National Army recruiters did no better than their British

---

[45] R. V. Comerford, 'Patriotism as Pastime: The Appeal of Fenianism in the Mid-1860s', *Irish Historical Studies*, 22 (1981), 239–43.

[46] Maura J. B. Murphy, 'The Role of Organized Labour in the Political and Economic Life of Cork City 1820–1899', Ph.D. thesis, Leicester University, 1979.

TABLE 16. *Occupations of National Army recruits, 1922 (% ages)*

|  | Provincial | 1926 Census | Dublin | 1926 Census |
|---|---|---|---|---|
| Sample | 3,842 |  | 690 |  |
| Farmer/son | 3 | 49 |  |  |
| Farm Labourer | 30 | 17 |  |  |
| Un/semi-skilled | 38 | 10 | 70 | 44 |
| Skilled | 17 | 9 | 18 | 23 |
| Shop Ass./clerk | 6 | 4 | 8 | 15 |
| Professional | 0.2 | 2 | 0.3 | 4 |
| Merchant/son | 1 | 4 | 0.3 | 5 |
| Student | 1 | 1 | 0.6 | 2 |
| Other | 3 | 4 | 3 | 6 |

*Source*: MA, Enlistment and Discharge Register, vols. 1–6. The sample includes both officers and volunteers.

predecessors.[47] The other outstanding characteristic of the 'Staters' was how proletarian they were. More than two-thirds had been labourers of one sort or another, on farms, docks, roads, or unemployed. Again, this fits the image and social background of the bulk of Irish recruits for the British army, a comparison anti-Treaty republicans were quick to make.

Compounding this lowly social status, the novice soldiers were young (their median age was 24 and many were under 20) and unmarried (95 per cent[48]). Moreover, 1922 also brought an economic slump, so work was scarce and wages were low. For such men, joining the army meant giving up little or nothing and gaining a year or two of steady employment—and possibly even respectability. Nor was it nearly as dangerous as joining the R.I.C. in 1921, let alone the British army in 1914 or 1915. Whatever the reasons, the result was that the two forces facing each other in 1922–3 possessed very distinct social as well as political identities.

## The Volunteer Type

The *Times* correspondent present at the collapse of the Easter Rising reported that there were essentially two kinds of rebel: 'Many...were

[47] See Martin Staunton, 'The Royal Munster Fusiliers in the Great War, 1914–19', MA thesis, University College Dublin, 1986, pp. 12–20, and Fitzpatrick, 'The Logic of Collective Sacrifice', 1017–30.

[48] From a sample of 2,106 men taken from the Army Census, Nov. 1922 (MA, Army Census, L/S/1).

unmistakeably of the rabble class to be found in every large town', but there was also a large complement of 'intellectuals', easily identifiable as 'young men with high foreheads and thin lips'. It was also obvious to him that the latter had led—or misled—the former into revolt, and that 'heavy is the responsibility of those who poisoned such men's minds'.[49] Six years later, General Cyril Prescott-Decie, a former Irish police commissioner, was still able to reduce 'I.R.A. types' to more or less the same two categories: 'the one the burly ruffian type; the other a moral and physical degenerate... these were the men with whom the Black and Tans had to deal.'[50]

These writers shared with their contemporaries the assumption that the Volunteers fell into 'types' who shared a distinct physical, as well as a social, anatomy: recognizable as well as categorizable. That there was such a thing as an I.R.A. type was as clear to friends as to foes. With political sympathy, however, came the rival image of a revolutionary 'new man': 'determined, steady, with a drilled uprightness of bearing... a Crusader of modern days.'[51]

Thin lips and fanatic brows aside, can a Volunteer typology be assembled from the data presented here? Catholic almost without exception, very likely unmarried and unpropertied, and probably under 30. Beyond that, the characteristics of the gunman become less predictable. Nevertheless, certain collective tendencies do stand out clearly enough to identify a prominent—if not dominant—I.R.A. 'type': urban, educated, skilled (and thus at least potentially socially mobile), and more or less at the beginning of his career. Such men were at the forefront of the struggle everywhere: in Dublin and all four provinces, in Britain, and in Sinn Féin as well. What was it that made republican activism so appealing to them? Can the social composition of the I.R.A. tell us something about its motivational composition as well?

Ideology offers one explanation. Perhaps prior exposure to cultural nationalism helped turn young men into guerrillas. Theirs was the first generation to have the Irish language taught widely in schools. This hypothesis is reinforced by the strong statistical correlation between the number of young male Irish-speakers, or the proportion of national schools teaching Irish in a county or city, and its level of I.R.A. activity.[52] There is an additional occupational congruence between the two movements. Turn-of-the-century observers often noted the prominent role played by shop assistants, clerks, and teachers in the Gaelic League, just

[49] *The Times*, 3 May 1916.   [50] Ibid., 18 July 1922.
[51] Mrs William O'Brien, *In Mallow* (London, 1920), 65, 68.   [52] See Ch. 2.

as others would a decade later with the I.R.A.[53] This is confirmed by a study of towns in county Cork, whose census records reveal that these occupations accounted for a majority of Irish-speaking young men in 1911. On the other hand, there is no statistical relationship between I.R.A. violence and the presence of shop assistants or clerks in an area.[54] Local research also shows that many Volunteers neither spoke Irish nor belonged to any cultural or political organization before joining. Finally, if we accept this connection, the question still remains: why did men with these jobs become language enthusiasts in the first place?

More generally, and in partial answer to the last two points, we might argue for the primacy of environment and organizational resources in producing activists of any sort. In towns, exposure to ideas, propaganda, and organizations would have been more continuous and intense than in the country. Newspapers, political literature, public meetings, and club rooms were all more immediately available. Working in offices, shops, or workshops meant constant contact with fellow workers, customers, and neighbours. Many farms, on the other hand, were comparatively isolated and removed from such everyday contacts. Towns and cities clearly offered greater organizational opportunities—to the language movement as well as to the I.R.A. Thus, even if one was not a member of any political or cultural group before 1916, one probably knew someone who was.

Why did urban labourers not respond in the same way? Most likely because, while they had the same potential exposure and access, they lacked the necessary personal resources. Republicanism (and Gaelicism) was consumed as well as believed. Newspapers, books, and political paraphernalia had to be bought and read, membership dues had to be paid, speeches had to be made. Greater disposable incomes and education made salaried workers better political consumers and entrepreneurs, especially after 1916, when republicanism was a new and improved product.

This did not necessarily mean that there was a deficiency of patriotism or republicanism in the countryside. Irish farms were even less likely than urban families to send their sons to fight in the British or National armies. Nor were countrymen any less supportive of Sinn Féin than townsmen when it came to votes or party membership.[55] It might be argued that the

---

[53] See Tom Garvin, *Nationalist Revolutionaries in Ireland 1858–1928* (Oxford, 1987), 86–90, and John Hutchinson, *The Dynamics of Cultural Nationalism: The Gaelic Revival and the Creation of the Irish Nation State* (London, 1987), 179, 287.

[54] See Ch. 2.

[55] See Ch. 2.

rural deficit which appears in the provincial membership figures (for both the I.R.A. and Sinn Féin) simply reflects the nature of the sources. Towns were better garrisoned, policed, and reported upon, so urban rebels were more likely to show up in arrest and prison records and newspaper accounts. By this reckoning, the drop in the percentage of countrymen in the samples after 1919 might be accounted for by the withdrawal of the R.I.C. from most of their rural barracks. This logic cannot explain the 1916 figures, however, and it breaks down again in 1922–3, when there were even fewer police in the countryside, yet the proportion of farmers and farm labourers in the provincial I.R.A. actually rose slightly.

There may be an additional explanation for urban–rural differences based on confrontation and risk. Sinn Féin and the Volunteers might have been better organized and supported most intensely in towns, but so were their opponents, whether the home rule party machine, ex-soldiers, unionists, or the police. The resulting polarization, experienced through arguments, street fighting, intimidation, arrests, raids, and surveillance, may have helped to radicalize urban republicans to a far greater extent than their country comrades. It may also have goaded them into greater levels of activism, by forcing them out of their homes and jobs under the threat of prison or death. Farmers' sons, because of where they lived and who their neighbours were, were less likely to face such a crisis.

Evidence for this theory can be found in the exceptionally detailed North Cork Brigade company records for 1921. These show that urban Volunteers had more than twice the chance of being arrested as their rural comrades, and were more than twice as likely to be 'on the run'. They were also 60 per cent more 'active'.[56] Which came first—the arrests or the activism—is debatable, but what is clear is that increased risk and increased militancy went hand in hand.

These explanations of the I.R.A.'s urban bias depend on a comparison between the gunmen and the general population. If we compare them to the members of other organizations, though, the question becomes, not why there were so few rural Volunteers, but rather, why there were so many. By the standard of the British and Irish regular armies, or the Fenians of the 1860s, the guerrillas actually did rather well in attracting rural recruits. Among their allies or enemies, only the R.I.C.—which took 60 per cent of its men from farming families—did better.[57]

---

[56] See Table 2.

[57] Brian Griffin, 'The Irish Police, 1836–1914', Ph.D. thesis, Loyola University of Chicago, 1991, p. 855.

Part of the answer may lie in the social circumstances of farm life. Family farms needed their sons' labour, so leaving to fight in Europe would often have been economically untenable. Joining the I.R.A. did not mean leaving home, though, and even offered the hope of preventing conscription. On the other hand, as violence escalated after 1918, so did the level of commitment and risk required of active Volunteers, and the likelihood of going on the run or to prison. The rising costs of revolution might, therefore, also account for the departure of so many farmers' sons after 1919. The farm exercised a pull on sons to stay, and politically hostile towns pushed republicans into greater activity, both to avoid risk. The same factors help to explain why Sinn Féin's paper membership and electoral support was predominantly rural while its activists tended to come from urban backgrounds.

## Family and Neighbourhood

Explanations for why shop assistants, skilled workers, or townsmen in general, were more likely to be revolutionaries do not tell us why particular individuals were. With the exception of a few long-time republicans, there was little or nothing to distinguish future guerrillas from their peers before they joined the movement. Who they were was not the sum of their vital statistics, however. Men did not simply join or participate as individuals, at a certain age, or as shoemakers or teachers. They joined in groups, with relatives or friends, and it was these relationships, as much as any common social background, that determined who became members and activists.

The informal networks that bound Volunteer units together can be seen from the beginning, in the Easter Rising. Using official reports, we can map the names and addresses of 914 captured or surrendered Dublin rebels deported to Britain between 30 April and 6 May 1916.[58] The results show that 17 per cent of these men had the same last name and lived at the same address as at least one other Volunteer. Presumably, the great majority belonged to the same family. Another 10 per cent with different names had shared a home with one or more fellow internees, and an additional 8 per cent lived adjacent to one or more rebels. In other

[58] See note on sources for Table 13.

words, more than a third of the sample can be grouped into definite family and residential clusters. And this, no doubt, understates the case. After all, many brothers and cousins lived apart but still volunteered together.

The same pattern is even more strongly evident in Cork city in the years after 1916. Here, 22 per cent of a sample of 588 guerrillas were brothers living together. Another 9 per cent shared an address, and 17 per cent lived next door to another Volunteer. So nearly half of the organization in Cork for whom names and exact addresses are known were family or next-door neighbours.

Nor was this clustering a peculiarly urban phenomenon. We might expect to find it to be even more prevalent in a small town or a country parish. And indeed, a close examination of the Behagh Company in West Cork reveals that, from 1915 to 1923, more than half of the members had at least one brother in the unit. Most of the men, and particularly the officers, were also immediate neighbours.[59] Many other such examples can be found. The pivotal Carnacross Company in Meath, for one, 'was almost a family affair with seven Farrelly brothers, five Dunne brothers, another family of four Dunnes, the Lynchs, the Dalys and two Tevlins making up most of the company'.[60] Nearly every county and city had its leading families: the Brennans and Barretts in Clare, the Sweeneys and O'Donnells in Donegal, the Hannigans and Manahans in Limerick, the Hales in West Cork, the Kerrs in Liverpool. Similar nuclei can be found in shops, offices, mills, and factories. Equally strong networks, less measurable but just as identifiable, were built around school and football or hurling team-mates. In these contexts, within families and neighbourhoods, being one of 'the boys' was at least as important as occupation or age.

## I.R.A. Identities

If we return to Yeats's opening allusion in 'Easter 1916', to Volunteer leaders working behind counters and desks, we can recognize it as a fair social assessment. The fact that they inspired 'a mocking tale or a gibe | to please a companion | around the fire at the club' also reflects the

---

[59] For further details, see *The I.R.A. and Its Enemies*, 220–5.
[60] Oliver Coogan, *Politics and War in Meath, 1913–23* (Dublin, 1983), 191.

condescension or even contempt accompanying such descriptions of rebel 'types'. Of course, such distinctions only mattered so long as motley was still worn. With rebellion came the birth of a terrible beauty and, for the rebels, a rebirth as heroes and martyrs. The question of who they were was now answered by what they had done for their cause.

The point is one that needs to be made for the whole period, and for the I.R.A. as a whole. We cannot answer the question only by cataloguing pre-revolutionary traits. The guerrillas' individual and collective identities were changed by the fact of their participation. The new Volunteers who joined after 1916 often spoke of their involvement in almost mystical terms, and the act of joining as a kind of conversion experience. Revolution became their vocation. The movement forged new bonds and attitudes. Urban Volunteers went on the run and on active service in the country. Provincial republicans went to Dublin or London. Thousands of men spent months or years in prison or in detention camps. For activists, their personal horizons both expanded with travel and new contacts, and contracted as the cause took over their lives. For the fighting men, what counted most was not social status but commitment and contribution: what you did, not where you stood on the social ladder. In this mobile, uncertain, politically charged, generally egalitarian new world, fellow revolutionaries became their primary reference group. For some, the identification with the comrades, the republic, with Ireland, was near-total.

Such conviction crossed all social boundaries. Nevertheless, while class, geography, religion, and family were not the only determinants of membership and activism, they were all highly influential. Nor did the 'new men' of the republic simply abandon old social attitudes. If anything, republicanism carried with it a heightened sense of respectability and community. Which brings us back to the issue of what I.R.A. members did or, more specifically, who they did it to. Who, among their neighbours and fellow countrymen, became their victims? The guerrillas too saw their enemies as 'types': 'corner boy' ex-servicemen, 'black' orangemen or freemasons, dirty tramps and 'tinkers', 'fast' women. People who were perceived as falling into such categories were the most likely to be denounced as 'informers' or 'enemies of the Republic' and shot, burned out, or intimidated. Thus, while knowing who the men behind the guns were is a vital question in itself, it can also tell us a great deal about who they were aiming at.

TABLE 17.  *Occupations of Volunteers by Province, 1917–1923 (% ages)*

| | Officers | | | Men | | | Census | |
| --- | --- | --- | --- | --- | --- | --- | --- | --- |
| | 1917–19 | 1920–1 | 1922–3 | 1917–19 | 1920–1 | 1922–3 | 1911 | 1926 |
| *Munster* | | | | | | | | |
| Sample | 510 | 332 | 150 | 1,019 | 1,525 | 899 | | |
| Farmer/son | 29 | 22 | 21 | 39 | 28 | 11 | 36 | 40 |
| Farm labourer | 5 | 4 | 8 | 11 | 12 | 24 | 26 | 17 |
| Un/semi-skilled | 4 | 5 | 9 | 10 | 16 | 25 | | 13 |
| Skilled | 21 | 26 | 28 | 16 | 20 | 23 | | 10 |
| Shop Ass./clerk | 20 | 22 | 19 | 10 | 13 | 11 | | 9 |
| Professional | 7 | 7 | 7 | 1 | 4 | 1 | | 4 |
| Merchant/son | 10 | 12 | 4 | 6 | 5 | 1 | | 4 |
| Student | 0.4 | 0.3 | | 1 | 1 | 0.4 | | 1 |
| Other | 3 | 4 | 3 | 2 | 2 | 3 | | 2 |
| *Connaught*[1] | | | | | | | | |
| Sample | 57 | 38 | | 246 | 126 | 97 | | |
| Farmer/son | 38 | 42 | | 52 | 39 | 35 | 67 | 74 |
| Farm labourer | 2 | 4 | | 6 | 12 | 11 | 15 | 7 |
| Un/semi-skilled | 2 | 3 | | 4 | 8 | 14 | | 4 |
| Skilled | 17 | 3 | | 12 | 12 | 23 | | 5 |
| Shop Ass./clerk | 13 | 6 | | 21 | 17 | 10 | | 3 |
| Professional | 20 | 29 | | 1 | 2 | 1 | | 2 |
| Merchant/son | 7 | 13 | | 4 | 5 | 2 | | 2 |
| Student | 2 | | | 0.5 | 5 | | | 0.4 |
| Other | | | | 0.5 | 1 | 3 | | 1 |
| *Leinster*[2] | | | | | | | | |
| Sample | 75 | 72 | | 132 | 216 | 93 | | |
| Farmer/son | 17 | 23 | | 22 | 32 | 10 | 44 | 35 |
| Farm labourer | 3 | 7 | | 18 | 13 | 24 | 43 | 23 |
| Un/semi-skilled | 3 | 5 | | 12 | 9 | 24 | | 12 |
| Skilled | 32 | 23 | | 12 | 16 | 17 | | 13 |
| Shop Ass./clerk | 15 | 19 | | 15 | 18 | 22 | | 5 |
| Professional | 13 | 15 | | 3 | 3 | | | 2 |
| Merchant/son | 12 | 6 | | 18 | 6 | | | 3 |
| Student | 1 | | | | | 1 | | |
| Other | 4 | 4 | | 1 | 2 | 3 | | |
| *Ulster*[3] | | | | | | | | |
| Sample | 40 | 20 | | 42 | 118 | | | |
| Farmer/son | 5 | 32 | | 12 | 28 | | 35 | 33 |
| Farm labourer | 8 | | | 9 | 13 | | 19 | 8 |
| Un/semi-skilled | 10 | 5 | | 12 | 19 | | | 21 |
| Skilled | 40 | 16 | | 29 | 18 | | | 20 |
| Shop Ass./clerk | 18 | 16 | | 18 | 18 | | | 7 |
| Professional | 15 | 21 | | 3 | | | | 2 |
| Merchant/son | 5 | 5 | | 18 | 6 | | | 5 |

(*continues*)

TABLE 17.   *(Contd.)*

| | Officers | | | Men | | | Census | |
|---|---|---|---|---|---|---|---|---|
| | 1917–19 | 1920–1 | 1922–3 | 1917–19 | 1920–1 | 1922–3 | 1911 | 1926 |
| Student | | 5 | | | | | | 0.2 |
| Other | | | | | | | | 3 |

*Notes:* [1] The samples for Connaught, Leinster, and Ulster do not include columns for officers in 1922–3 because the sources do not state ranks. [2] Not including Dublin District. [3] The census data include Protestants, who dominated the professions and skilled trades. As the I.R.A. drew exclusively on the Catholic population, this means that these occupational groups were even more over-represented in the I.R.A. than the above figures suggest.

# PART III
# Guerrillas Abroad

# 6

## Operations Abroad:
## The I.R.A. in Britain

From the 1790s onwards, Hibernian revolutionary endeavours have invariably spanned the Irish Sea. Indeed, if rebellions are measured in bullets and bombs, it was Britain, not Ireland, that was the main battlefield in nineteenth-century struggles to establish a republic. Whatever yeast was lacking in the Fenian rising of 1867, for example, was more than made up for in England, where the Manchester Martyrs and the Clerkenwell bombers left a rich legacy of corpses, anthems, and anniversaries. The greatest of the 'bold Fenian men', William Lomasney, died not by a Saxon bullet on an Irish hillside, but by the Thames, blown up by his own bomb.[1]

The Easter Rising finally produced a republican insurrection in Ireland in 1916, which continued in various forms until 1923. However, this realization of the Fenian dream also saw the culmination of the terrorist tradition in Britain, where Irish Republican Army guerrillas mounted the most destructive campaign yet seen, and prior to the 1990s. Man for man, and operation for operation, the Liverpool, Manchester, Tyneside, and London I.R.A. outperformed many Irish brigades. Nevertheless, the men of this British underground laboured in the shadows and stayed there, even after their comrades in flying columns and squads became heroes.

[1] See Leon O'Broin, *Fenian Fever: An Anglo-American Dilemma* (London, 1971); K. R. M. Short, *The Dynamite War* (Atlantic Highlands, 1979); Charles Townshend, *Political Violence in Ireland*, 158–66.

Michael Collins himself declared that, 'After all, in a manner of speaking, our people in England are only the auxiliaries of our attacking forces'.[2]

They deserve historical attention. The I.R.A.'s activities in Britain between 1920 and 1923 may have been a sideshow to the troubles, but they were much more extensive and effective than is usually assumed in the absence of detailed research.[3] The British government and police did not dismiss the threat they posed; quite the contrary. Indeed, the official response it provoked is as fascinating as the republican underground itself, as these were uniquely British guerrillas.

## Organization

The I.R.A. units active in Britain were formed in 1919 and 1920, several years after the new movement took shape in Ireland. Companies of the Irish Volunteers (the original, official title of the I.R.A.) had been estab-lished in several British cities before, at the height of the home rule crisis in 1914, but they dwindled into near-nothingness after the outbreak of the Great War. Those that remained collapsed in 1916, when most of the active members departed to avoid conscription and take part in the Easter Rising.[4]

The Liverpool Volunteers were the first to be re-established, in May 1919. One company covered the city and its neighbours (Bootle, most importantly), with a subsidiary unit in St Helen's.[5] Another was

---

[2] M.[ichael Collins] to L. [Art O'Brien], 6 June 1921 (NLI, Art O'Brien Papers, MS 8430).

[3] See Steven Fielding, *Class and Ethnicity: Irish Catholics in England, 1880–1939* (Buckingham, 1993), 102–3; Iain D. Patterson, 'The Activities of Irish Republican Physical Force Organisations in Scotland, 1919–21', *Scottish Historical Review*, 72 (1993); David Fitzpatrick, 'A Curious Middle Place: The Irish in Britain, 1871–1921', in Roger Swift and Sheridan Gilley, *The Irish in Britain 1815–1939* (London, 1989), 42; Tom Gallagher, *Glasgow: The Uneasy Peace* (Manchester, 1987), 90–7.

[4] For these men and their activities, see the following articles in *An tOglach*: Seamus Reader, 'Irishmen in Scotland, 1916' (St Patrick's Day 1962, Easter 1963, Summer 1964) and 'Volunteers From Scotland' (Easter 1965); John T. ('Blimey') O'Connor, 'Some Have Come From a Land Beyond the Sea' (Autumn 1966); Ernie Nunan, 'The Irish Volunteers in London' (Autumn 1966) and 'The Kimmage Garrison, 1916' (Easter 1967). See also 'An Rathach', 'London Volunteers', *Irish Democrat* (Apr. 1948); Piaras Beaslai, *Michael Collins and the Making of a New Ireland* (Dublin, 1926), i. 68–71.

[5] Tom Craven to Michael Collins, 25 May 1919 (UCD, Richard Mulcahy Papers, P7/A/1). See also Col. M. 'Iron Mike' O'Leary, 'The History of the Liverpool Battalion and the Story of the Burning, in 1920, of the Liverpool Docks', *An tOglach* (Autumn 1966); Interview with Hugh Early (UCD, Ernie O'Malley Papers, P17b/110). These interviews will hereafter be referred to with the interviewee's name only, followed by the location in the O'Malley Papers.

established independently and without sanction a year later, but appears to have done nothing thereafter.[6] At about this time, a group of Londoners wrote to Michael Collins—as adjutant-general of the I.R.A.—to propose the formation of an 'I.R.A. Division in England'. Collins was cautiously acquiescent, and men began to be enrolled there as well in October 1919.[7] One company soon became four, quartering the city.[8] Other areas were slower off the mark. A Tyneside unit was formed in September 1920 by 'men anxious to start corps of the I.V. in this district'.[9] Within a year this had splintered into a chain of companies, anchored in Newcastle.[10] The first official Manchester company was also affiliated in September, but a separate, unofficial, group of local enthusiasts had already started their own, again after contacting Collins. A third was added in 1921, and members in outlying towns acquired separate status by 1922.[11] Further fledgling units appeared in Birmingham and Sheffield in the spring of 1921.[12]

Scottish republicans followed a divergent path. Two companies existed in Glasgow at the beginning of 1919, with a third requesting affiliation in April, each at odds with the others. Collins thereupon sent an organizer from Dublin, Joe Vize, to sort things out. Order and discipline proved elusive, but there was no shortage of new recruits: five companies' worth by the middle of June.[13] By September 1920 Collins was declaring that 'the Volunteers there are excellent'.[14] Other cities proved less fertile ground, but a company was finally established in Edinburgh in February 1920. One leading officer, John Carney, claimed that twenty-one

---

[6] Neil Kerr to Michael Collins, 7 July 1920; Collins to Kerr, 8 July (Mulcahy Papers, P7/A/2).

[7] This undated, unsigned letter can be found in the Irish Military Archives (MA, A/0457). See also Sean McGrath to Collins, 7 Oct. 1919, in the same file and Collins to McGrath, 9 Oct. (A/0312).

[8] A useful summary history entitled 'London Battalion I.R.A.' (although such a battalion never officially existed) can be found in the O'Malley Papers (P17a/51).

[9] Sean McGrath to Michael Collins, 7, 14 Sept. 1920 and subsequent correspondence (Mulcahy Papers, P7/A/8); Collins to Neil Kerr, 23 Sept. 1920 (P7/A/3).

[10] For details of this—and all—British units, see Director of Engineering [D/E] Rory O'Connor's memos to Chief of Staff [C/S] Richard Mulcahy: 'Reorganizing Britain', 9 Sept. 1921, and 'Report on Visit to Britain September 1921', 15 Oct. 1921 (Mulcahy Papers, P7/A/24, 29).

[11] Paddy O'Donoghue to Michael Collins, 29 Sept. 1920, and subsequent correspondence (Mulcahy Papers, P7/A/9); Memo. to O/Cs, Manchester Area, 24 April 1922 (Trial Exhibits, O'Brien Papers, MS 8442); Manchester Evening News, 27 Apr. 1921.

[12] D/E memo: 'Report on Visit to Britain'.

[13] Joe Robinson to Michael Collins, Feb. 1919; John Carney to Collins, 12 Apr.; Joe Vize to Collins, 19 Apr., and subsequent correspondence (Mulcahy Papers, P7/A/11).

[14] Collins to Art O'Brien, 17 Sept. 1920 (O'Brien Papers, MS 8430).

companies existed in Scotland in August 1920. This total rose through 1921, but fell back to seven in 1922.[15]

The number of men in these units varied enormously and changed constantly. Liverpool's company had forty when it began in 1919, perhaps 150 in November 1920, thereafter falling to about 100. The split over the Anglo-Irish Treaty in December 1921 and subsequent Civil War reduced this to thirty-five by the end of 1922. St Helen's maintained a steady membership of twenty men.[16] The London companies doubled in size, from 120 to about 200 nominal members in all over the course of 1920, declining to around 100 by the July 1921 Truce.[17] Several hundred joined in Newcastle and outlying areas, although many did so after the Truce. The Manchester and Salford Volunteers never reached a hundred all told, and could only assemble a few dozen men by mid-1921. Birmingham and Sheffield fielded a similar number apiece.[18] Glasgow began with fewer than 100 Volunteers in 1919, but reorganization there and elsewhere in Scotland produced a potential force of 600 men by August 1920. Post-Treaty divisions brought the total back to 138 in 1922.[19]

So, all told, there were perhaps a thousand men enrolled in British I.R.A. units in the crucial twelve months between July 1920 and July 1921. How many of these were actually reliable, 'available for duty', or active at any given time, was a different matter. Turn-out varied with risk and commitment. Scores of I.R.A. men were jailed or deported after November 1920, and the prospect of losing one's livelihood, freedom, or life further thinned the ranks. Only very rarely were whole units mobilized for an operation, whereupon many so ordered failed to turn up. In Denis

[15] John Carney ('O/C Scotland') to C/S, 22 Feb. 1922 (NLI, Sean O'Mahoney Papers, MS 24,474). See also John McGallogly Statement (UCD, P60).

[16] Tom Craven to Michael Collins, 25 May 1919; Hugh Early (O'Malley Papers, P17b/55, 110); Anon. (P17b/128); Free State intelligence list of 'principal active irregulars' c.1923 (P17a/182).

[17] Here, estimates vary—as did company rolls. See Billy Aherne (O'Malley Papers, P17b/99); 'London Battalion' history; D/E memo: 'Reorganizing Britain'.

[18] For each of these centres, see D/E memo: 'Reorganizing Britain'. For Manchester, see also *Manchester Evening News*, 27 Apr. 1921; *Manchester Evening Chronicle*, 4 May 1921.

[19] For the 1919 figure, see Joe Robinson to Michael Collins, Feb. 1919 (Mulcahy Papers, P7/A/11). For 1920, see John Carney to C/S, 22 Feb. 1922 (O'Mahoney Papers, MS 24,474). For 1922: list of members, Scottish Brigade (O'Malley Papers, P17a/182). Much larger estimates are cited in Patterson, 'The Activities of Irish Republican Physical Force Organisations', 52–3. These match the alarmist police estimates in a memo from Basil Thomson, 18 Oct. 1920 and the report by the Procurator-Fiscal on Sinn Féin in Glasgow, 30 Nov. 1920 (S[cottish] R[ecord] O[ffice], HH 55/62, 69). These reached even the cabinet: memo. on illegal drilling in Scotland by the Sec. for Scotland, 18 Oct. 1920 (PRO, CAB 24/112, C.P.1978).

Brennan's West London company, for example, only half of his two-dozen men 'at the best' could be counted on.[20] Young Irishmen in Britain were also a highly mobile group, which meant that Volunteers often simply moved out of their unit's territory. The result was a continuous turnover in membership. In September 1921 it was estimated that half the original Liverpool I.R.A. had departed and been replaced by new men since the previous November.[21]

Even these 400 or so genuinely aspiring guerrillas still had to wait for a campaign to commence. For most of 1919 and 1920, initiation into the underground world of orders and oaths meant only meetings, the extraction of weekly dues, and occasional parades or sessions of drill.[22] 'Operations' as such were still the preserve of the Irish Republican Brotherhood, the conspiratorial heart of the republican movement in Britain as in Ireland.

The history of 'the Organization'—as the I.R.B. was known to its members—like that of the Volunteers, was a succession of ups and downs. Dubbed 'Fenians' in their Victorian heyday, the membership in Lancashire alone numbered in the thousands.[23] By 1914 these men were long gone: England as a whole claimed only 117 paying I.R.B. members, and Scotland 250 (as opposed to 1,660 in Ireland), each belonging to a 'circle' of fellows, led by a 'centre'. In Glasgow, at least, there may also have been a few hundred more sympathizers working for the revolution on the sly, but here the I.R.B. faced the same problems later encountered by the I.R.A.: 'as a result of the migratory nature of work of the Irish in Scotland, it was very difficult to keep circles together. A circle might disappear in a few months.'[24] Outside Glasgow, and spread between London, Liverpool, and Manchester, the Brotherhood was stretched very thin. A residue of middle-aged and elderly brethren reduced the active element even further, so that the departure to Dublin in 1916 of many dynamic young men who were also Volunteers left most circles moribund.

---

[20] Denis Brennan (O'Malley Papers, P17b/100).

[21] D/E: 'Report on Visit to Britain'. For a social profile of the membership of the British I.R.A., see Ch. 5.

[22] See e.g. Edward M. Brady, *Ireland's Secret Service in England* (Dublin, 1929), 22–4. Although much criticized upon publication by some of his former comrades, this—the sole published memoir by a British I.R.A. veteran—holds up as generally accurate when compared to other sources.

[23] W. J. Lowe, 'Lancashire Fenianism, 1864–71', *Transactions of the Historic Society of Lancashire and Cheshire*, xxvi (1977), 126, 156–85; Fitzpatrick, 'A Curious Middle Place', 31.

[24] Patrick McCormick Statement (NLI, MS 15,337).

These same qualities paradoxically made the British I.R.B. more valuable to the revolutionary cause in the years that followed. Its leadership in Ireland was still determined upon rebellion, and sought weapons. These were available in Britain, and could be smuggled out by the Organization's experienced old hands, along routes used since the 1860s. Having a widely dispersed network of sedentary members and sympathizers was suddenly an advantage. Michael Collins, once a London Irishman but now a reverse émigré building a revolutionary career in Dublin, knew these men and was perfectly positioned to put the pieces back together and keep the money, information, and arms moving. The same networks were used to provide safe houses and escape routes for wanted men and women fleeing Ireland.[25]

In 1919 Collins also began to call upon his Organization men for more energetic operations. The most famous of these was the ingenious rescue of Eamon de Valera and others from Lincoln jail in February 1919. Equally successful was a second break-out of republican prisoners from Strange-ways prison in Manchester in October. Both involved Collins personally, as well as the combined forces of the Liverpool and Manchester circles. In true secret society fashion, the full apparatus of coded messages, keys baked into cakes, and disguises was employed, and everyone seems to have enjoyed themselves immensely.[26]

The ever-growing demand for guns, ammunition, and explosives, and the infusion of young blood into the republican movement, led the I.R.B. to recruit new members from among the growing ranks of the Volunteers. The I.R.A. in turn drew on recently formed Sinn Féin clubs, and both recruited from the Irish Self-Determination League, a front for repub-lican activities of all kinds in England and Wales, also founded in 1919. The Organization controlled them all from the start. Enthusiastic novices may have provided the initiative to start companies, but it was often established I.R.B. men who ended up in charge. Uninitiated officers and activists were then almost always inducted into the Brotherhood. As many as half of the reliable Volunteers in London thereby became Organization men.[27] 'In so far as London was concerned, I.R.B. and I.R.A. were interchangeable terms.'[28]

---

[25] See Art O'Brien's memoir of the Organization in London (O'Brien Papers, MS 8427); Sean McGrath and Paddy Daly (O'Malley Papers, P17b/100, 136). For gun-running through Britain, see Ch. 7.

[26] Beaslai, *Michael Collins*, i. 262–93, 360–74; Tim Pat Coogan, *Michael Collins* (London, 1990), 98–101.

[27] Denis Brennan (O'Malley Papers, P17b/100).

[28] Art O'Brien memoir (O'Brien Papers, MS 8427).

By 1921, therefore, most I.R.B. members belonged to the I.R.A., most of whose members had first joined Sinn Féin or the I.S.D.L. And behind the political clubs were their social and cultural counterparts, the Gaelic Athletic Association, the Gaelic League, and associated clubs and societies, which provided much of the social milieu in which the activists operated: the water—or alphabet soup—for the fish. As in Ireland, the Army was one part of a composite movement, with layers of overlapping membership. It was not unusual for all these organizations to meet in the same hall or rented rooms. Behind this elaborate organizational façade, however, lay a simpler reality, as much of the work was done by a small number of people in each city who ran nearly everything. In Liverpool the key players were Neil Kerr and his sons, Steve Lanigan, Peter Murphy, Paddy Daly, Hugh Early, and Denis and Patrick Fleming; in Manchester, Paddy O'Donoghue and William McMahon. In London they were Sean McGrath, Reginald Dunne, Denis Kelleher, and Sam Maguire, often depicted as Michael Collins's political godfather. And in a category of his own was Art O'Brien, described by one London republican as 'the god of our small world'.[29] From his numerous offices in London, O'Brien presided over the Gaelic League, the I.S.D.L., Sinn Féin, the Dáil loan, a host of republican charities, and numerous bank accounts. He had been in the Volunteers up to 1916, and was an influential member of the I.R.B.[30] Almost all of these men were in personal contact with Collins.

The first British I.R.A. units to act as such were the London companies, in the spring of 1920. Their inaugural 'operation', however, cast them in the role of victims—of mob violence directed at an otherwise peaceful protest. The occasion was the mass hunger strike of Irish prisoners in Wormwood Scrubbs in April. Sympathizers, organized and otherwise, would gather every day in front of the prison to show their support. They, in turn, attracted hostile crowds, so the Volunteers were covertly drafted in to meet them, under the guise of the I.S.D.L. The young republicans were eager to face a challenge, and confrontations amounting to riots were the daily result.

The demonstrations were called off at the end of the month, after—as Art O'Brien put it—'terrible experiences . . . when our comparatively small

[29] Letter from London, 22 Jan. 1922 (NLI, Beverly and Dorothy Carter Correspondence, MS 20,721[2]).
[30] See O'Brien to Editor, *Daily Herald*, 10 Oct. 1919 (O'Brien Papers, MS 8433)—which lists his organizational affiliations—and O'Brien to Michael Collins, 14 Apr. 1921 (Mulcahy Papers, P7/A/14)—which describes the history and duties of his London office.

band sustained over 50 serious casualties.' He blamed the trouble on 'the criminal hooligan element which was being imported in increasing numbers every evening' but praised 'the courage and devotion to duty of the men forming the cordons, the guards and the flying column'.[31] Sean McGrath, the chief arms organizer and O'Brien's right-hand man, wrote to Michael Collins in the same spirit, but with more pointed meaning: 'Our Volunteers behaved magnificently this last week at the Scrubbs. It was a test for them and they came through it well.'[32] A second test for the London flying column came in August, once again in support of a hunger strike. Terence MacSwiney was dying in Brixton prison, demonstrators were again summoned, and this time the police were the main enemy. Combatants on both sides were injured in the ensuing battles, and several Volunteers were arrested.[33]

Everywhere I.R.A. and I.R.B. members met that summer, the men talked expectantly, impatiently, of doing something for Ireland. In Glasgow, Liverpool, and Manchester local plans were eagerly forwarded to G.H.Q. in Dublin, usually proposing large-scale sabotage.[34] 'After a number of such meetings a few of the men became impatient for "something to do"', one Liverpool activist recalled. 'Only official or Headquarters' control restrained immediate action.'[35]

## Plans

As Terence MacSwiney's ordeal set off riots in Brixton, it also spurred the G.H.Q. staff in Dublin into action—or at least into considering action. Their first idea was to take hostages, to be exchanged for MacSwiney's release. In early September Michael Collins told Art O'Brien to 'go ahead with finding that place for a hostage'. A week later O'Brien wrote back about the 'apartments'.[36] As MacSwiney's condition worsened, this became an assassination plot: Lloyd George's death in exchange for

---

[31] Memo. to I.S.D.L. branches from Art O'Brien, 1 May 1920 (O'Brien Papers, MS 8428).

[32] Sean McGrath to Michael Collins, 1 May, 1920 (O'Brien Papers, MS 8426).

[33] Protests and fighting also took place in Manchester following MacSwiney's death: Fielding, *Class and Ethnicity*, 102.

[34] Joe Vize to Michael Collins, 11 June 1920 (Mulcahy Papers, P7/A/11); Paddy Daly (O'Malley Papers, P17b/136); John McGallogly Statement.

[35] Brady, *Ireland's Secret Service*, 24.

[36] Michael Collins to Art O'Brien, 7 Sept. 1920; O'Brien to Collins, 13 Sept. (O'Brien Papers, MSS 8430, 8426).

MacSwiney's. The rest of the cabinet were soon included as well. Gunmen were sent from Dublin and Cork to prepare several elaborate plans; some stayed for months.

MacSwiney died on 25 October. When Sean McGrath went to Ireland for his funeral, for 'the first time I saw Michael Collins really upset. He talked then about shooting in England.'[37] Nevertheless, no one was shot. The killings were eventually, quietly, called off, presumably after it was realized that they would—at the very least—be politically counter-productive.

These, however, were only the first of a series of plots over the following months, directed at the British government. All followed essentially the same pattern. High-profile targets would be selected, their movements tracked, and their kidnapping or murder arranged—only to be called off in the end. The proposed victims included Lloyd George (again), his cabinet (again, in a separate plan), M.P.s of several parties (to be 'arrested' and shot if Sinn Féin T.D.s were harmed), Basil Thomson, the head of the Special Branch, Field-Marshal Henry Wilson, the chief of the Imperial General Staff, and Lord Fitzalan, the lord-lieutenant of Ireland. The initiative, the plans, and the men usually came from Dublin. Their objective, always, was retribution for some past or expected British outrage.[38]

Michael Collins was usually aware of or involved in planning these escapades (and was always kept informed by 'his' Organization men in Britain), but never acted alone, contrary to his reputation as 'the man who won the war'. In fact, it was he who was responsible for curbing over-zealous gunmen and for shutting several of the operations down. Cathal Brugha, the republic's minister of defence, on the other hand, was responsible for some of the most bloodthirsty proposals and pursued them ardently and independently. In 1918 he had even moved to London to oversee the massacre of the government's front bench by members of the Dublin I.R.A. should conscription be enforced in Ireland, playing billiards and looking after his baby daughter while he waited.[39]

---

[37] Sean McGrath (O'Malley Papers, P17b/100).

[38] For accounts of these plans, see Pa Murray, Billy Aherne, Denis Brennan, Sean McGrath, Frank Thornton, Denis Kelleher, Liam Tobin (O'Malley Papers, P17b/88, 100, 107). See also letter from Florence O'Donoghue to *Sunday Press*, 25 Jan. 1959; Bat Keaney Statement: MA.

[39] The best account, by one of the men who went with Brugha from the Dublin I.R.A., is Joe Good, *Enchanted by Dreams: Journal of a Revolutionary* (Dingle, 1986), 130–44. See also Sean McGrath: O'Malley Papers, P17b/100, Leo Henderson (P17b/105) and Fintan Murphy (P17b/107). Collins disagreed with this, along with several of his later, similar, schemes.

This phoney war had two sides, as British police forces and intelligence services worked to ward off the attacks which never came. Reports and rumours of assassins being sent from Ireland frequently reached the cabinet and individual M.P.s, often through Basil Thomson himself.[40] Bodyguards were assigned to fifty people in London, and policemen were stationed behind newly erected barricades in Westminster and Whitehall: an embarrassment and a huge waste of resources.[41]

The attack that was actually launched—and which itself launched the I.R.A. campaign in Britain—had little to do with this Dublin–London shadow boxing, and involved local, not imported, gunmen. Only the motive and rationale were the same: to 'do something' and take revenge for British actions in Ireland. In particular, it was felt that police reprisals demanded counter-reprisals against English property. The man charged with organizing these 'operations abroad' in August 1920 was Rory O'Connor, the G.H.Q.'s director of engineering and unofficial 'O/C Escapes' (he referred to himself as 'Director of Jail Deliveries'[42]). To these titles he now added the equally informal 'O/C Britain'.

O'Connor had already been involved in several abortive prison-breaks in England in 1920, as well as the smuggling of explosives, so he knew many of his new subordinates.[43] In early November I.R.A. and I.R.B. officers in Liverpool and London were summoned by headquarters to a conference in Manchester to meet 'our representative' and discuss operations.[44] O'Connor and his staff—notably Jack Plunkett—took the proposals made then and previously by the locals, and synthesized them into a multi-sited catastrophe.[45] The primary targets selected were the

---

[40] See letter to Basil Thomson, 27 Mar. 1920 (House of Lords Record Office, Lloyd George Papers, F46/9/4); Thomson to Alexander Maxwell (F/45/6/37); L. [Art O'Brien] to Michael Collins, 9 Nov. 1920 (O'Brien Papers, MS 8430). See also Directorate of Intelligence (Home Office) Report on Revolutionary Organizations in the United Kingdom [hereafter RRO], 9 Dec. 1920, 23 June 1921 (CAB 24/116, 125, C.P. 2273, 3074).

[41] See the correspondence between Lloyd George and W. Horwood, Commissioner of the Metropolitan Police (Lloyd George Papers, F/28/1/1–5); Report of the Commissioner of Police of the Metropolis for the Year 1921 (Parliamentary Papers, 1922, Cmnd. 1699; Minute from Cabinet Sec. to PM, 25 Nov. 1920 (CAB 23/23, C.66(20), App.1); and Home Secretary Shortt's comments in the House of Commons: House of Commons Debates, 143, col. 582.

[42] D/E to C/S, 28 Feb. 1920 (NLI, Count Plunkett Papers, MS 11,410[5]).

[43] See Art O'Brien to Michael Collins, 8 Apr. 1920 (O'Brien Papers, MS 8426); Collins to O'Brien, 17 Apr. and to Sean McGrath, 26 Apr. and 17 May 1920 (MS 8430); Collins to D/E, 26 Apr. 1920 (Plunkett Papers, MS 11,410[8]).

[44] Michael Collins to Neil Kerr, 10 Nov. 1920 (Mulcahy Papers, P7/A/3).

[45] Jack Plunkett memoirs (Count Plunkett Papers, MS 11,397), and statement (MS 11,981), fos. 40–2.

Liverpool docks and the Stuart Street power station in Manchester, partly because of their economic importance, but also because there were sympathizers working in both who could help the guerrillas. In Liverpool, dock gates and pumps were to be blown up, power stations wrecked, and warehouses burned, while in Manchester, the station was to be systematically demolished and then burned down.[46] Less ambitiously, the London Volunteers were to burn timber yards. All units were to be well armed with revolvers and pistols, out of the stocks held for shipment to Ireland.[47]

All that month O'Connor inspected and addressed I.R.A. companies, and toured canals, warehouses, and docks.[48] Unfortunately for his gran-diose schemes, however, the I.R.A. chief of staff's files had just been captured in Dublin, and among them were two memoranda detailing the Manchester and Liverpool plans. These were communicated to local police forces and subsequently released to the press. This was done to discredit the republican cause, but the attempted public relations coup rebounded against the government when, three days later—on the night of 28 November—the I.R.A. struck against the Liverpool warehouses anyway. Squads of armed guerrillas, numbering well over a hundred men in all, fanned out across the docklands, attacking twenty-three build-ings and burning nineteen of them, causing hundreds of thousands of pounds of damage. The Manchester men were supposed to act simultan-eously, but failed to do anything.[49] The night before, an arson attempt on a timber yard in London was only just foiled by the police.

Panic and shock was the result, rather than the indignation intended by the official revelations. If anything, the image of the I.R.A. as a sinister and powerful force was enhanced by their ability to mount such a large operation in the face of an already alerted government and in the midst of a great English city.[50] This public reaction was reinforced by the guerrillas' aggressiveness. They were determined and willing to shoot

[46] See the captured plans printed in *The Times*, 25 Nov. 1920, and also 'I.O.' (C. J. C. Street), *The Administration of Ireland 1920* (London, 1921), 444–7.

[47] Michael Collins to Sean McGrath, 17 Nov. 1920; McGrath to Collins, 25 Nov. (Mulcahy Papers, P7/A/8).

[48] See the ongoing correspondence between Kerr and Collins, 16–21 Nov. 1920: Mulcahy Papers, P7/A/3; Brady, *Ireland's Secret Service*, 25–8.

[49] Paddy O'Donoghue to Michael Collins, 23 Nov., 3 Dec. 1920 (Mulcahy Papers, P7/A/10); Collins to Neil Kerr, 27 Nov. (P7/A/3).

[50] *The Times*, 29 Nov. 1920. See also the Special Reports to Cabinet, 28 Nov. 1920 (CAB 24/115, C.P.2187) and RRO, 2 Dec. 1920 (CAB 24/115, C.P.2222), in which the alarm is evident.

when challenged, killing one civilian watchman. The unarmed police suddenly appeared overmatched.

Scotland—or more specifically, Glasgow—was not included in these plans and events, despite the comparatively large I.R.A. presence there. That city's Volunteers did raid a colliery for explosives on the same weekend as the Liverpool fires, and had previously attacked an army arsenal in October and an Orange Order rifle club earlier in November (resulting, respectively, in a policeman being badly wounded and a vicious riot).[51] These, however, were incidental acts of violence, aimed at equipping needy rebels in Ireland rather than matching Black and Tan outrages. Nor did the Scottish guerrillas ever mount more than a few isolated operations in the months that followed (see Tables 18 and 19).

What had happened to the Volunteers Michael Collins had described as 'excellent' only a few months before? In a June 1921 report, Rory O'Connor explained that, 'acting on orders no operations were carried out in Scotland or Wales'.[52] In fact, neither the headquarters staff nor the English underground seem to have had much contact with, let alone control over, either the I.R.A. or the I.R.B. in Scotland (Wales never had an I.R.A. unit). In an earlier memo, O'Connor admitted that 'I have no knowledge of Glasgow but from the reports which have been received it is clear that they have no military instincts, and apparently no training'.[53] Collins's own comments after 1920 were a litany of despairing complaints. In March, for example, 'the Organization in Scotland . . . seems to be an indefinite thing. We never hear from them.' In June, affairs were still 'very disorganized at the present moment'.[54] In fact, after 1916 the Scottish movement was consumed by an indecipherable mesh of personality clashes, ideological splits, and factional in-fighting.[55] When the I.R.A. acted north of the border, they did so on their own and to little effect.

---

[51] *The Times*, 29 Oct. 1920; 30 Nov. 1920; RRO, 13 Nov. 1920 (CAB 24/114, C.P.2089).

[52] D/E to C/S, 3 June 1921 (Mulcahy Papers, P7/A/19).

[53] From a captured, undated, memo entitled 'Operations Abroad', most likely written soon after the Liverpool fires: *Irish Times*, 22 Feb. 1921.

[54] Collins to L. [Art O'Brien], 19 Mar., 15 June 1921 (O'Brien Papers, MS 8430).

[55] John McGallogly Statement; John Carney correspondence (NLI, Sean O'Mahoney Papers, MS 24,474). See also Patterson, 'Activities of Irish Republican Physical Force Organisations', 46–55.

## Operations

British officials at all levels feared that the Liverpool 'spectacular' was only the beginning of an onslaught, but it turned out to be almost the last I.R.A. operation in England in 1920, as just one arson attack was mounted in December. January saw only five attacks against commercial targets in Manchester and London. The latter incidents still attracted anxious public and cabinet attention, though, as they involved gunfights and again left a policeman wounded.

There were several reasons for this lull. In the immediate aftermath of the November operations, the newly blooded guerrillas were cowed by the swift response of the police forces concerned. Mass arrests and deportations hit the Liverpool men particularly hard, as key leaders such as Tom and Neil Kerr and Steve Lanigan were picked up along with other activists. Paddy Donoghue of Manchester reported that '*They* seem to have gotten most of *the* people in Liverpool, unfortunately'.[56] Drill and meetings were suspended, many fair-weather volunteers dropped out, and for most of the rank and file the organization was—temporarily—'for all intents and purposes dead'.[57]

As with strong units in Ireland, however, new men stepped in and the work of the revolution continued, their attitude summed up by the 2 December message from replacement I.R.B. chief Paddy Daly to Michael Collins: 'if you say carry on it is carry on.'[58] However, even after the shock had worn off and reorganization had begun, British units were hampered by their uncertainty as to the wishes of the Dublin G.H.Q. and their hesitation to act without that authority. According to Daly, 'that was a big drawback to us for we had many and many a job ready to put into action and now we were told to wait up a while'.[59] The Headquarters men had initially thought of the November plan as a one-time operation, and were then themselves distracted by the advent of martial law and a new British counter-insurgency campaign. This in turn prompted them again to seek retribution on their enemies' home soil, but their thinking was still

---

[56] Paddy Donoghue to Michael Collins, 3 Dec. 1920 (Mulcahy Papers, P7/A/10). See also *The Times*, 1 Dec. 1920; C. Desmond Greaves, *Liam Mellows and the Irish Revolution* (London, 1971), 225–7.

[57] Brady, *Ireland's Secret Service*, 32.

[58] Paddy Daly to Michael Collins, 2 Dec. 1920 (Mulcahy Papers, P7/A/3). Daly replaced Neil Kerr as the head of the Liverpool I.R.B.

[59] Hugh Early (O'Malley Papers, P17b/110).

encumbered by a devotion to over-elaborate schemes. The Liverpool men complained that 'always we had to wait for London and Manchester—it held us up for they wanted things to come off simultaneously'.[60] Rory O'Connor was especially prone to this, and he never did give up his dream of pulling off a truly massive act of destruction. Much preparation went into a variety of bizarre schemes, from truck-bombing the Houses of Parliament to blowing up a bridge to poisoning horses in Buckingham Palace, none of which came close to being realized.[61]

The sustained campaign which followed, from February to the 11 July Truce, may have emerged out of these ongoing plans, but it took a very different—and more British—course. Dublin retained some control in 1921 but the initiative, plans, and guerrillas were now firmly local.

The London I.R.A. began this phase on the night of 6 February. Two farms on the outskirts of the city, one near Croydon and another near West Molesley, were attacked in direct response to the British army's new martial-law policy of destroying civilian property as punishment for ambushes.[62] The targets were random: 'We were to burn anything we could set fire to.'[63] Over £3,000-worth of produce was destroyed. A week later Manchester was the scene of a concerted incendiary effort, mounted simultaneously against warehouses and factories in the centre of the city and against cotton mills on the outskirts.[64] The night following this, Lancashire was again the scene for industrial sabotage, as factories and cotton mills were set on fire in Stockport, Oldham, and again Manchester.[65] On the subsequent weekend, as if by routine, Irish arsonists were at work in both Lancashire and Cheshire. Ten farms over a 25-mile area lost barns and produce worth between £15,000 and £20,000.[66]

At the same time, the Liverpool Volunteers, who 'were again growing restive from a sense of inactivity',[67] devised a plan in support of the new republican policy of discouraging emigration.[68] 'I am organizing a raid on one or two lodging-houses here where the emigrants usually 'put up', Paddy Daly informed Michael Collins on 15 February. 'I think we could do very much here.'[69] Collins wondered what 'the exact idea' was, and found out a few days later when the raids, in which the Volunteers posed as

[60] Id. (O'Malley Papers, P17b/55).

[61] Billy Aherne; Denis Kelleher (O'Malley Papers, P17b/99, 107).

[62] The Times, 8 Feb. 1921; Townshend, The British Campaign in Ireland, 149–50.

[63] Billy Aherne (O'Malley Papers, P17b/99).

[64] The Times, 4 Feb. 1921.      [65] Ibid., 4 Feb. 1921.      [66] Ibid., 21 Feb. 1921.

[67] Brady, Ireland's Secret Service, 38.      [68] The Times, 21 Feb. 1921.

[69] Daly to Collins, 15 Feb. 1921 (Mulcahy Papers. P7/A/4).

policemen to seize tickets and documents from America-bound 'desert-ers', made Irish and British headlines.[70] After this incident *The Times* paid uncharacteristic tribute to the raiders' 'wonderful organization and excep-tional executive ability'.[71] Daly exulted that 'the morale of the local company is very good', and was soon repeating the familiar refrain that they were 'very impatient at not getting some work to do', followed by the declaration that 'we are going to imitate our Manchester friends by doing some "farm-work" until there is something more important to do'.[72] In other words, the British rebels were no longer going to wait for those in Ireland (or Rory O'Connor) to tell them what to do, to which Michael Collins simply replied: 'your idea...appeals to me very strongly.'[73] As successive units adopted this attitude, and began to copy—and compete with—one another, the campaign was palpably acquiring its own momen-tum. Sir Hamar Greenwood, the chief secretary for Ireland, warned the House of Commons that 'the Sinn Féin conspiracy has spread to England and I urge the House to remember that it will spread farther. The troubles in this country are commencing.'[74]

The events of February set the basic operational and geographic pattern for the rest of the campaign. The methods used by the I.R.A. remained the same throughout. Individual attacks were planned in advance by local commanders, very occasionally prompted or specifically directed by orders from Dublin. Members would then be contacted, and units mobil-ized on the appropriate day (often meeting in Irish club rooms or halls), issued with arms and necessary equipment (stored in garages or flats) and then sent on their way. There seems to have been no shortage of weapons (invariably revolvers and pistols), and these groups usually outgunned the police. The basic tools for arson and sabotage were wirecutters, paraffin, gasoline, and fuses, all easily available.[75] Explosives and heavier weapons were hardly ever used, as these were needed more urgently in Ireland.

Despite the simplicity of these requirements, the conduct of operations was often rather sloppy or haphazard, although it must also be said that some were very efficiently executed as well. The guerrillas were fre-quently—and surprisingly—unprepared for a confrontation with the

[70] Collins to Daly, 17 Feb. 1921 (Mulcahy Papers, P7/A/4).
[71] *The Times*, 21 Feb. 1921.
[72] Paddy Daly to Michael Collins, 22 Feb., 4 Mar. 1921 (Mulcahy Papers, P7/A/4).
[73] Collins to Daly, 9 Mar. 1921 (Mulcahy Papers, P7/A/4).
[74] HC Debates, 1921, 138, cols. 631–3; *The Times*, 22 Feb. 1921.
[75] Brady, *Ireland's Secret Service*, 28–9, includes a photo of I.R.A. equipment captured by the police.

police, often carried incriminating or secret documents, and sometimes lacked determination in seeing a job through. All these things were complained of by the G.H.Q. and local leaders, but much the same could be, and was, said of many units in Ireland.[76]

A complete narrative of the 1921 campaign would be unnecessary and repetitive, but certain events and developments should be pointed out. The greatest mass assaults on private property after the Liverpool dock fires occurred on the nights of 9 and 26 March and 23 May, when, respectively, thirteen, forty and thirty separate farms were attacked. The first operation took place in a wide arc around Liverpool, caused damage of at least £15,000, and featured a gunfight between an arson squad and an irate farmer. One gunman was wounded and taken prisoner—the farmer was later attacked again as a reprisal.[77] The second event was a truly impressive feat of organization which stretched from the Tyne to the Tees, and 'lit up the district for miles around' in 'extraordinary bursts of illumination'.[78] Over £100,000-worth of produce, buildings, and machinery were destroyed. The last operation of this type again took place in the Tyneside area, but this time it was not just farms that were targeted. In Jarrow, a theatre and a garage were destroyed and gas mains were blown up, cutting off the city's light. An attempt was also made to blow up part of a shipyard. In nearby Wallsend and Durham, a factory and two railway stations were damaged. In contrast to these extensive and carefully planned operations, though, most attacks took place against only one or two farms or buildings at a time.

Until April remarkably few people had been hurt or killed, but the potential for serious violence was shown on the second of that month in Manchester. On that night an elaborate plan to destroy hotels, office buildings, and warehouses in the city centre degenerated into a series of encounters with terrorized civilians, and ended with a ferocious battle around an Irish club in which four policemen were shot and several I.R.A. men were killed or wounded.[79] Two days later the body of an English spy, Vincent Fovargue, was discovered on a golf course in Middlesex with a note pinned to his jacket saying: 'Let Spies and traitors beware—I.R.A.'

[76] In the 'Operations Abroad' memo. (*Irish Times*, 22 Feb. 1921), the author stated that 'the Volunteers abroad could not be relied upon absolutely to undertake operations on a large scale with success'.

[77] For an estimate of the cost, see *The Times*, 16 Mar. 1921. For details of these events, see ibid., 10, 11 Mar. 1921; Brady, *Ireland's Secret Service*, 38–43.

[78] *The Times*, 28 Mar. 1921.

[79] Ibid., 4 Apr. 1921.

He had been planted in the Dublin I.R.A. (probably on the orders of Basil Thomson) after a faked escape, and had travelled to London in order to penetrate the republican underground there. Michael Collins's intelligence organization had, true to form, discovered his mission. He was taken from an Irish dance and executed by a team of local gunmen.[80]

The first deliberate attack on British policemen came on 4 May. In a replay of the 1867 rescue mission which created the 'Manchester Martyrs', a Glasgow prison van containing Frank Carty, a former commander of the Sligo Brigade who had famously escaped from prison in Derry and been recaptured in Scotland, was held up in broad daylight by a dozen armed men. They killed a police inspector and wounded a detective, but failed to get him out. The convulsive police reaction which followed brought mass arrests in Irish districts and produced the only serious confrontation between an Irish community and British police (Glasgow and Liverpool had already seen numerous sectarian gang fights). Crowds in the east end of the city rioted and stoned the police after a priest was jailed. The army was called in, and most traffic out of the city was halted in the search for the would-be rescuers.[81]

On 14 May a country-wide operation was carried out which again displayed a new ruthlessness. For months the I.R.A. had gathered the home addresses of British ex-officers acting as auxiliary policemen in Ireland. In reprisal for their collective record of outrage, at least fifteen of these addresses were simultaneously attacked in Liverpool, St Albans, and London. Five people—relatives of auxiliaries—were shot on their doorsteps (one of whom later died) and many of the houses were burned. A few homes missed were later attacked individually.[82]

---

[80] Denis Brennan, Frank Thornton, and Denis Kelleher (O'Malley Papers, P17b/100, 107); *The Times*, 4 Apr. 1921. For Fovargue's 'escape', see *Irish Times*, 2 Feb. 1921 and for further revelations, 6 Apr. 1921. Brady, *Ireland's Secret Service* (p. 12), also has something to say. The British intelligence effort against the I.R.A. is discussed in Eunan O'Halpin, 'British Intelligence in Ireland, 1914–21', in Christopher Andrew and D. N. Dilks (eds.), *The Missing Dimension* (London, 1984), 54–77, and Christopher Andrew, *Secret Service: The Making of the British Intelligence Community* (London, 1985), 246–58. Unfortunately, neither of these discusses the I.R.A. in Britain.

[81] Frank Carty (O'Malley Papers, P17b/128); Glasgow Chief Constable's Report, 4 May 1921 (SRO, HH 55/63); *The Times*, 5, 6 May 1921. See also Greaves, *Liam Mellows*, 232, and Douglas Grant, *The Thin Blue Line: The Story of the City of Glasgow Police* (London, 1973). Carty himself was severely beaten by his guards after the rescue attempt.

[82] *The Times*, 16 May 1921. See also Brady, *Ireland's Secret Service*, 63–6; 'I.O', *The Administration of Ireland 1921*, 23–7. Also of interest are Charles Dalton, *With the Dublin Brigade 1917–1921* (London, 1929), 89–92, and the captured documents printed in *The Times*, 14 Mar. 1921.

The other major evolution in the conduct of the campaign was that communications—particularly railway, telegraph, and telephone lines—became a major object of attention. The first such operation was carried out in and near Jarrow on 9 April, when a number of telegraph poles were sawn through and knocked down, and wires were cut in surrounding districts. Railway stations became targets as well in following weeks, and June brought an unprecedented wave of such incidents. These began on 2 June in and around Liverpool, when telephone lines were cut and poles chopped down all around the city, disrupting services for a week. Just as these were returning to normal, the saboteurs struck again, cutting over 300 telegraphic and telephone wires around Liverpool, and more in Cheshire. The Liverpool police, already on the alert, 'rushed to the scene in motor conveyances of every description and scoured the district', provoking several skirmishes with retreating I.R.A. squads.[83] Again, telephone and telegraph services to many other cities were completely cut off for days.

On this last occasion, however, the damage was not just confined to Liverpool. In the belt of country ringing outer London, and as far afield as Eastbourne, Bristol, and Brighton, hundreds more lines were disabled, and dozens of poles were toppled in a massive display of energy and organization. The I.R.A. had cut a swathe of destruction through the telecommunications network of southern and north-western England, prompting an anxious government to call out the army to patrol telegraph lines around London. This new offensive continued through the month, along with industrial sabotage, and reached its peak on 16 June with a final great effort. In what was described as 'a wild Sinn Féin outbreak in the suburbs of London', ten separate railway signal boxes were either damaged or destroyed, along with all nearby telegraph wires.[84] These attacks were pressed home with great determination, and any civilians who got in the way were liable to be held up or shot (one workman was wounded). In a battle with the police, one I.R.A. man was also seriously injured. Two days later a similar series of raids were carried out around Manchester where, again, a watchman was shot.

Finally, a rather mysterious episode must be mentioned. For two weeks in April a wave of window-smashing and cutting spread through English, Welsh, and Scottish cities. The attacks began in central London on the night of the 16th, directed against shops and other businesses in an apparently premeditated and well-organized plan of destruction. They

---

[83] *The Times*, 9 June 1921.          [84] Ibid., 18 June 1921.

soon spread out from the capital to Birmingham, Swansea, Cardiff, Hull, Worcester, and elsewhere, so that thousands of windows were being damaged or broken night after night, despite the best precautions of the police. Then, just as suddenly, after 28 April the attacks stopped.[85]

Were the I.R.A. responsible? Edward Brady, a Liverpool officer, states that they were not, although it was widely accepted at the time that they were.[86] When the Free State government compiled a list of I.R.A. operations for compensation purposes, only some of the London incidents were accepted as being 'probably attributable to Irish agency'.[87] However, a close reading of newspaper accounts reveals a previous incident in Liverpool on 1 April, when exactly the same thing happened on a much smaller scale. This was itself taken as an I.R.A. act and, if we accept it as such, it provides a clue to the later occurrences. A plausible explanation for what happened runs as follows: the Liverpool I.R.A. carried out the first operation, and the London men decided to emulate it on a grander scale. This resulted in the first controlled effort on 16 April. The I.R.A. may have had a hand in the nightly sabotage which followed, but the scale of the actions, which staggered police authorities, was certainly beyond the capacity of the Irish underground to mobilize. The only explanation is that other unknown people spontaneously joined in, in a remarkable display of copycat contagion.

The last act of the campaign took place on 1 July in London, when an attempt was made to blow up some Ministry of Pensions buildings in Regent's Park.[88] After this, and until the Truce of 11 July, the republican leadership in Dublin were deeply involved in negotiations with the British government, and wanted to avoid disrupting or complicating the process. This restraint only took effect in Dublin and England where G.H.Q. influence over individual units was strongest.

## Truce, Treaty, and Civil War

As in Ireland, the Truce was seen by British militants as a chance to prepare for the next round. The back room gun-runners redoubled their

[85] Ibid., 19–28 Apr. 1921.
[86] Brady, *Ireland's Secret Service*, 81–2. See also *The Times*, 22 Apr. 1921, and RRO, 28 Apr. 1921 (CAB 24/122, C.P.2891).
[87] Summary police reports, claims for compensation in respect of damage to property in England by Irish forces during the war (NA, FIN 576/42).
[88] *The Times*, 2 July 1921.

arms buying and smuggling efforts to the point where over a ton a week of arms, ammunition, and explosives was flowing across the Irish Channel. The actual production of arms in Britain ended at the end of July, however, when an incendiary bomb factory—a rented garage in Greenwich—was itself incinerated, killing one Volunteer and injuring another.[89] The police did not connect this episode to the I.R.A., so neither it nor the other underground activities disturbed the political atmosphere until nearly the end of negotiations. Then, on 18 and 22 November, to the accompaniment of tremendous publicity, large quantities of weapons were stolen from two regimental barracks in London.[90] These were quickly recovered and the raiders—sent from Ireland rather than local men— apprehended, but in the following week another minor crisis occurred when customs officers discovered a shipment of Thompson submachine guns in Liverpool. This one was kept secret, on the strength of Michael Collins's promise that it would not happen again.[91]

Rory O'Connor toured English cities in September (at Cathal Brugha's direction), 'for the purpose of organising and perfecting plans for an Active offensive to be carried out on the resumption of hostilities', but was 'not particularly optimistic of anything being done on a large scale'.[92] New units in Sheffield and Newcastle appeared to hold the most promise, while old-guard Liverpool and Manchester he found to be very disappointing. His proposed solution was to establish a British G.H.Q. and divisions along Irish lines, but this typically overambitious idea did not appeal to the men in Dublin. Tentative plans were made to undertake assassinations, further attacks on the homes of Black and Tans, and another sabotage campaign, and these became more elaborate and concrete in later months. Some proposed victims were shadowed, and targets reconnoitered, at least in London. Reggie Dunne, O/C London, explained in October that 'the last time you met my officers they were not exactly prepared to give details of possible operations without reports in hand. They would be now in a somewhat better position. The number of intended operations is greatly increasing.'[93]

[89] Dir. of Chemicals's Report, 1 Aug. 1921; D/E to C/S, 31 Oct. 1921 (Mulcahy Papers, P7/A/23, 27); *The Times*, 30 June 1922.

[90] *The Times*, 23, 24 Nov.; 3, 8 Dec. 1921. See also Rex Taylor, *Michael Collins* (London, 1958), 168–9; Margery Forester, *The Lost Leader* (London, 1971), 240–3; Tim Pat Coogan, *Michael Collins*, 249.

[91] Paddy Daly to Collins, 1 Dec. 1921; Collins to Daly, 5 Dec. (Mulcahy Papers, P7/A/7).

[92] D/E memos: 'Re-Organising Britain'; 'Report on Visit to Britain September 1921' (Mulcahy Papers, P7/A/24, 29).

[93] O/C London to D/E, 24 Oct. 1921 (Mulcahy Papers, P7/A/27).

For front-line guerrillas like Dunne, the Truce was a somewhat uncertain period, unrelieved by the sense of victory and recognition accorded their Irish comrades. They still had to be careful of the police, they received no greater support from their 'people' or from the G.H.Q., and few new recruits (outside Glasgow). Most devastating was an upsurge in unemployment, which demoralized units everywhere. Art O'Brien told Collins that 'It is coming up against us now on all sides, and is going to cause a great deal of mischief, annoyance and unpleasantness'.[94] These frustrations led Dunne to assert the primacy of the I.R.A. and demand money and help from the I.S.D.L. and G.A.A., which led him into squabbles with the equally assertive Cumann na mBan and with O'Brien, who complained that 'such childish acts are heading us for a fiasco'.[95] Dunne also fruitlessly solicited Dublin for aid and official acknowledgement. When he first went in person in August he failed to get a meeting with Michael Collins, but this was rectified a few weeks later, and O'Brien reported that Dunne's 'attitude seems to have changed for the better'.[96] This failed to translate into actual help, however, as the men in Britain were kept at a distance. Particularly revealing of this semi-detached status was Chief of Staff Richard Mulcahy's remark that 'it is very difficult to know what to say in the case of men about whom one knows absolutely nothing'.[97] Dunne's last hope was that, if operations were resumed, he would be authorized to raise money through robberies. This interestingly anticipated later forms of urban guerrilla warfare, but the British Volunteers never got a chance to mount their projected financial campaign.

The Treaty of 6 December split the republican movement in Britain as thoroughly as in Ireland, with pro- and anti-Treaty camps rapidly being established on either side of an uncertain middle ground. I.R.A. members were found in all three groups. A few left for Ireland to enlist on one side or the other, and most simply dropped out altogether. Art O'Brien, an opponent of the Treaty from the outset, won a pyrrhic victory as he and his followers managed to maintain control of the I.S.D.L., but found themselves with almost no one left to lead.[98] O'Brien did retain the use of a

---

[94] L. [Art O'Brien] to Michael Collins, 22 Aug. 1921 (O'Brien Papers, MS 8430).
[95] Art O'Brien to 'RMG' [Michael Collins], 20 July 1921 (O'Brien Papers, MS 8430).
[96] 'L' to 'RMG', 10 Aug. 1921 (O'Brien Papers, MS 8430).
[97] C/S to D/E, 31 Oct. 1921 (Mulcahy Papers, P7/A/27).
[98] e.g. out of seventy branches in South Wales, only three or four were left by early 1923. See *The Times*, 14 Mar., 31 May 1923. The decline of the I.S.D.L. is somewhat gleefully charted in the weekly Reports on Revolutionary Organisations: 1, 14 June; 6, 13, 27 July (CAB 24/137, 138).

considerable sum of money, however.[99] And eventually, as in Ireland, frustration, anger, and a desire for revenge against old enemies led to violence. Thus was precipitated the assassination of Sir Henry Wilson on 22 June by Reggie Dunne and another London veteran, Joseph O'Sullivan.

Ironically, while this is by far the best known and most controversial incident in the history of the British I.R.A., it was an isolated, even desperate, act carried out by the killers alone.[100] There is no evidence that Dunne and O'Sullivan were the tools of a conspiracy or of Michael Collins in particular, as biographers and historians continue to suggest. Wilson, former chief of the Imperial General Staff and current Ulster Unionist M.P., had been on previous I.R.A. hit lists (not, apparently, of Collins's devising), but so had much of Britain's political elite. His status as a target derived from widespread nationalist rage at the treatment of Catholics in Northern Ireland, whose government he vociferously defended. It was this, and Dunne's deep desire for unambiguous patriotic action to remove his political and personal dilemmas, that drove the assassins to seek revolutionary justice. Both men were caught—after wounding three pursuers—and hanged on 10 August. A rescue was mooted by their comrades, but disorganization and division prevented it being attempted.

The Wilson affair was very nearly the last act of violence by members of the I.R.A. in Britain. When Scotland Yard went in search of what they presumed to be a formidable murder conspiracy, all they found was a few small guns and bombs, and an anonymous blueprint for an 'Irish Expeditionary Force' to be recruited from former Volunteers.[101] Even the reliably alarmist Special Branch dismissed remaining republicans as 'cranks and roughs'.[102] The I.R.A. itself seemed to have disappeared.

Elsewhere, as well, only residual networks remained. Eight Lancashire collieries were raided for explosives by armed men on 3 June—presumably St Helen's activists operating on behalf of the anti-Treaty forces. Despite a massive police search, no one was ever caught, but nor were the daring robberies repeated.[103] In Liverpool a few dozen republicans still met occasionally in basements and pubs, nominally under the command of

[99] See J. J. McElligot to Art O'Brien, 5 Apr. 1932; O'Brien to McElligot, 3 May 1932 (O'Brien Papers, MS 8461).

[100] For the assassination and a survey of the evidence and arguments concerning its origins, see Ch. 8.

[101] *The Times*, 4, 27 July 1922.

[102] RRO, 6 July 1922 (CAB 24/137).

[103] *The Times*, 5 June 1921; RRO, 14 June 1922 (CAB 24/137).

Denis and Patrick Fleming, but Home Office intelligence reported that 'there are at present no instructions to attack persons or property in this area'.[104] On 8 July a group of Midlands militants were caught in the act of robbing an ammunition factory in Birmingham. Thereafter, the republican underground in Britain returned to its pre-1920 existence as an arms pipeline and escape route.

The idea of a second British campaign was revived briefly in the winter of 1923. Liam Lynch, the I.R.A.'s uncompromising chief of staff, was searching for secret weapons, foreign aid, or some other miraculous method to turn the tide of defeat, and became determined to open up a second front on what he still considered enemy soil.[105] A veteran Cork city guerrilla, Pa Murray, had already been asked to be the new 'O/C Britain' the previous autumn, although he was sceptical of the mission:

'To take charge of London' is rather vague. If I were to go there I would like to know what I am expected to do. The reason I ask this question is—very little was done in England when everyone was with you. Now you have very few on your side—what do you propose to do there? Burn houses—shoot people— what is expected? If a definite plan was drawn up and considered carefully by men who knew the difficulties of England, I have no doubt but I would go.[106]

No proper plans were ever made, but Murray went anyway, followed by three other Corkmen, specialists in explosives and engineering, and they concentrated on acquiring arms and chemicals. Suddenly, in February, Murray was informed that 'We are considering active hostilities in England owing to the advanced development of the situation here. Activities would mean general destructive policy.' Then came the order that 'activities in England, as arranged, would start at once'.[107]

Nothing happened. Murray, a hard and devoted worker, had been able to reassemble an organization in skeletal form, but he could not reanimate it without the indigenous aggressive spirit of 1919–21.[108] In any case, the orders were apparently cancelled by Moss Twomey, Lynch's deputy

---

[104] RRO, 27 July 1922 (CAB 24/138).

[105] See Florence O'Donoghue, *No Other Law* (Dublin, 1954), 281; Sean Cronin, *The McGarrity Papers* (Tralee, 1972), 132–5.

[106] Pa Murray to Adj., 1st Southern Div., 30 Sept. 1922 (O'Malley Papers, P17a/51).

[107] Portions of Lynch's intercepted correspondence are reprinted in the *The Times*, 13 Mar. 1923.

[108] For Murray's activities, see his interview with Ernie O'Malley (O'Malley Papers, P17b/88) and his correspondence with Art O'Brien (O'Brien Papers, MS 8429, 8461). See also Michael Hopkinson, *Green Against Green*, 254–5.

(later to be involved in the English bombing campaign of 1939–40), 'for he was a good staff officer who had a sense of reality'.[109] Mass arrests followed in March, but again all the police found was some old guns and a paper army. The government wished to present their findings as a serious threat only just nipped in the bud, but one judge took a more realistic view when he let off one suspect with a fine of 20 shillings for possessing a revolver, and the comment that these were 'a lot of young and foolish people . . . who did not mean to do any harm'.[110] Twomey told Lynch on 5 April that 'I am afraid the chances of operations in Britain are now negligible if not altogether impossible'.[111] Lynch was shot by Free State soldiers on 10 April, and the plan died with him.

## Counting the Cost

Tables 18 and 19 measure I.R.A. activity by area and month over the course of the British campaign. A few operations have been omitted as unclassifiable, such as the raids on emigrants in Liverpool and window-breaking in general. On average, from January to July I.R.A. incidents were taking place twice a day in Britain, concentrated in and around London, Liverpool, Manchester, and Newcastle. As Table 19 shows, the guerrillas in the first two centres ran the course; the latter two faded in the stretch. This geography of violence was not foreordained by the presence or absence of Irish communities or I.R.A. units. Scotland had a large first- and second-generation 'Irish' population and many Volunteer companies, but saw little violence. Parts of Wales had seen sizeable immigration, but the immigrants and their descendants eschewed armed republicanism. As in Ireland, it was factors other than the size of the movement or its potential support that determined the level of activity.

    I.R.A. operations in Britain also followed a pattern similar to that in Ireland (and particularly its cities), in that they were usually carried out by people living near the targets, operating from their own homes. The fact that most Volunteers also had jobs helps account for the timing of attacks, which generally took place at night and on weekends. Although Irish communities as a whole were definitely not involved, they did provide the basic social context in which the I.R.A. operated. In this sense, the

---

[109] Pa Murray (O'Malley Papers, P17b/88).     [110] *The Times*, 16 Apr. 1923.
[111] Twomey to C/S, 5 April 1923: O'Malley Papers, P17a/51.

TABLE 18.  *I.R.A. operations in Britain, October 1920–July 1921*

| | Arson | | Sabotage | Robbery | | Shootings | |
|---|---|---|---|---|---|---|---|
| | Buildings | Other | Telegraph | Arms | Explosives | Police | Other |
| London | 22 | 36 | 38 | 2 | | | 7 |
| Liverpool | 52 | 4 | 41 | | | | 1 |
| Manchester | 51 | 12 | 1 | | | 5 | 1 |
| Tyneside | 15 | 54 | 4 | | | | |
| Teesside | 7 | 21 | 2 | | | | |
| Lancashire | 2 | 1 | | | 2 | | |
| Yorkshire | | | | 2 | 2 | | |
| Birmingham | | 2 | | 1 | | | |
| Scotland | 5 | 10 | 5 | 3 | 13 | 3 | |
| TOTAL | 154 | 140 | 91 | 8 | 17 | 8 | 9 |

*Sources*: The data for Tables 18, 19, and 20 were collected from a daily survey of the London *Times* and the *Irish Times*, from the weekly Reports on Revolutionary Organizations in the United Kingdom presented to the cabinet by the Home Office Directorate of Intelligence, and from the summaries of police reports contained in the Irish Department of Finance file on 'Claims for Compensation in respect of damage to property in England by Irish forces during the war' (NA, FIN 576/42). These latter were themselves scrutinized by Free State military intelligence, whose own report is contained in Sec., Dept. of Defence to Dept. of Finance, 28 Jan. 1925, in the same file. Also useful was a D/E report on operations to C/S, 3 June 1921 (Mulcahy Papers, P7/A/19). 'London' includes the suburban and rural areas surrounding the city proper. These figures do not include events before October 1920 or after July 1921.

TABLE 19.  *The I.R.A. campaign in Britain, 1920–1921*

| Operations | 1920 | | 1921 | | | | | | | Total | % age of total operations |
|---|---|---|---|---|---|---|---|---|---|---|---|
| | Nov. | Dec. | Jan. | Feb. | Mar. | Apr. | May | June | July | | |
| London | 1 | | 2 | 4 | 20 | 13 | 10 | 51 | 1 | 102 | 24 |
| Liverpool | 30 | | | | 15 | 1 | 10 | 42 | | 98 | 23 |
| Manchester | | 1 | 3 | 43 | 7 | 7 | 2 | 5 | | 68 | 16 |
| Tyneside | | | | | | 26 | 12 | 41 | | 79 | 19 |
| Teesside | | | | 14 | 7 | 9 | | | | 30 | 7 |
| Lancashire | | | | | 3 | 2 | | | | 5 | 1 |
| Yorkshire | | | | | | | 2 | | | 2 | 0.5 |
| Birmingham | | | | 2 | | | | | | 2 | 0.5 |
| Scotland | 2 | 1 | 1 | 4 | 1 | 11 | 16 | 1 | | 37 | 9 |
| TOTAL | 33 | 2 | 6 | 51 | 85 | 54 | 90 | 101 | 1 | 423 | |

characteristics of the campaign were not those of modern terrorism, but of low-level guerrilla warfare.

The choice of targets also reflects the importance of locality. When particular collieries were raided for explosives, or arsenals for arms, it was usually because the I.R.A. had members or contacts who worked inside them. The planned attacks on the Liverpool docks and the Manchester power station in 1920, for example, both required such local knowledge. The most common targets were in isolated and deserted places: farms or warehouses at night, telephone and telegraph lines along lonely roads.

Incidentally, one plausible scenario for the violence—that it was carried out by seasonal labourers coming from Ireland—is not borne out by the evidence. Very few of those arrested worked in agriculture or had recently come from Ireland, and in any case, the demand for Irish labour was at a very low point in 1921 for both political and economic reasons. Finally, seasonal labourers typically did not arrive in England until the spring, which does not coincide with the chronology of violence.[112]

How much damage did the campaign do? Thanks to compensation negotiations between the British and Irish governments in the 1920s, we have an extraordinarily precise figure for its financial cost: £672,169. This is a considerable underestimate, however, as it merely represents the total amount of liability admitted by insurance companies where claims were made.[113] Not all insurance figures were available to the police, by no means all property affected was insured, and admitted liability rarely covered all damages. For example, the November attacks in Bootle and Liverpool cost insurance companies a little over £400,000 but estimates for the total cost ranged from £950,000 to £1,200,000.[114] In fact, this episode created tremendous alarm in the British insurance industry, which immediately raised its fire rates and refused to cover any damages resulting from politically inspired arson except under new and very expensive policies.[115]

So the total bill for damages undoubtedly lay somewhere upwards of a million pounds (the amount of compensation initially agreed upon by the

---

[112] See P. E. Dewey, 'Agricultural Labour Supply in England and Wales During the First World War', *Economic History Review*, 28 (1975), 103, and E. J. T. Collins, 'Migrant Labour in British Agriculture in the Nineteenth Century', ibid. 29 (1976), 38–59.

[113] The police summaries provided to support the British government's compensation case are itemized and include financial estimates (NA, FIN 576/42).

[114] For estimates, see *The Times*, 29 Nov.; 30 Dec. 1920.

[115] There were even questions in Parliament about possible government help. See HC Debates, 1921, 139, col 1737; *The Times*, 30 Nov., 1 Dec. 1920; 7 Feb. 1921.

two governments[116]). This destruction was not, of course, on a scale that would have a significant impact on the British economy as a whole, but in personal or business terms, particularly in the north of England, the damage was sometimes very severe. Even the extra costs involved in compensation and police and legal services could impose a strain on many municipal and county budgets.[117]

Table 20 charts the direct human costs of the campaign: ten people killed (including the two men executed) and twenty-four wounded due to I.R.A. activity. The figures are divided into the periods before and after 11 July 1921.

I.R.A. losses themselves must also be measured in terms of people arrested, jailed, and deported. Police and legal statistics—as reported in newspapers—are partial, but it is clear that, between 1920 and 1923, several thousand men and women were forcibly detained for questioning (which could easily last several days), many more than once. According to *The Times*, 317 people were formally arrested and charged in connection with political violence between October 1920 and April 1923, 165 of these in the period from December 1920 to the Truce. This only represents a minimum number: the real total could easily have been as high as 400 and 200 respectively, and was quite possibly higher.

The number of convictions is equally unclear. *The Times* reports show forty-five people convicted during the campaign, but when an amnesty was declared for pre-Truce political prisoners in February 1922, over sixty

TABLE 20.  *Victims of the Irish Revolution in Britain, 1920–1921*

|  | Police | | I.R.A. | | Civilians | | Total | |
|---|---|---|---|---|---|---|---|---|
|  | K | W | K | W | K | W | K | W |
| 1920–July 1921 | 1 | 7 | 2 | 6 | 3 | 6 | 6 | 19 |
| July 1921–2 |  | 2 | 3 | 1 | 1 | 2 | 4 | 5 |
| TOTAL | 1 | 9 | 5 | 7 | 4 | 8 | 10 | 24 |

*Note*: K = killed; W = wounded.

[116] See the correspondence in NA, FIN 576/42; also *The Times*, 18 Apr. 1923, *Irish Times*, 18–19 Apr. 1923.

[117] *The Times*, 29 Mar.; 5 Sept. 1921.

were released.[118] Of course, some were jailed before the campaign began. Even so, Michael Collins was immediately bombarded with appeals from I.S.D.L. branches and Sinn Féin clubs in England and Scotland regarding up to seventy further prisoners who were deemed by the Home Office not to have political status. These included men convicted of arson who had declared themselves to be 'soldiers of the I.R.A.'[119] The total number of convictions for 1920–3 was at least 200, most of which were for sentences of two to ten years.

Moreover, emergency legislation covering both Britain and Ireland allowed the government to circumvent the necessity of charging and convicting suspects. Anyone merely suspected of being a threat to law and order in Ireland could be deported and interned there indefinitely on the orders of the Home Secretary. By extension, this was applied to members of Irish or allied organizations suspected of breaking the law in Britain. The full power of this legislation was displayed in March 1923, when 110 Irish men and women (still British citizens) residing in England were rounded up and shipped *en masse* to prisons in Dublin, but liberal use of these measures was made before this as well. It was reported in the House of Commons that from 6 January to 21 May 1921 twenty-two 'Irishmen living in England' were interned, and more were also interned both before and after these dates.[120] But how were 'Irishmen living in England' defined? Did this include sons and daughters of immigrants, as many in the I.R.A. were? It seems safe to assume that the number interned before the Truce reached at least fifty, as is indicated by other sources.[121] Thus, the likely total of people arrested and either charged, convicted, or interned on I.R.A.-related suspicions or offences between late 1920 and the Truce was well over 200, and over 500 by early 1923.

## Policing the British Troubles

These two sets of figures, for I.R.A. arrests and operations, illustrate the achievements and limitations of the British counter-insurgency effort.

---

[118] *Ibid.*, 15 Feb. 1921. The cabinet deliberations are found in CAB 23/29, c.6(22), 30 Jan. 1922. Concern over this issue had been expressed at the Irish Race Conference held in Paris in January 1922: see its *Proceedings* (Dublin, 1922), 33.

[119] See the correspondence in the Ministry of Home Affairs file (NA, H12/1), and particularly: Sec., Leeds I.S.D.L. No. 5 branch to Collins, 28 Feb. 1922; Pres., Sinn Féin cumann, Dunfirmline to Collins, 8 Mar. 1922.

[120] HC Debates, 1921, 142, cols. 1075–6.

[121] See Greaves, *Liam Mellows*, 231.

Some police forces were able to catch I.R.A. guerrillas in considerable numbers, either in the act or soon afterwards. What they were not able to do was to stop the campaign or even prevent it from intensifying. The I.R.A. was far from being defeated in July 1921, and loomed as a greater threat if the Truce were to break down.

This combination of local success and overall failure was in large part due to the division of state action into two distinct organizational levels: on the one hand, the Special Branch and the Directorate of Intelligence responsible to the Home Office (and united under the control of Basil Thomson until his removal in November 1921), and on the other, individual municipal and county police forces responsible to local governments.

It was the latter which formed the front line of the counter-insurgency effort. In each affected area, the pattern of the official response was essentially the same, although it varied in intensity. Most of the time police forces relied on normal criminal procedures, although because they were dealing with a well-established target group—the Irish—they were probably more severe than usual. The one major departure was that raiding parties, guards, and patrols began to arm themselves in large numbers in late 1920. Nevertheless, it still remained common for I.R.A. men with guns to be confronted by constables without.[122] I.R.A. operations were occasionally broken up when routine police patrols challenged guerrillas who were acting suspiciously, but the authorities typically only acted after the fact. Once a shooting or arson attack took place, a manhunt—sometimes of vast dimensions—would be launched. Homes, offices, and clubs would be raided and suspects rounded up for questioning until, if possible, specific charges could be laid. Some forces, particularly in Scotland, took an unsubtle view of Irish political activism, and detained 'suspicious' people of all sorts for weeks and months at a time (the maximum then was an astonishing 110 days without trial).[123] For example, after a Lanarkshire constable was shot twice by Volunteers attempting to raid a drill hall in October 1920, it was reported that: 'a rigorous roundup of known Sinn Féiners is now in progress with a view to ascertaining their movements and whereabouts at the time of the outrage.

---

[122] Liverpool City Police Report on the Police Establishment and the State of Crime for Year Ending 31st Dec. 1921 (Liverpool Record Office); Minute from Lord Polwaite, Prison Commission for Scotland, 10 Nov. 1921 (SRO, HH 55/66); Robert W. Gould and Michael J. Waldren, *London's Armed Police 1829 to the Present* (London, 1986), 86–94.

[123] See the discussion in CAB 23/29, c.6(22), 30 Jan. 1922.

A large number of young men, known to be of pronounced Sinn Féin sympathies, have been interrogated by the police, and a number have been taken into custody.'[124]

The local police were concerned with catching the perpetrators of specific crimes and not with defeating the I.R.A. as an organization. They do not seem to have attempted to infiltrate republican organizations, to identify their members *en masse*, or to gather intelligence through systematic surveillance. They did not have the training or experience to do so. Because of this, the policemen were fortunate that the I.R.A. were equally parochial and stayed in their homes and jobs to be arrested. A great deal of local effort also went into preventative measures, usually hastily arranged in the immediate aftermath of an attack. In Liverpool in 1920 the army was called out to protect the docks.[125] In rural areas of Lancashire and Cheshire elaborate rocket signalling and telephone warning systems were instituted in early 1921 to alert county policemen and residents of I.R.A. raids.[126] Later, in London, military guards were assigned to railway and telegraph lines, and armed motor patrols operated in the city centre while road-blocks were established in the outer boroughs to search cars.[127] In Scotland troops were assigned to protect an oil pipeline along the Forth and Clyde canal after a failed I.R.A. sabotage attempt, while explosives stores and other potential targets also received military guards.[128] None of these measures lasted very long, being short-term expedients rather than long-term solutions. Nor do they seem to have had any substantial effect on I.R.A. actions. On the contrary: guerrillas often judged the success of their operations by the scale of the response.

The most effective police force was Liverpool's. They had the best intelligence and used it well: no fewer than four successive captains of that city's I.R.A. company—along with a good number of other activists— were arrested between late November and early June.[129] This may have

---

[124] *The Times*, 29 Oct. 1920.    [125] *Irish Times*, 30 Nov. 1920.

[126] Memo. from Lancashire Chief Constable, 25 Feb. 1921: Lancashire County Record Office, Lancashire Constabulary Memo. Book; *The Times*, 8, 14 Mar. 1921.

[127] *The Times*, 9 June 1921, and RRO, 7 July 1921 (CAB 24/126, C.P.3115); Gould and Waldren, *London's Armed Police*, 87.

[128] J. Rose, Scottish Office to ? Hogg, 9 May 1921; Protection Sub-Cttee Minutes, 27 June 1921 (SRO, HH 55/62).

[129] See Hugh Early and Patrick Daly (O'Malley Papers, P17b/110, 136), and Michael Collins's correspondence with a succession of Liverpool I.R.B. leaders over this period (Mulcahy Papers, P7/A/1–6).

been a result of the force's acute consciousness of 'Irish' crime, which was even enumerated separately in its annual reports.[130] In any case, as Table 19 shows, the Merseyside Volunteers soldiered on despite their vigorous opponents. The Manchester I.R.A., on the other hand, never recovered from the April debacle which saw twenty men arrested with weapons, one of whom was willing to testify against his former comrades. This disaster, and the disarray that followed, had more to do with internal problems than with brilliant police work, however. The Glasgow police were at least as aggressive as in Liverpool—as demonstrated by their reaction to the Bothwell arms raid and the Carty rescue attempt—but never faced the same systematic violence. Nor can I.R.A. inactivity there be attributed to police efficiency. The underground units remained intact throughout: as in Manchester, the main problem was internal, not external. In London, the Metropolitan Police simply failed to come to grips with their foes, so much so that several guerrillas later commented on the surprising lack of arrests in 1921. It may well be that the London detectives and divisions were ill-served by the more political agencies above them who were waging their own war against Irish republicanism.

The I.R.A. came to the attention of Scotland Yard and Scotland House as part of their post-war struggle against 'subversion' and revolution. Growing popular unrest and the perceived menace of Bolshevism had prompted the development of counter-revolutionary policies and organizations (along with a remarkable counter-revolutionary consciousness) in the Home and War Offices.[131] Among these were Basil Thomson's Special Branch (heavily staffed with men of Irish birth or descent) and his new Directorate of Intelligence (located in Scotland House), which included the I.S.D.L. and the I.R.A. in Britain among the 'revolutionary organizations' to be watched.[132] Information on their activities was collected and sent to cabinet in weekly reports, composed in an appropriately

---

[130] See Liverpool City Reports on the Police Establishment and the State of Crime for 1920 and 1921; Mike Brogden, *On the Mersey Beat: Policing Liverpool Between the Wars* (Oxford, 1991), 130–7.

[131] See Bernard Porter, *Plots and Paranoia: A History of Political Espionage in Britain 1790–1988* (London, 1989), 120–69; Keith Jeffery, *The British Army and the Crisis of Empire, 1918–1922* (Manchester, 1984), 11–30; Andrew, *Secret Service*, 224–45.

[132] The category was conceived rather broadly, as even demonstrations of the blind were included. For Thomson's own account, see his preface (also in French) to the French edition of Edward Brady's book: *Le Secret Service Irlandais en Angleterre* (Paris, 1933), 7–47. Unfortunately it is only occasionally enlightening, but it does portray a Lloyd George fearful of assassination. Whether we can believe Thomson on this is another matter.

racy style. The Branch and Directorate worked closely with Dublin Castle, even sharing the services of spies.[133]

With the commencement of the I.R.A. campaign, Scotland Yard and Scotland House developed an active, pre-emptive policy, based on the counter-espionage and later counter-revolutionary organizations and techniques built up during and after the war. These combined aggressive intelligence-gathering, using Special Branch surveillance, spies, raids, and systematic interception of mail, with a vigorous use of deportation and internment as allowed by the Defence of the Realm Act (made permanent in 1920 as the Emergency Powers Act) and the Restoration of Order in Ireland Act.[134] The key regulation enacted under the latter, and derived from the former, was number 14b, which could be applied to any 'person who is suspected of acting or having acted or being about to act in a manner prejudicial to the restoration or maintenance of order in Ireland'.[135] The exercise of such draconian powers in wartime, or during a period of insurrection (as in Ireland and Britain up to July 1921), was controversial enough, but their use in peacetime and in the absence of political violence, as in 1922 and 1923, was a profound extension of the powers of the state. It did not take place without resistance in the courts and in Parliament, but it nevertheless remained effectively unchallenged, even after Regulation 14b was declared illegal in 1923.

Basil Thomson took a personal interest in the fight against the I.R.A., as he did with many other matters, and even played a part in interrogating suspects.[136] This personal involvement was merely one aspect of the wider gradual intervention of the whole counter-subversion apparatus. Special Branch detectives and agents operated all over the country, gathering intelligence, making arrests, and aiding and supervising the efforts of local police. As a result, all Irish republicans came under pressure, especially those of the I.S.D.L., who were frequently raided and detained.

---

[133] See O'Halpin, 'British Intelligence in Ireland', 74, 76. For some typical reports by Thomson's agents, see RRO, 19 Nov. 1920 (CAB 24/115, C.P.2116) or 21 Apr. 1921 (CAB 24/122, C.P.2859).

[134] See Andrew, *Secret Service*, 174–202; Porter, *Plots and Paranoia*, 120–50; Nicholas Hiley, 'Counter-Espionage and Security in Great Britain During the First World War', *Ante*, 101 (1986), 635–70.

[135] The regulation is quoted in full in *The Times*, 28 June 1921.

[136] Brady was himself interrogated by Thomson. For both sides of the encounter, see Brady, *Ireland's Secret Service*, 113–4, and, in the French edition, 32, 37–8. Of Thomson, Brady said: 'for courtesy and gentlemanly conduct I do not know his equal.' Thomson called Brady 'charming' and 'well-behaved'.

This centralization and intensification of anti-I.R.A. measures involved the War Office as well as the Home Office. Irish activities did not occasion much alarm in these quarters until late 1920, when the plans for attacks on Liverpool and Manchester were captured in Dublin. An emergency committee of cabinet then recommended undertaking special protection measures for the Houses of Parliament, government offices, and ministers and officials potentially threatened by Irish violence, and these were immediately put into place after 28 November. Armed bodyguards were assigned to scores of potentially vulnerable men, from Lloyd George on down, the public galleries in the Houses of Commons and Lords were closed to the public, barricades were put up in Downing Street, and 150 Metropolitan policemen (some armed) were posted around key buildings in London.[137]

The I.R.A. threat was also incorporated into the army's internal security planning—itself a recent innovation—as units in the London area became involved in these protection duties. This was the precursor to the permanent 'Whitehall Defence Scheme' used in the General Strike of 1926. Military forces had been deployed several times on an ad hoc basis in Liverpool, London, and Scotland but, after the Truce much more extensive preparations were made in case it broke down. Units all over the country were detailed to protect vulnerable points and vital installations on receiving the code-word RESUMPTION from the War Office.[138] All these precautionary measures continued in force until January 1922, when they were cancelled in the wake of the Treaty's acceptance in Ireland. They were all immediately reinstituted after Wilson's assassination, which caused a minor parliamentary furore over the withdrawal of his bodyguards.[139]

The army also included Art O'Brien and the I.S.D.L. among the targets of its own short-lived domestic surveillance programme, run by the specially formed 'A2' Branch of G.H.Q. Great Britain. Branch agents (themselves military personnel) placed within the Soldiers', Sailors' and Airmen's Union were in close contact with Art O'Brien and, through him, with Michael Collins and other republican figures in Ireland. This information was shared with Thomson and the Special Branch, but as 'A2'

[137] *The Times*, 30 Nov. 1920. See also *the Report of the Commissioner of Police of the Metropolis For the Year 1921*, 8, 14, 24, and the cabinet decisions recorded on 25 and 29 Nov. 1920 (CAB 23/23).

[138] See Keith Jeffery, 'The British Army and Internal Security', *Historical Journal*, 24 (1981), 387.

[139] See Appendix 1 of the 23 June 1922 cabinet minutes (CAB 23/30).

ceased operations in February 1920, it did not take part in the active campaign against the I.R.A.[140]

The central agencies actually intensified their efforts after the Truce, relegating local police to a supporting role. The pressure on the I.R.A. and I.S.D.L. continued in the form of surveillance, arrests, and trials, and the militarized protection schemes remained in force until 1923. This pressure culminated in March 1923 in the arrest, deportation, and internment in Ireland of 110 men and women under the notorious Regulation 14b, by order of Home Secretary Bridgeman. The whole operation was meticulously and massively planned. The suspects were taken in simultaneous nocturnal raids across the country, and rushed to waiting destroyers. By morning they were in Free State custody. The move was prompted by a Scotland Yard report stating that the I.R.A. in Britain were 'gathering their forces so as to put their full weight behind the blow to be struck against the Free State this spring'.[141] This report in turn was based on information gathered by the Special Branch about Liam Lynch's fantastical plans to win the war, backed up by detailed but alarmist reports from Free State intelligence.

Such an operation, with its secrecy and use of hundreds of police as well as the armed forces, was an extraordinary public display of Britain's security apparatus, and it was soon apparent that many, if not most, of the deportees had committed no offence other than supporting the Irish republican cause.[142] Moreover, many had been born and lived their lives in Britain, only to find themselves deported to a (newly) foreign country. The uproar which erupted as soon as the news was announced did not die away, but gradually blew up into a major political crisis, with the Bonar Law government and the not-particularly-nimble Bridgeman being put decidedly on the defensive. The evidence he put forward was sketchy and ambiguous, consisting mainly of intercepted letters discussing a resumption of I.R.A. violence, some of which were quite dated.[143]

---

[140] The 'A2' Branch was formed to combat Bolshevism in the army, but under the command of Lt.-Col. Ralph H. Isham, an expatriate American and virulent anti-communist, it quickly extended its reach to spying on civilian organizations, including the I.L.P. and the *Daily Herald*. A large volume of 'A2' files can be found in the Ralph H. Isham Papers, Group No.1455 in the Yale University Library manuscript collections.

[141] RRO, 8 Mar. 1923 (CAB 24/159). See also the presentation of the government's case in court, as reported by the *The Times*, 24 Apr. 1923, and Paul Canning, *British Policy Towards Ireland 1921–1941* (Oxford, 1985), 79–80.

[142] *The Times* editorialized: 'at first sight, arrests of so summary a kind are suggestive of methods foreign to this country', but went on to approve of them: 13 Mar 1923.

[143] *The Times*, 13 Mar., 10 May 1923.

The crisis soon became a disaster, as the Court of Appeal declared Regulation 14b invalid and the deportations illegal. The government appealed this judgement to the House of Lords and were again rebuffed, leaving them no alternative but to bring back the deportees and face the humiliation of compensating the victims. The total amount came to £64,200.[144] The government tried to recoup some of its losses by rearresting and trying fourteen of the deportees, about half of whom were eventually convicted, but it was combating a threat which had long since dissipated.[145] Irish republicanism, and the I.R.A. in Britain, had been in decline since early 1922, and the militants put on trial were not a new vanguard but rather the few remaining members of a nearly vanished movement.

## Success or Failure?

Does the British failure to halt the I.R.A. in 1920–1 mean that its campaign was therefore a success? In one very direct sense the answer is: yes. The first objective of any guerrilla campaign is to maintain its organization and keep fighting. Survival itself, therefore, represented a kind of victory over the government, just as in Ireland. The fact that operations did not inhibit the flow of arms through the vital British pipeline—as some rebel leaders feared—was further proof of the underground's capabilities and resilience.

Another way of judging the I.R.A.'s performance in Britain is to compare it to that of Irish units over the same period. In Irish terms, the twenty or so English companies, with their approximately 400–500 members, were the equivalent of a weak brigade or a strong battalion. As such, they come out rather well—not in the premier division but still well up in the movement's tables. Their record of eleven shootings between the end of November 1920 and the beginning of July 1921 outdid that of many full brigades, such as Carlow's, Westmeath's, or either of Waterford's. The 149 buildings burned in England also far outstripped the combined total of all these units. And the hundreds of lesser attacks were at least comparable to the number of raids on mails, bridges destroyed, and the like which formed the standard repertoire of every Irish unit.[146] The fact that the boys of London, Liverpool, and elsewhere

---

[144] *Ibid.*, 15 May 1923, 7 Mar. 1924.  [145] *Ibid.*, 29 May 1923.  [146] See Ch. 2.

accomplished what they did in the face of casualties and arrests as heavy as those faced in many parts of Ireland must also be taken into account. Thus, despite differences in context, it is fair to say that the record of the Liverpool and London companies in particular can match that of their most committed Irish counterparts.

Finally, we can ask whether the campaign achieved the guerrilla's own objectives. What was the British I.R.A. trying to achieve in 1920–1? In fact, violence in Britain was driven not so much by stratagem or calculation as by urge or instinct: to retaliate against British violence in Ireland. This was true both for those nominally in control in Dublin, and for the men on the ground. One arson squad in Manchester, for example, told their victims that 'We are doing to you what you are doing to Ireland'.[147] As such, events in Britain can be seen as an extension of the escalation of violence in Ireland, which was driven on both sides by the same reprisal principle, and where the destruction of property and the shooting of civilians was rising rapidly after November 1920.

Beyond this lay the rather vague idea—again, held at both the Head-quarters and local level—that violence in England would force the British public to focus their attention on Ireland, and thereby put political pressure on the government to pull out. Hence the emphasis in the 1920 planning on creating the most dramatic impact, although there were different views as to what sort of operations would be most effective in this regard. Denis Kelleher, adjutant of the London I.R.A., recalled that 'Michael Collins was more for the publicity which an undertaking would create, but Rory O'Connor more for the spectacular event and he did not care about human life'.[148] Certainly, the operatives themselves were quite conscious of their attention-getting role. When Thomas O'Sullivan was convicted of conspiracy to commit arson and the possession of fire-arms in London, he declared that 'There was a lot of damage being done in Ireland. Protest meetings have been held here, but the general public took no notice, and we wanted to force them to take notice.'[149] Equally clear was the shock value of violence occurring in England, and of the importance of good headlines: 'the man in the street knew there was something on. The papers played up our litle acts tremendously.'[150]

The problem with this sort of armed propaganda was that it conflicted with the I.R.A.'s presentation of themselves as soldiers engaged in a war against their oppressors—crucial to their international propaganda as well

---

[147] *The Times*, 4 Apr. 1921.     [148] Denis Kelleher (O'Malley Papers, P17b/107).
[149] *The Times*, 19 Feb. 1921.     [150] Denis Brennan (O'Malley Papers, P17b/100).

as their self-image. This conflict helps to account for the ultimate reluctance to assassinate politicians, and for the initial orders to avoid shooting people while on operations. It also meant that the Dublin G.H.Q. never officially acknowledged the British campaign or units. They were not mentioned in *An tOglach*, the I.R.A.'s in-house journal, and British units never communicated directly with Headquarters. This ambiguous status was a permanent source of annoyance to the British activists.

If success is measured in terms of public and governmental attention and alarm, the guerrillas achieved what they set out to do. The I.R.A. threat was the subject of numerous cabinet reports and discussions. It was raised regularly in the House of Commons. It provoked an unprecedented and highly visible internal security regime. Most importantly, it made headlines. On average, *The Times* ran a story on the British I.R.A. every second day in 1921 from January onwards, often with dramatic and substantial reportage.[151] The perceived seriousness of the threat can be gauged by the extent of the government's reaction when a second campaign was feared in 1923. As such, it may have added a small but perceptible weight to the scales of British decision-making on Ireland over the course of the revolution.

It is its identity as much as its violence which makes the I.R.A. in Britain historically significant, however. For this was as much a British as an Irish movement, largely composed of people who had been born or brought up in England and Scotland, or who had settled there as employed and permanent residents. Many activists in the I.R.A., I.R.B., I.S.D.L., and Sinn Féin were also active in left-wing politics, as communists, socialists, or trades unionists, and as such their commitment can be seen as an extension of British post-war radicalism as much as of Irish republicanism. All of these organizations had also internalized a very British sense of localism, with the movement as a whole split at the Scottish border, and further divided between mutually suspicious northern England and London. The I.R.A. in Britain was thus a very rare phenomenon: a guerrilla movement arising from an immigrant population as part of a struggle against the host country's rule of their 'native' land. Its existence raises fascinating questions about the guerrillas' ethnicity, social backgrounds, political ideas and motives, and the sources of their violence, which can do much to illuminate both the place of these people within British society and the nature of the Irish revolution as a whole.

---

[151] Stories appeared in November and December 1920, on every fourth and every third day, respectively.

# 7

## The Thompson Submachine Gun in Ireland Revisited

In 1967 *The Irish Sword* published a pioneering article by J. Bowyer Bell on the early history of the Thompson submachine gun and its acquisition by the Irish Republican Army in 1921. Bell was one of the first historians to deal with guns and gunmen in a scholarly fashion, and in doing so also uncovered an extraordinary story 'involving Irish agents, British spies, inscrutable Japanese, aborted smuggling', and the first ever use of the Tommy gun in action.[1] Due to the lack of available documents at the time, however, much of this story remained untold, particularly the details of the 'aborted smuggling', how and when the guns reached Ireland, and what happened to them after the Truce of 1921. Fortunately, since Bell's article was first published a full history of the Thompson gun has appeared[2] and a large amount of relevant material has come to light in Irish and British archives. Armed with this new information, we can trace

---

[1] J. Bowyer Bell, 'The Thompson Submachine Gun in Ireland, 1921', *The Irish Sword* (Winter 1967), 108. It has recently been reprinted in Bell, *The Gun in Politics: An Analysis of Irish Political Conflict, 1916–1986* (New Brunswick, 1987). Unless otherwise specified, page references to Bell's work are to the former article.

[2] W. J. Helmer, *The Gun that Made the Twenties Roar* (New York, 1970), which includes a detailed chapter on the purchase and smuggling attempt discussed in this article. Also of interest is John Ellis, *The Social History of the Machine Gun* (New York, 1975), 149–64. Since I first wrote this essay, a third substantial article has appeared: Patrick Jung, 'The Thompson Submachine Gun During and After the Anglo-Irish War: The New Evidence', *The Irish Sword*, 21: 84 (1998), 191–218.

the tangled—and occasionally bizarre—history of the Thompson gun in the Irish revolution.

## Buying the Guns

The submachine gun was the brainchild of General John T. Thompson of the United States Army. Thompson was keen to develop a rapid-fire weapon suitable for the special conditions of trench warfare, but his work did not bear fruit until after the 1918 Armistice and his retirement. Produced in prototype in 1919 and 1920 by Thompson's Auto-Ordnance Company (of Hartford, Connecticut), the new gun aroused some professional interest but lacked an institutional buyer until one was found in the Irish Republican Army.[3]

Investigators from J. Edgar Hoover to J. Bowyer Bell have been unable to piece together the exact chain of events by which Irish revolutionaries became Auto-Ordnance's first customers.[4] Did the company seek out clandestine buyers or did the revolutionaries take the initiative? Speculation has inevitably centred on Thomas Fortune Ryan, an Irish-born millionaire and veteran contributor to nationalist causes who also happened to be General Thompson's main financial backer.[5] Was Ryan the secret broker behind the deal? This air of mystery is somewhat reduced, however, by the fact that the guerrillas may simply have been responding to Auto-Ordnance's aggressive publicity campaign, which reached Irish newspapers in December 1920.[6]

---

[3] The weapon's prehistory is described in Helmer, *The Gun*, 26–52, which supersedes Bell's earlier account.

[4] Hoover, fresh from his triumphs over 'Bolshevism', participated in the US Dept. of Justice smuggling investigation described below (Helmer, *The Gun*, 61).

[5] Bell has suggested that Ryan was 'an influential member of Clan na Gael' (p. 98; see also Helmer, *The Gun*, 55) but this may be doubted. Ryan receives no mention in the papers of leading Clansmen John Devoy and Joseph McGarrity, nor did he take any part in the Clan's factional squabbles. On the other hand, he was known as a contributor to mainstream organizations such as the Irish Party and the American Committee for Relief in Ireland. See Alan J. Ward, 'Frewen's Anglo-American Campaign for Federalism', *Irish Historical Studies* (Mar. 1967), 259–61; Francis M. Carroll, *American Opinion and the Irish Question 1910–23* (Dublin, 1978), 275.

[6] See the *Cork Examiner*, 30 Dec. 1920. Michael Collins also noticed an article on the new gun in *Popular Mechanics* in January 1921: Sean Cronin, *McGarrity Papers* (Tralee, 1972), 98–9. Since writing the above, I have been able to read the Michael Collins–Harry Boland correspondence in the De Valera Papers (UCD, P150/1665). This includes a letter from Boland to Collins on 10 Dec. 1920 (probable date) including an article on the gun and stating that an order for 100 had already been placed.

Whatever the combination of patriotic and commercial interests involved, the company were as eager as the Irish to make a deal, with no questions asked. The I.R.A. had been importing small amounts of American weapons for some time, but by the end of 1920 the rebels were feeling an increasingly urgent need for greater firepower. The Munster brigades in particular were pestering their headquarters to provide them with more arms, and had begun to smuggle in their own. The Thompson gun had not only the virtue of easy availability (thanks to Auto-Ordnance and US gun laws) but also apparently packed a formidable punch. Enthusiastic at the prospect of outgunning British forces for the first time, I.R.A. General Headquarters gave the go-ahead to start buying as soon as they saw the gun in action in May 1921.[7]

What they did not count on was the even greater enthusiasm of their American agents, Harry Boland, Liam Pedlar, and Larry de Lacy, who operated in a whirl of secret societies, front organizations, and political and financial intrigue. Boland was the representative of the Irish Republican Brotherhood in the United States; Pedlar and de Lacy were political exiles and activists still dedicated to the cause. Acting on their own initiative, Boland and his comrades had already placed orders for 653 Thompsons and ammunition through sympathetic middlemen in New York. The money—$132,634 in certified cheques—was cadged from the Trustees' Reserve of the Dáil Éireann external loan, quite possibly without official permission.[8] When called to task for this impropriety by the ever-censorious Minister of Defence, Cathal Brugha, Boland professed amazement: 'Am I to understand... that you did not authorize me to purchase 653 Thompson Sub-Machine guns? Where did you think I could get the money to pay cash on the nail for these!... I accepted a certain responsibility feeling sure that the Defence Dept. would welcome such a splendid weapon.'[9]

---

[7] See Tom Barry, *Guerilla Days in Ireland* (Dublin, 1949), 193, and Tim Pat Coogan, *Michael Collins*, 168.

[8] H. Boland to C. Brugha, 21 July 1921 (UCD, Ernie O'Malley Papers, P17a/158). This did include a 20% discount off the list price, however. See Boland to Collins, 14 Apr. 1921 (De Valera Papers, P150/1665). John T. Ryan later reported that: 'Sean N[unan] said Harry wrote to Mick [Collins] asking for permission to use certain funds to purchase the articles required and that Mick sent back word to use said funds.' Ryan to Joseph McGarrity, 26 Jan. 1924 (National Library of Ireland, Joseph McGarrity Papers, MS 17,637[2]).

[9] H. Boland to C. Brugha, 19 July 1921 (O'Malley Papers, P17a/158). In his next letter, Boland apologized: 'I regret very much if my action has caused you any embarrasment, and will be more careful in future in doing unauthorized work.' Boland to Brugha, 21 July 1921. By this point,

Although it had been planned to ship the arms over in small quantities, in late May or early June the decision was taken to send the entire lot to Ireland in one go. The opportunity was provided by the relief organization the Irish White Cross, which had chartered a ship, the S.S. *East Side*, to carry coal to Dublin.[10] This impatient decision to put all the eggs in one basket would prove to be costly.

The saga of the *East Side* began on 8 June 1921, when the ship was moved from New York to Hoboken, New Jersey.[11] Once there it lost its engine crew to an engineers' strike, after the men (who had been on strike but had re-entered service) received threats. Two days later an official of the shipping line which leased the pier offered the services of an unknown chief engineer and replacement crew.[12] Not coincidentally, there were a great many Irishmen in the New York Engineering and Fireman's Union.[13]

On 11 June Pedlar, de Lacy, Joe McGarrity, and half-a-dozen others moved the bulk of the arms and ammunition from a warehouse in the Bronx to a hotel in Manhattan owned by McGarrity. The next day it was delivered to the *East Side* in Hoboken. This shipment of 495 guns, spare parts, and cases of ammunition had been sewn into sacks and labelled as legs of lamb in an attempt to evade attention, but the scheme backfired when they were unaccountably left lying about on deck all that after-noon.[14] As Liam Pedlar later admitted, 'there was a snag...somebody did something wrong'.[15] A curious cook opened one of the sacks and reported his astonishing find to the stewards, who left the ship on the 13th and told the pier superintendent.[16] After an exhaustive search of the ship he finally

Boland had—by his own account—already recouped more than half the money from wealthy American donors. See also Boland to Collins, 21 July 1921 (De Valera Papers, P150/1665).

[10] Liam Pedlar (O'Malley Papers, P17b/94).

[11] Hoboken was a perennial center for arms-smuggling, for groups as diverse as the Ku Klux Klan and the Irgun. See the *New York Times*, 25 Feb. 1923; Robert I. Friedman, *The False Prophet: Rabbi Meir Kahane* (New York, 1990), 36.

[12] This account is primarily based on the *New York Times*, 16, 17, 18 June 1921, and on the chronology presented in a memo from the British Consul-General, New York, to Ambassador, 16 June 1921 (PRO, FO 115/2674), which reports an interview with two officials of the Cosmopolitan shipping line.

[13] Liam Pedlar (O'Malley Papers, P17b/94); C. Desmond Greaves, *Liam Mellows*, 200.

[14] For the smuggling operation, see Liam Pedlar (O'Malley Papers, P17b/94) and Marie Veronica Tarpey, *The Role of Joseph McGarrity in the Struggle for Irish Independence* (New York, 1976), 140.

[15] Liam Pedlar (O'Malley Papers, P17b/94).

[16] Despite contemporary and subsequent claims otherwise, there were no 'British spies' involved in the discovery of the guns.

discovered the guns in the engine room, where they had been belatedly hidden. The whole shipment was impounded and placed in the pier strong room. The new chief engineer and his men promptly vanished.

As their plans began to unravel, the conspirators took increasingly desperate measures to recover their cargo. A clumsy attempt to impersonate customs officers was easily foiled, and a belligerent visit to the Manhattan offices of the shipping line was also rebuffed. At the last minute, however, more conventional political wire-pulling in New Jersey worked. On the night of 15 June, just as customs officials were about to take the Thompsons into custody, a squad of Hoboken policemen arrived with a warrant stating that the guns had been stolen. The warrant had been sworn out by Larry de Lacy, using the name 'Frank Williams' (Boland subsequently claimed that 'we ourselves reported the guns on board in order to save them'[17]). Over the startled protests of the customs men, the shipment was re-seized and transported to the Hoboken police station.

A short but sharp legal battle now ensued between Hoboken, backed by the well-connected Irishmen, and Washington, under considerable pressure from the British embassy to stop the guns leaving the United States.[18] As the story broke, newspapermen also flooded in. The *New York Times* gleefully described the scene on June 16:

Customs officials, Department of Justice agents, Hoboken detectives, U.S. district authorities, representatives of Williams [de Lacy], Williams himself, and reporters thronged the corridors of the Hoboken police station all day...a day replete with mystery, rumour, denials and counter-denials. Government agents stared with suspicion at representatives from other Federal departments and refused to give their names to reporters or discuss their interest in the case.

Asked if he was Irish, 'Williams' replied: 'Surely you must be mishtayken.'[19]

At this point the Department of Justice, the Customs Bureau, the State Department, the US Shipping Board, and a posse of US Marshals were all conducting investigations, trying to support the federal government's

---

[17] Undated report (O'Malley Papers, P17a/158). Patrick Jung argues that there was a Frank Williams (n. 29), but the evidence remains unclear.

[18] Irish influence in New Jersey's political machinery is mentioned in Liam Pedlar (O'Malley Papers, P17b/94) and in Consul-General, New York, to Ambassador, 16, 17 June 1921 (FO 115/2674). See also Luke Dillon to J. McGarrity, 11 Nov. 1925 and Percy Landsdowne to J. McGarrity, 19 Nov. 1925 (McGarrity Papers, Ms. 17,530[1]). British communications with the US State Department can be found in the same file. See also Carroll, 170.

[19] *New York Times*, 17 June 1921.

claim to the weapons. 'A chronological narration of the events connected with the legal developments is as possible as an account giving in sequence the incidents of a street fight', wrote one baffled observer.[20] In the end a federal judge in Newark allowed customs agents to take possession due to alleged violations of the Neutrality Act.[21] The legal contest continued, but the guns stayed put.

## Gun Running

Thus, the Tommy guns went the way of nearly all the I.R.A.'s large-scale arms-smuggling ventures. As a disaster, the *East Side* ranked somewhere below the failure of the *Aud* in 1916, but was on a par with the repeatedly frustrated attempts to buy and ship arms from Italy in 1920 and 1921, and from Germany in 1921, 1922, and 1923. These continental affairs were more colourful, involving as they did Fascists, Communists, *Freikorps*, and Nazis, and not a little bickering, fraud, and embezzlement, but they were nearly as futile. Only two small boatloads of obsolescent arms were eventually landed in Ireland from Hamburg after the Truce.[22] Contrary to J. Bowyer Bell's assertions, the 'skills' of the Dublin G.H.Q. were not terribly 'impressive' when it came to such projects.[23]

Much more reliable was the small but steady trickle of weapons from the black markets of England and Europe, and from the gun shops of America, carried laboriously along old and well-tested smuggling routes. This was an ancient organization dating back to the previous century, operated by the Irish Republican Brotherhood and inherited by the I.R.A. The shipments might be small—usually no more than half-a-dozen weapons at a time—but the cumulative results were actually impressive: in the two years before the 1921 truce, 289 handguns, 53 rifles, 24,141 rounds of ammunition, and 1,067 pounds of explosives were shipped

---

[20] Ibid., 17 June 1921.

[21] The Customs Bureau's original charge that the guns were not included in the ship's manifest and did not have State Department authorization was declared spurious because the *East Side's* next port of call was actually Norfolk, Virginia.

[22] Published accounts of the extraordinary German adventures may be found in Charlie McGuinness, *Nomad* (London, 1934), and Robert Briscoe, *For the Life of Me* (London, 1958), but these conceal as much as they reveal. The McGarrity and O'Malley Papers tell a great deal more of the story. See especially the memoranda contained in the O'Malley Papers, P17a/4 and 155. For the Italian escapade, see Mick Leahy's statement in the Florence O'Donoghue Papers (NLI, Ms. 31,421[8]).

[23] Bell, *The Gun in Politics*, 32–4.

through Liverpool alone.[24] These networks ran at their own speed, depending more on seasoned operators (who were frequently also commercial smugglers) and local (often familial[25]) initiative than on I.R.A. organizers for their efficiency. Attempts to speed them up or streamline them usually came to grief.[26]

Indeed, many arms flowed into Ireland almost by osmosis, guided by demand and prices rather than by the I.R.A.'s director of purchases. The market was a relatively free one. The G.H.Q. had to compete with units and individuals in southern and western counties while, on the supply side, a lot of items were moved purely for profit—by entrepreneurial sailors and the like. Buyers in England often complained that competition was forcing the prices sky-high.[27] It is to these more informal networks that we must turn for the next chapter in our story.

The US government did not discover all the Thompson guns: 495 were seized from the *East Side*, but a total of 653 had been purchased. The remainder, by a lucky delay, had been late in arriving and so were saved.[28] Almost immediately they were rerouted into the regular American shipments to Liverpool, through which most of the Irish arms traffic flowed. The Thompsons travelled on the S.S. *Baltic* and her sister ship, the *Celtic*, couriered by a Mr Rees. Arms from the United States also travelled via London and Irish ports, but surviving records make no mention of Thompsons arriving by this route.

[24] These figures have been assembled from the individual reports contained in the Mulcahy Papers, P7/A/1–7.

[25] Key smuggling families included the Carrs in London and the Kerrs in Liverpool.

[26] See e.g. the correspondence between the Chief of Staff and the Director of Purchases in the Mulcahy Papers (UCD, P7/A/17). First-hand accounts of gun buying and smuggling in England can be found in Patrick Daly (O'Malley Papers, P17a/136), in Martin Walsh and Tom McCormick (P17a/154), and in Col. M. O'Leary, 'The History of the Liverpool Battalion', *An tOglagh* (Autumn 1966 and Winter 1967).

[27] See the memos from Sean McGrath (in charge of arms purchases in London) to Michael Collins in the Art O'Brien Papers (NLI, MS 8426). McGrath complained that 'these people [are] coming over here and interfering with my buying and as a result the prices are going up' (McGrath to Collins, 3 Jan. 1921 [Mulcahy Papers, P7/A/8]). See also the Director of Purchases' general statement for 1922–3 (O'Malley Papers, P17a/49).

[28] There is still some uncertainty as to the number of guns bought. Harry Boland stated definitely that 653 was the total paid for, but it may be that not all of these had been delivered by 16 June. A memo in the McGarrity papers states that 'an additional 108 guns were included in the S.S. allotment too late for inclusion', which would bring the total to 603 (McDevitt memo, 1 Oct. 1934, MS 17, 530[3]). The other fifty weapons apparently constituted a separate order from another group of Irishmen in New York, whose connections with Pedlar, de Lacy, and Co. are unclear. See the *New York Times*, 2 Oct. 1921; Helmer, *The Gun*, 57.

In Liverpool the guns were received by Patrick Daly and his small band of dockside gun-runners. These men were helped by the blind eye usually turned to smuggling by their co-workers, and by the fact that the docks were still largely populated by sympathetic Irishmen.[29] The Liverpudlians found that the machine guns required special handling: 'Thompson[s] with their magazines and supplies of ammunition were rather bulky, and therefore taking them out of the docks to our dump and back again increased the risk of discovery so we decided with the help of our friends amongst the crew to transfer them directly to the Irish boats. This involved a fairly long trek inside the docks.'[30] The 'Irish boats' were those of the B&I line. In Dublin the guns were taken off the ships and past customs and police by the dockers and seamen of 'Q' Company.[31] Here again, though, the I.R.A. still depended on well-established smugglers and smuggling routes rather than any new organization or skills. Many of the men involved were well past middle age.[32]

The first lot of three Thompsons, three drums, and twelve magazines arrived in early May—a month before the Hoboken incident—and were sent on to Dublin on 12 May.[33] It was presumably these guns that were tested by Michael Collins before the G.H.Q. officially authorized the purchase. Collins wrote that he was 'very glad that those Thompsons have come', and Patrick Daly of Liverpool replied that 'Mr. Reis [sic] goes tomorrow. It seems there will be a regular supply.'[34] The disastrous plan to move the Thompsons all at once now intervened, so the next shipment did not arrive until the beginning of July. Four more were dispatched to Dublin from Liverpool on 6 July. This time, however, there had been 'great difficulty getting them away as the Customs were unusually active. Reis has got the wind up.' The other side of the story was supplied when Collins got a letter from New York complaining that 'our messenger was very angry at the way he was treated on last trip. He says if it happens again he'll quit. The men were two hours late for the

[29] Patrick Daly (O'Malley Papers, P17b/136).       [30] Ibid.

[31] British interdiction efforts were almost completely ineffective. When a special unit of cadets was recruited to work in Irish harbours, Collins confidently reported that 'the new force searching the boats does not make any difference. Most of it is newspaper talk. One of the old "G" crowd would be worth 20 of them.' Collins to P. Daly (Mulcahy Papers, P7/A/5).

[32] See William Nelson, '"Q" Company', *An tOglagh* (Winter 1967), and 'The John (Archie) Kennedy Story', ibid. (Summer 1971).

[33] Patrick Daly to Michael Collins, 12 May 1921 (Mulcahy Papers, P7/A/5). Daly later recalled that the first shipment consisted of seven Thompsons (O'Malley Papers, P17b/136).

[34] Collins to Daly, 13 May 1921; Daly to Collins, 17 May (Mulcahy Papers, P7/A/5).

appointment, and caused our man considerable embarrassment.' Daly promptly received the standard Collins lecture on punctuality.[35]

The 11 July Truce and the easing of British controls on Irish ports brought a rapid increase in arms traffic. Amongst the wide assortment of weapons now entering Ireland was a steady stream of Thompsons. This continued until disaster struck again on 27 November, when ten of the guns were found by British customs officers in a random search of the S.S. *Baltic*. The incident was also a potential diplomatic disaster, as the Irish had previously agreed to halt arms imports. Collins was ready to take full responsibility if necessary, but news of the capture did not reach the press and there was no rupture in the peace negotiations.[36] The Treaty was signed only a few days later.

Most of the guns went from Liverpool to Dublin, but others were sent to Cork (although the exact number is unclear) and probably also to Dundalk.[37] As often happened with scarce weapons, squabbling broke out over who was to get Thompson guns almost as soon as they arrived.[38] Not surprisingly, the Dublin Brigade got them first, and were the first to use them in combat.[39] Some may even have been surreptitiously commandeered by one of the provincial units, who usually felt neglected by the Dublin-oriented G.H.Q. Paddy Daly certainly thought so, and blamed a 'certain active area'; this probably meant the Cork brigades, the most enterprising when it came to acquiring arms.[40]

---

[35] Daly to Collins, 6 July 1921; Collins to Daly, 8 July (Mulcahy Papers, P7/A/6).

[36] Thompsons were sent to Dublin via Liverpool in July (fifteen had been shipped from New York by 29 July), on 23 August, 6, 7 and 20 September, and 4 October. For details of the capture, see Daly to Collins, 1 Dec. 1921; Collins to Daly, 5 Dec. (Mulcahy Papers, P7/A/7).

[37] It had apparently been planned that the *East Side* would smuggle some of its cargo into West Cork. See Liam Deasy, *Towards Ireland Free*, 288, and Tom Barry, *The Reality of the Anglo-Irish War 1920–21 in West Cork* (Dublin, 1974), 48. Bell quotes several Cork city officers as saying that thirty Thompsons arrived there before the Truce: see Bell, 104–5 and Bell to Florence O'Donoghue, 17 May 1967 (NLI, O'Donoghue Papers, MS 31,317[1]). Con Neenan, another officer of the 1st Cork Brigade, remembers getting only six (out of an expected seven) before the Truce: Con Neenan (O'Malley Papers, P17b/112). Jung devotes much of his article to the supposed shipment of thirty guns to Cork in April 1921, but in my research on the Cork I.R.A. I came across no reference to this having taken place. If they had them, they kept them entirely secret and never used them.

[38] See e.g. C/S to O/C 1st Eastern Div., 22 July 1921 (Mulcahy Papers, P7/A/22). See also the memo 'Allocation of the new Machine Gun' (P7/A/18).

[39] See Bell, 106–7.

[40] Patrick Daly (O'Malley Papers, P17b/136).

## Impact

By 31 October, forty-nine submachine guns were in the hands of units all over the country.[41] Fourteen went to southern brigades, nine went to western units, and the remaining twenty-six were divided between northern and eastern units. Not surprisingly, the Dublin Brigade got the most of any single unit: seven guns. Large numbers of men had been trained in their use at camps set up in September, and manuals, copied by hand, were widely distributed.[42] Faith in the power of the new weapons was unbounded: 'The I.R.A. is the first fighting force to make use of it in actual warfare ... not only is it the latest and finest machine gun made but, in addition, has proved to be especially well adapted for use in the particular form of guerrilla operations in town and country.'[43] The I.R.A. headquarters staff was expecting a great return on its investment if combat was resumed, but the split in army ranks over the Treaty dictated that the guns would be used against former comrades rather than against British forces.

Both the pro- and anti-Treaty forces used Thompson guns, but these much-heralded weapons were not nearly as effective as originally expected. Indeed, they had very little impact. Their presence made no recorded difference to the outcome of any Civil War engagements in Cork, for example.[44] Out of fifty-nine battles in Ireland in which the I.R.A. were said to have used the submachine gun (along with other weapons) between July 1922 and June 1923, thirty-four (58 per cent) drew no Free State casualties and six (10 per cent) resulted in only 'slight' or 'light' wounds. In the remaining nineteen (32 per cent) encounters,

[41] Only two more Thompsons had arrived by 17 December, not including the ten which were intercepted in Liverpool in November.

[42] The September training camps, and the open delivery and display of 'a small sized machine gun of American pattern', are described in R.I.C. monthly County Inspector's reports for Armagh, Cavan, South Tipperary and Kerry (PRO, CO/904/116). All the original manuals supplied with the guns (440 of them) had been seized in Hoboken. A handwritten copy can be found in the Count Plunkett papers ( NLI, MS 11,410[12]).

[43] 'Notes on the Thompson sub-machine gun', n.d. (Mulcahy Papers, P7/A/32). When Denis McCullough was released from the Ballykinlar internment camp in Dec. 1921, the first thing he was shown on his way home to Belfast was 'one of the first Thompson guns' (NLI, Leon O Broin Papers, Ms. 31,653). See also C. S. Andrews, *Dublin Made Me* (Cork, 1979), 194; 'Notes on the tactical employment of the Thompson sub-machine gun in guerrilla warfare' (P7/A/28) and Charles Townshend, *The British Campaign in Ireland*, 181.

[44] Based on a survey of Cork Command operations reports from November 1922 to May 1923 (MA, CW/OPS/13). See also the February 1923 Report of the District Justice for Carlow, Leix and Kilkenny (NA, Dept. of Justice Records, H5/1307).

National Army losses averaged 2.9 killed or seriously wounded per incident, close to the average for I.R.A. ambushes as a whole.[45]

This poor record was partly due to the gun's inherent limitations, compounded by the way it was employed. General Thompson had intended his invention (which he nicknamed the 'trench broom') to be used for clearing trenches at very short range, and it simply was not suitable for use against the elusive targets of Irish country ambushes.[46] The Thompson was inaccurate and had little hitting power beyond a few hundred yards. Irish troops on both sides were reluctant to fight at such close quarters, and the guns were almost never brought together to provide massed firepower. When such an opportunity did present itself, as at the infamous Clones ambush of 11 February 1922 or the attack on Wellington Barracks in Dublin in November of the same year, the effect was devastating. However, the targets in these cases were either trapped in a railway carriage or lined up on an open parade ground.[47]

On top of this, many of the I.R.A.'s guns were rendered useless because of poor maintenance and chronic shortages of ammunition.[48] As of October 1921, most units had an average of only 100 rounds per gun, which was not nearly enough for these rapid-fire weapons.[49] These minimal reserves were augmented by further shipments from the United States over the course of 1922, but the problem was never really solved.[50]

[45] These figures are based on a day-by-day survey of the *Freeman's Journal* and the *Irish Times* for this period. It should be noted that many of these men may have been hit by weapons other than Thompson guns. Also, nearly one-third of these serious casualties occurred in a single attack on unarmed Free State soldiers in November 1922 (see below). The average casualty rate for all I.R.A. ambushes in county Cork in the same period (including only those engagements which resulted in death or serious injury) was 2.2 killed or wounded per incident.

[46] See Ellis, *Social History*, 149.

[47] For the Clones ambush (of Ulster Special Constables), see Patrick Shea, *Voices and the Sound of Drums* (Belfast, 1981), 78–9. Interestingly, the first use of Thompson guns in combat was against a slow-moving British troop train (see Bell, 107). For the Wellington Barracks attack, see the *Irish Times*, 9 Nov. 1922. In this case, Lewis machine guns were also used.

[48] G.H.Q. inspectors were frequently shocked at the state of firearms in country units. For a typical complaint about Thompson gun maintenence, see O/C Dublin Bde. to C/S, 26 July 1921 (Mulcahy Papers, P7/A/22).

[49] Statement of munitions, Oct. 1921 (MA, A/0606). It is quite possible that the main ammunition shipment had been successfully smuggled in before the *East Side* venture, only to be captured in Dublin in May 1921. On 26 May Sir Hamar Greenwood, the Irish secretary, reported that 13,608 rounds of American .45 calibre 'rifle ammunition' had been seized by British forces. *Hansard*, vol. 142, col. 291.

[50] In June 1922, according to captured I.R.A. Director of Purchases accounts, the S.S. *Baltic* and her sister ship were delivering up to 800 rounds of Thompson gun ammunition a week; such amounts would soon have been exhausted (NA, Dept. of Justice Registered Files, C/R/FM5). See also the *New York Times*, 2 Aug. 1922; Cronin, *The McGarrity Papers* (Tralee, 1972), 134.

In September 1922, for instance, the West Limerick Brigade's two Thompson guns were idle for lack of ammunition, while in February 1923 the 4th Cork Brigade had only fifty rounds for its two weapons.[51] Twenty-two thousand rounds did get through in March 1923, too late to make any difference.[52] 'The Thompson gun', a Free State intelligence officer observed, 'is practically worthless to them.'[53]

Despite its poor performance, a legend quickly grew up around the Thompson gun, and the anti-Treaty I.R.A. was eager to acquire more. Liam Pedlar remembers sending 'a few over on and off during the Civil War', but the full extent of these deliveries is unclear.[54] At least five were shipped from the United States before April 1923, one of which disappeared in England.[55] These had probably been left over from the eighty-odd still in republican hands in New York at the time of the Treaty. In May (after the I.R.A. ceasefire that effectively ended the Civil War) the Liverpool police captured the following letter: 'Send to Dublin the remaining Thompson locking pieces in your possession. Send 2000 rounds to Cork. Divide remaining Thompsons between Sligo and Dublin. 1500 rounds each. For the present avoid sending anything north of the border. Anything you can send South.'[56] Seventy-six machine-gun silencers and 3,500 rounds of .45 calibre ammunition were also seized. Thompsons were still moving through Liverpool in October of the same year.[57]


## After the Revolution

But what of the 495 guns taken from the *East Side*? These were held in the seizure room of the Brooklyn army base until November 1925, when they were handed over to the 'owner's agent' (as nominated by the elusive 'Frank Williams'), Joseph McGarrity. No one had been brought to trial for trying to ship the guns, and there was actually nothing illegal about

---

[51] O/C West Limerick Bde. to Quartermaster, 1st Southern Div., 13 Sept. 1922 (MA, A/0991/5); 4th Cork Bde. arms list, *c.* Feb. 1923 (Cork Archives Institute, Siobhan Lankford papers, U169b/32).

[52] Dir. of Purchases accounts (C/R/FM5). Aside from this, 9,000 to 10,000 rounds were captured before they could be distributed to units. See also, *Irish Times*, 12 May 1923.

[53] Cork I/O Report, 16 Oct. 1922 (O'Malley Papers, P17a/169).

[54] Liam Pedlar (O'Malley Papers, P17b/94).

[55] Dir. of Purchases accounts (C/R/FM5).

[56] NLI, Political Prisoners Committee Collection, MS 8483[7].

[57] See the fragmentary letters to M. O'Callaghan in the O'Malley Papers, P17a/51.

owning several hundred submachine guns, so the Irish republicans had gone to court to get them back. Apart from eight pieces which had gone missing, this miniature armoury was placed in the care of the Manhattan Storage and Warehouse Company (where McGarrity got a 20 per cent discount for dealing in volume).[58]

McGarrity, an occasionally successful Philadelphia businessman and diehard republican, was the I.R.A.'s chief American fund-raiser. He had an unwavering faith in the efficacy of violence and still intended the guns to be used in Ireland. In 1931, with the I.R.A. reorganizing and facing new threats and new opportunities, hundreds of the long-awaited Thompsons were shipped across the Atlantic.[59] Exactly how many is unknown. Tom Barry remembers fully 500 coming ashore in Cork, Stephen Hayes remembers 400, and William Helmer believes that 300–400 were smuggled into Cork by way of Galway.[60] One thing is certain: not all 487 guns made it to Ireland. A few were handed out to Irishmen in Boston, New York, Chicago, and perhaps other places as well.[61] Some—directly or indirectly—found their way into the hands of 'unauthorized persons' in criminal gangs. In 1933 Justice Department investigators were able to match the serial numbers of 'underworld' guns to those found on the *East Side* in 1921.[62] It is unknown whether McGarrity was aware of this traffic, but it is interesting to speculate on the extent to which I.R.A. guns were used in the American gang wars of the 1920s and '30s.

Once in Ireland, the arms were not, as in 1921, widely distributed to individual units.[63] Most of them ended up in dumps in and around

---

[58] McGarrity Papers, MSS 17,530[1], [2], and [3].

[59] The last bill from the warehouse company that survives is dated 19 September 1931 (McGarrity Papers, MS 17,555).

[60] Barry, *The Reality of the Anglo-Irish War*, p.48; Stephen Hayes memoir, *The People*, 11 Nov. 1962; Helmer, *The Gun*, 180–1.

[61] The receipts are in the McGarrity Papers (MSS 17,478; 17,530[1]).

[62] See the *New York Evening Post*, 29 June 1933. It is possible that among these were the eight guns that went missing in 1925. Possession of a submachine gun was not made a felony in New York State until August 1933. The federal Justice Department did not even require that such weapons be registered, as they claimed that the National Rifle Association code had already 'virtually checked procuring of new machine guns by gangsters and racketeers' (*New York Times*, 26 Oct. 1933). This may have been so, but it did not stop criminals from procuring the I.R.A.'s guns, and Irish and other revolutionaries still managed to buy large numbers of new Thompson guns in the 1930s. Indeed, one aspect of the eternal US gun control debate which has gone unremarked is the extent to which an open market in weapons has helped to arm foreign rebellions.

[63] A few did reach Cork and Kerry, as well as northern units. See Ronnie Munck and Bill Rolston (with Gerry Moore), *Belfast in the Thirties: An Oral History* (Belfast, 1987), 170.

Dublin, where ten years' worth of old grease had to be laboriously cleaned off.[64] Even when ready to fire, once again there was almost no ammunition available for them. The main shipment of magazines had been captured in Dublin soon after it had arrived.[65] This may help account for the seemingly extraordinary fact that so many weapons had so little impact on the turbulent Irish scene of the 1930s.

Whatever the case, the original supply of Thompson guns in New York was exhausted by 1936. At this time, with a new I.R.A. campaign in the offing, McGarrity bought forty brand new guns, which made it to the Dublin Brigade in 1937.[66] The proposed assault on Northern Ireland was derailed by internal disputes and by McGarrity's pet scheme of bombing England, however, so the guns went back into storage—often buried in oil drums—where many were eventually seized in government arms raids during the Emergency.[67] A few of the weapons did finally see action in the border campaign of the 1950s, by which time Tommy guns were once more being smuggled into Ireland from New York docks.[68] Here again, they failed to give the I.R.A. the hoped-for edge over the 'B' Specials and the Royal Ulster Constabulary. Nevertheless, the Thompson gun remained a key part of both Provisional and Official I.R.A. arsenals until well into the 1970s, when it was superseded by the Armalite and the AK-47.[69]

In the long run, perhaps the most important consequence of the I.R.A.'s brand loyalty lay not in Ireland but in America. The rebels were

[64] Ned Gargan, *The Great Betrayal* (Dublin, 1989), 46. Gargan, who was assistant quartermaster general of the I.R.A. at the time, never says exactly how many guns there were, but remembers having 200 in his house at one time.

[65] Ibid. 64–6; Hayes memoir. According to Hayes, it was this shortage of ammunition which prompted the famous Magazine Fort raid in December 1940. See also J. Bowyer Bell, *The Secret Army: The I.R.A. from 1916–*(Cambridge, 1983), 172.

[66] The receipt is in the McGarrity Papers (MS 17,544[2]). McGarrity's correspondence on the subject with Sean Russell, the I.R.A. quartermaster-general, can be found in MS 17,485.

[67] See e.g. the police reports contained in Dept. of Justice Registered Files, A.6/7/36 and S.9/40. Helmer (151) states that 108 were captured in one raid in Mayo alone, in 1942. According to Jung's meticulous accounting, sixty-six were seized by the R.U.C. after 1921 and 199 by the Garda between 1935 and 1981 (pp 209–10). For an interesting account of the symbolic importance of the Tommy gun to one 1930s I.R.A. unit—and of its ultimate irrelevance—see Jack Holland, *The American Connection: U.S. Guns, Money, and Influence in Northern Ireland* (New York, 1987), 67–9.

[68] For the border campaign, see Bell, *The Secret Army*, 292–8. For renewed smuggling activity in the 1950s, see Holland, *American Connection*, 71–4.

[69] See Holland, *American Connection*, 69; Patrick Bishop and Eamonn Mallie, *The Provisional I.R.A.* (London, 1987), 183; Lt.-Col. Michael Dewar, *The British Army in Northern Ireland* (London, 1985), 65.

apparently the biggest single customer for the submachine gun before the Second World War, and their early and continued support probably helped keep it in production.[70] The I.R.A. thus has an important place in the history of the Thompson gun, even if the reverse is not necessarily true.

## Image and Reality

John Ellis has called the Thompson gun a 'contemporary icon' because of its identification with gangsters in American popular culture, and this description is true for Ireland as well.[71] In both countries it remains a symbol of the romanticized 1920s, and of the power of rebellion and violence. If this chapter helps to fill in the reality behind this image, it will have achieved its purpose. Beyond this, however, the story of the gun also raises several important historical issues. The romanticization of the Thompson gun went hand in hand with the myth of the guerrilla campaign as an essentially military affair of flying columns and roadside duels with the Black and Tans. In fact, this idealized notion had about as much to do with the reality of the revolution as Hollywood gangster movies did with the reality of criminal violence in the United States. No 'Tans' ever 'flew' from 'the rattle of a Thompson gun', nor did many—if any—National Army soldiers or R.U.C. policemen. Shotguns killed far more people in this period than submachine guns ever did, and even rifles often took second place to pistols and revolvers. 'Executions'—assassination and murder—were much more common than battles, and death was more likely to come at point-blank range, on doorsteps and in ditches, than in a firefight.

Such was the nature of guerrilla warfare in Ireland, waged on both sides by small groups of men who were as much predators as warriors, British death squads being as active in this regard as the I.R.A. In county Cork in 1921, for example, only one-third of the I.R.A.'s victims—and less than a third of those shot by Crown forces—were killed or wounded in actual combat. As the Thompson guns were being purchased and as the G.H.Q. began to set up the first I.R.A. divisions in the spring of that year, brigade flying columns all over Ireland were rapidly being disbanded or destroyed.

---

[70] For the poor sales record of the gun, see Ellis, *Social History*, 149–50. It did not become a success until it was bought by the American and British armies in the Second World War.

[71] Ibid. 164.

Indeed, for all the Dublin G.H.Q.'s visions of well-armed military forma-tions implied by its investment in expensive arms and elaborate organiza-tion, these anonymous killers and their simple weapons were more efficient than the columns—and even less amenable to central control. Ambushes and sniping attacks were risky, wasteful of precious ammuni-tion, and generally fruitless. A handful of bullets or slugs used against a 'soft target' were usually much more effective.

The real technological advance made by the I.R.A. in 1921 came not with the acquisition of submachine guns but with the successful use of industrial explosives as mines. These posed a far more dangerous threat to British—and eventually National Army—convoys and patrols. We need only compare the impact of the first Thompson gun attack in Drumcondra on 16 June with the mining of another troop train in Armagh a week later. The former wounded one soldier seriously. The latter killed four men, wounded another three, and caused the deaths of thirty cavalry horses.[72] And several weeks before that, a bomb hidden in a culvert had nearly wiped out a British regimental band near Youghal, causing twenty-nine casualties—the bloodiest single ambush of the entire campaign.[73] Here lay the real future of guerrilla warfare in Ireland.

Revolutionary logistics followed the same pattern, as we have seen. In gun-running, as in killing, handguns and gelignite were clearly superior. While shipment after shipment of Thompsons and their ammunition were being captured, hundreds of pistols and revolvers and hundreds of sticks of explosives were quietly smuggled into Ireland from Britain, one package at a time. Such shipments were almost never intercepted: a result, not of G.H.Q. planning, but of the ability of small, tight-knit groups in London, Liverpool, and elsewhere to evade detection and keep the guns moving—the same sort of networks of friends, neighbours, and relatives, in fact, that became guerrilla units in Ireland. What gave the I.R.A. its strength was not its overt layer of bureaucracy, but rather its mobilization of deep communal and personal loyalties. In both the manner of its arrival and in its ultimate irrelevance, therefore, the Thompson gun illustrates in a small way the primacy of localism and informal networks in the Irish revolution.

[72] *Irish Times*, 25 June 1921.    [73] Ibid., 1 June 1921.

# 8

# Michael Collins and the Assassination of Sir Henry Wilson

On the morning of 22 June 1922, Field-Marshal Sir Henry Wilson left his home in London to unveil a war memorial at Liverpool Street railway station. When he returned at 2.30 that afternoon two young men, Reginald Dunne and Joseph O'Sullivan, were waiting for him. What happened next is best described in Reggie Dunne's own words:

Joe went in a straight line while I determined to intercept him (Wilson) from entering the door. Joe deliberately levelled his weapon at four yards range and fired twice. Wilson made for the door as best he could and actually reached the doorway when I encountered him at a range of seven or eight feet. I fired three shots rapidly, the last one from the hip, as I took a step forward. Wilson was now uttering short cries and in a doubled up position staggered towards the edge of the pavement. At this point Joe fired once again and the last I saw of him he (Wilson) had collapsed.[1]

Dunne and O'Sullivan subsequently shot three pursuers (two policemen and a civilian) in their attempt to escape but, fatally slowed by Joe O'Sullivan's wooden leg, they were caught shortly thereafter. They were tried, convicted, and, on 10 August, hanged in Wandsworth Prison.

This ruthless killing of the Unionist M.P. and former Chief of the Imperial General Staff shocked and infuriated Britain and its government,

[1] Excerpted from Dunne's (apparently genuine) official report, smuggled out of prison and first published in the *Sunday Press*, 14 Aug. 1955.

and was one of the key precipitants of the Irish Civil War. However, while the consequences of the assassination were and are clear, its origins remain shrouded in mystery. This is not due to any lack of speculation; many attempts at explanation have been made, but they have only added to the confusion. Indeed, the history of investigations into the affair resembles nothing so much as a hunt for clues in a particularly baffling murder mystery, with plenty of suspects, dead ends, and red herrings. Despite this, a great deal of relevant material does exist, much of it only recently available to the public. Using this evidence we can now recover many of the missing pieces in the puzzle and, perhaps, even 'solve' the murder of Sir Henry Wilson.

## Theories and Facts

At the time of the assassination two simple and plausible explanations were put forward. On the basis of documents captured with the killers, the British government hinted darkly at the existence of a conspiracy connecting the Irish Republican Army Executive, which was adamantly opposed to the Anglo-Irish Treaty, with the assassination. This argument was used primarily as a lever to force the Provisional Government into taking action against the anti-Treaty 'Irregulars'.[2] Once the Civil War had begun it was quietly dropped, and did not figure in the murder trial. The other public explanation came from Dunne and O'Sullivan themselves. Although not allowed to make a formal statement in court, they managed to smuggle one out for publication. In this Dunne declared that they 'joined voluntarily for the purpose of taking human life' because they believed Wilson to be a threat to both the cause of Irish independence and the beleaguered Catholics of Belfast. Wilson was an outspoken Unionist and an adviser to the Northern Ireland government, and was widely blamed for the Belfast 'pogroms' by Irish nationalists.[3]

Dunne concluded his statement with the assertion that 'you cannot deprive us of the belief that what we have done was necessary to preserve the lives, the homes and the happiness of our countrymen in Ireland'. No affiliation with any organization was claimed, nor did any group claim them. Both the Provisional Government and their opponents disclaimed

---

[2] Conclusions of a Conference of Ministers, 22, 23 June 1922 (PRO, CAB 23/30, c.36[22] and c.38[22]).

[3] See *Freeman's Journal*, 6, 8, 12 June 1922.

any responsibility for the killing. Eoin O'Duffy, the chief of staff of the Provisional Government army, emphatically denied that the men were even members of the I.R.A.[4] By their own account, Dunne and O'Sullivan acted alone and for patriotic and humanitarian reasons.[5]

Amid the confusion and violence that reigned over all parts of Ireland in 1922 neither version seemed unlikely. The British government's interpretation was widely accepted in Britain while the Irish public easily believed Dunne's portrayal of himself and his companion as martyred patriots, responsible for their own acts.[6] 'These men fought for their faith', was a typical conclusion.[7]

In the years after the assassination a series of conspiracy theories began to circulate among I.R.A. veterans, in the Irish press, and in biographies and histories of the period. Most importantly, from the late 1920s on a number of ex-revolutionaries and acquaintances of Dunne and O'Sullivan have claimed that neither of the above explanations was true. They declared that the two men were simply loyal soldiers following orders, and that the man who gave the order to kill Wilson was Michael Collins, hero of the Irish revolution and first chairman of the Provisional Government. This verdict was endorsed by Frank O'Connor and Rex Taylor, biographers of Collins, and has been incorporated—with varying degrees of caution—into most scholarly accounts.[8] The most important recent contribution has come from Michael Hopkinson, who upholds and elaborates upon the idea of a Collins conspiracy in his history of the Irish Civil War.[9]

---

[4] *The Times*, 23 June 1922.

[5] A copy of Dunne's statement is in the Art O'Brien Papers (NLI, MS 8442). Dunne's few words in court echo this defence of his actions on the grounds of personal principle. See Rex Taylor, *Assassination: The Death of Sir Henry Wilson and the Tragedy of Ireland* (London, 1961), 167–71.

[6] See the *Irish Independent*, 11 Aug. 1922. For the widespread British belief in a conspiracy, see the *Morning Post*, 24 June 1922 (which accuses members of the Provisional Government) and C. E. Callwell, *Field-Marshal Sir Henry Wilson: His Life and Diaries* (London, 1927), ii. 349.

[7] This was the statement of a Mr O'Leary, who was praying for Dunne and O'Sullivan outside Wandsworth Prison on the day of their execution. *The Times*, 11 Aug. 1922.

[8] See F. S. L. Lyons, *Ireland Since the Famine* (London, 1973), 460–1; Charles Townshend, *Political Violence in Ireland*, 383; Joseph Lee, *Ireland 1912–1985* (Cambridge, 1989), 62, and R. F. Foster, *Modern Ireland 1600–1972*, 510. Joseph Curran is more circumspect in *The Birth of the Irish Free State* (University of Alabama, 1980), 224–5. Frank O'Connor's *The Big Fellow* (London, 1937) should be compared to the revised edition published in 1965. Richard Mulcahy made some interesting comments on these revisions (University College Dublin, Mulcahy Papers, P7/D/66). Taylor's somewhat muddled conclusions are presented in *Assassination*.

[9] Michael Hopkinson, *Green Against Green* 112–14.

The figure of Michael Collins is a natural focus for such conspiracy theories. His leadership of the clandestine Irish Republican Brotherhood (I.R.B.), his activities as director of intelligence for the I.R.A., and his involvement in so many aspects of the Irish revolution have created an indelible aura of intrigue and power as well as the myth that his hand was behind every secret endeavour. This image of Collins as the man who knew and did everything, so irritating to his colleagues, is still cultivated today and lends automatic credence to any conspiracy theory which implicates him. Taylor and others make full use of this element of mystery to add weight to their arguments and to tantalize their audiences.

The key question has now become: did Michael Collins order the assassination of Sir Henry Wilson? Before assessing the evidence for and against, however, we should first examine the assassins themselves and their personal histories. By setting up Collins as the main actor in this drama, the conspiracy theorists have diverted attention away from Dunne and O'Sullivan. These, the actual participants, deserve our attention.

In the summer of 1922 Reggie Dunne and Joe O'Sullivan were both 24, unmarried, and still living with their parents. Both had been born and raised in London, both had volunteered for service in the British army (Dunne's father was an ex-serviceman), been wounded, and had been invalided out with good records. O'Sullivan lost a leg in France in 1918. Dunne was an unemployed teaching college drop-out, while O'Sullivan worked as a messenger for the Ministry of Labour. Both men were devout Roman Catholics.[10]

Neither Dunne nor O'Sullivan had been politically active before or during the war (Dunne, in fact, had joined the army after the Easter Rising), but they displayed the zeal of converts once they became committed to the cause of an Irish republic. They joined Sinn Féin and the Gaelic League, but there was no real focus for their energies until a branch of the Irish Volunteers (soon to be known as the I.R.A.) was formed in London in 1919.

Several companies of Volunteers had existed in London in 1914 and 1915, and much of their active membership, including Michael Collins, had fought in Dublin in 1916.[11] The organization in England collapsed

---

[10] These details have been gathered primarily from: Taylor, *Assassination*, 106–10; statements taken in the case of *Rex* v. *Connolly and O'Brien* (the names first given to the police by Dunne and O'Sullivan) (HLRO, Lloyd George Papers, F/97/1/30); 'Shooting of Sir Henry Wilson' (report of a speech by Sean McGrath), *Irish Democrat*, Feb. 1948; and Dunne and O'Sullivan's farewell letters to their parents (NLI, Art O'Brien Papers, MS 8442; Mulcahy Papers, P7b/146).

[11] Ernie Nunan, 'The Irish Volunteers in London', *An tÓglach* (Autumn 1966), 4; 'An Rathach', 'London Volunteers', *Irish Democrat* (Apr. 1948).

with the Rising. Its rebirth followed the usual Irish pattern. Small groups of young men calling themselves Volunteers began to join together on their own initiative, with the encouragement of a few older I.R.B. activists. These new militants were impatient with Sinn Féin-style politics and were eager to emulate the budding guerrilla campaign in Ireland.

Dunne and O'Sullivan emerged as leaders among these early expatriate enthusiasts when they wrote to Michael Collins (in his capacity as adjutant-general of the Volunteers) in mid-1919 to suggest the formation of a Republican 'division' as a fifth column in Britain. The leaders in Dublin and London decided that it would be better to control these 'young wild chaps' than have them act on their own, so the first official I.R.A. companies were established in London in October 1919.[12] Dunne and O'Sullivan were eventually sworn into the I.R.B. (which still dominated the movement in Britain) in late 1920.[13]

Dunne was soon elevated to the command of the London I.R.A., a position he was to occupy until his death. O'Sullivan remained an ordinary Volunteer, albeit a highly dedicated one. He was one of the few in London willing to carry out I.R.A. 'executions'.[14]

There was little for the I.R.A. to do, apart from street fighting, hiding fugitives, and running guns, until the autumn of 1920. At that time the Dublin G.H.Q. decided to organize a series of 'operations' in Britain in reprisal for the destruction of property by Crown forces in Ireland. In 1921 these attacks evolved into a wholesale campaign of arson and sabotage aimed at farms, factories, hotels, and rail and telegraph lines. A few 'spies' and relatives of Irish policemen were also shot, but the British I.R.A. generally shied away from murder.

The absence of political assassinations did not mean that there were no assassination plots. In fact, beginning in 1918, these became quite numerous. The potential victims included the Prince of Wales, Lloyd George and his cabinet ministers, Lord Fitzalan (the last viceroy of Ireland), Sir Basil Thomson (the head of the Special Branch at Scotland Yard), various Unionist M.P.s, and Sir Henry Wilson. These men were never targeted as part of any plan or strategy, but rather were chosen at different

---

[12] Sean McGrath to Michael Collins, 7 Oct. 1919 (MA, A/0457). The proposal to form a 'division' is in an undated letter to the adjutant-general in the same file. For the affiliation of the London companies, see Collins to McGrath, 1 Apr. 1920 (O'Brien Papers, MS 8430).

[13] Sean McGrath to Collins, 1 Oct. 1920 (Mulcahy Papers, P7/A/8). For the role of the I.R.B., see the interview with McGrath in the Ernie O'Malley Papers (UCD, P17b/100). See also Art O'Brien's memoir of the organization in London (O'Brien Papers, MS 8427).

[14] It was O'Sullivan, along with another man, who shot the spy Vincent Fovargue in April 1921. Denis Kelleher (O'Malley Papers, P17b/107).

times in response to some British action. Wilson, for example, was probably first singled out because, as Chief of the Imperial General Staff and a well-known ardent Unionist, he was held responsible for the executions carried out by the army in Ireland.[15]

Of all these potential targets—and there were others as well—only Wilson met his death, and he was not shot until 1922. Some of the planned attacks were bungled, such as the one on Lord Fitzalan. Some, like the plan to take Unionist M.P.s hostage in early 1921, were called off because the rationale disappeared, in this case because the British army stopped carrying hostages in their vehicles. Others simply faded away, like the elaborate scheme to kill Lloyd George after the deaths of Terence MacSwiney and Kevin Barry. Common sense finally prevailed over the thirst for revenge.

Several of these projects were shelved in the run-up to the Truce of July 1921 so as not to disrupt the negotiations.[16] They were incorporated into a master plan to be carried out by the I.R.A. in Great Britain if hostilities resumed. Amongst other things, the plan called for the assassination of selected 'individuals', one of whom was Sir Henry Wilson. Preparations were made to carry out the scheme, but they were abandoned after the signing of the Anglo-Irish Treaty in December 1921.[17] What was Michael Collins's role in these affairs? Joe Dolan, a gun-wielding member of Collins's intelligence directorate, summed up the universally accepted view of the 'big fella': 'all orders for major executions were issued by the Director of Intelligence who was Michael Collins.'[18] This appeal to the myth of Collins as the secret mastermind has been repeated again and again in the debate over Wilson's death. In fact, whenever Collins contemplated such major 'stunts' as assassinations, prison rescues, and kidnappings, he faithfully consulted the G.H.Q. staff and other republican leaders. Such plans were even vetoed on occasion.[19]

---

[15] Most of our knowledge of these plans comes from the O'Malley Papers. See Pa Murray (P17b/88), William Aherne (P17b/99), Denis Brennan, Frank Thornton, and Liam Tobin (P17b/100) and Denis Kelleher (P17b/107). Also important is a letter from Florence O'Donoghue in the *Sunday Press*, 25 Jan. 1959. See also Collins to Art O'Brien, 7 Sept. 1920 and Sean McGrath to Collins, 18 Dec. 1920 (O'Brien Papers, MS 8430); and O'Brien to Collins, 13, 20 Sept. 1920 (MS 8426).

[16] William Aherne (O'Malley Papers, P17b/99).

[17] 'Report on a Visit to Britain September 1921' [by Rory O'Connor] (Mulcahy Papers, P7/A/29).

[18] Letter to the *Sunday Press*, 25 Oct. 1953.

[19] See Collins to Sean McGrath, 26 Apr. 1920 ('Unfortunately we have not been allowed to go ahead with this plan') and 17 May 1920 ('I have been trying to get this matter taken up but I have not been very successful. *The others* are very much opposed.') (O'Brien Papers, MS 8430). For

Moreover, not all such plans were hatched by Collins and his men. Cathal Brugha, the minister of defence, was responsible for several of the most bloodthirsty ideas, while the decision to avenge MacSwiney and Barry was a corporate one.[20] Indeed, Collins opposed carrying out some of the wilder schemes, often to the frustration of the gunmen involved.[21]

Rory O'Connor, the G.H.Q. director of engineering, was put in charge of operations in Britain in late 1920.[22] It was he who proposed and planned avant-garde operations like the truck-bombing of the House of Commons and the poisoning of horses in Buckingham Palace.[23] It was also O'Connor who put Wilson on the agenda for a renewed campaign of violence in 1921.

Collins retained a personal hold over the English I.R.A. because of his long cultivation of the mainland networks and his I.R.B. connections (he was chairman of the Supreme Council and knew most of the British leaders personally). He maintained separate lines of communications to many republican activists, and it is possible that he met Reggie Dunne more than once. However, it was O'Connor, not Collins, who dealt personally with Dunne and O'Sullivan in 1920 and 1921.

Another characteristic of the I.R.A. assassination plans of 1920 and 1921 was the number of people who knew about or participated in them. All involved lengthy and elaborate preparations, with an emphasis on escape routes. Virtually all the active I.R.A. and I.R.B. men in London were drawn in, and often delegations from Dublin and Cork as well, as the Londoners were felt to be timid when it came to actual gunplay. I.R.A.

---

examples of Collins's collaboration with Rory O'Connor and Cathal Brugha, see Collins to McGrath, 17 Apr. 1920 (MS 8430) and McGrath to Collins, 13 Sept. 1920 (MS 8426).

[20] Brugha's first assassination plan in 1918 is described by Sean McGrath (O'Malley Papers, P17b/100), Leo Henderson (P17b/105), and Fintan Murphy (P17b/107). His attempt to revive the plan in 1921 was blocked by Collins and Richard Mulcahy. See the accounts given by Mulcahy and Sean MacEoin (Mulcahy Papers, P7/D/3). For the attempt to revenge MacSwiney's death, see Florence O'Donoghue's letter to the *Sunday Press*, 25 Jan. 1959, and Pa Murray (O'Malley Papers, P17b/88).

[21] Pa Murray (O'Malley Papers, P17b/88) and Denis Kelleher (P17b/107).

[22] O'Connor's own account of his activities is 'Reorganising Britain' (Mulcahy Papers, P7/A/24). Collins's continued authority is clear from his correspondence with agents in London and Liverpool (Mulcahy Papers, P7/A/4–7).

[23] See the list of 'Operations Contemplated' appended to the 'Report on Visit to Britain'. For some startling details of various O'Connor projects, see Tom MacMahon (O'Malley Papers, P17b/86), William Aherne (P17b/99), Denis Brennan (P17b/100), and Denis Kelleher (P17b/107). Not surprisingly, some of O'Connor's comrades doubted his sanity.

men in other English cities were usually in the know, as were many republicans who happened to be in London on a mission or on the run.[24]

When Wilson's assassination was first contemplated in 1921 it followed the normal rituals of consultation and preparation. As a result, many people knew about it and would report later that the idea had originated in Dublin. This is in stark contrast to 1922, when only two men were involved, no one else in London was informed, and no escape plans were made.

## The Evidence

Let us now consider specific conspiracy theories. The original British charge that anti-Treaty rebels were responsible for Wilson's death was based on I.R.A. documents found in Dunne's possession. These turned out to be irrelevant to the assassination, and the Special Branch's murder investigation concluded that the killers acted on their own.[25] The home secretary informed Lloyd George that: 'We have no evidence at all to connect them, so far as the murder is concerned, with any instructions from any organised body. They were both undoubtedly members of the I.R.A., but that was not known until their arrest.'[26] For its part, the diehard I.R.A. executive denied the accusation immediately, and its denial has stuck.[27] This theory has rarely resurfaced. At one point (as discussed below) Denis Kelleher, a London I.R.A. officer, suggested that Collins and Rory O'Connor (the leader of the rebels) were jointly responsible, but his account is shaky at best and he contradicts himself elsewhere.

A more substantial report comes to us from Frank Martin, who claimed to be a pro-Treaty volunteer in the London I.R.A.:

In June 1922, I was approached by the Captain, Reggie Dunne. He asked me would I be willing to take part in the action he had been ordered to carry out,

---

[24] See e.g. Charles McGuinness, *Nomad* (London, 1934), 166 and the unpublished memoirs of Commandant Bat Keaney and John Sherlock, deposited in the Irish Military Archives and the F. S. Bourke Papers (NLI, MS 9873) respectively.

[25] For the documents, see Conclusions of a Conference (CAB 23/30, c.36[22]), esp. Appendix 3; L. Curtis to Lloyd George, 1 July 1922 (Lloyd George Papers, F/10/3/14), and Eoin Neeson, *The Life and Death of Michael Collins* (Cork, 1968), 94. For the conclusions of the Special Branch, see Assistant Commissioner, S.B., to Commissioner, Metropolitan Police, n.d. (PRO, MEPO 2/1974).

[26] Notes dictated by the Home Secretary, n.d.[Aug. 1922] (Lloyd George Papers, F/45/6/42).

[27] Ernie O'Malley, *The Singing Flame* (Dublin, 1978), 85.

namely the execution of Sir Henry Wilson. He said it had been decided upon by the [anti-Treaty] Four Courts people, the calculation being that this would force a direct British attack on them, and that 'Portobello' [the Free State Army headquarters] could not look on and see comrades attacked directly by the British, but would have to join with them, and so re-union would be achieved.[28]

Martin is a problematic source, as there is no proof that he was ever actually in the I.R.A. and his statement became public only after he died.[29] There is no other evidence to corroborate his story or to support the idea that the assassination was an anti-Treaty plot. Other witnesses have said that Reggie Dunne was in touch with Rory O'Connor but O'Connor's own notebooks of the time make no mention of Dunne or of an assassination plan (although they do contain plans for other operations in England).[30] A conspiracy linking Rory O'Connor with the murder does have a certain prima facie plausibility. As their former superior he knew Dunne and O'Sullivan, he was familiar with earlier plans to shoot Wilson (and perhaps even gave the orders), and in June 1922 he was intent on restarting the war with Britain. O'Connor had the means, the motive, and the opportunity, but we have no solid evidence of his involvement, so the case must rest until some appears. It should be noted that Martin's account, although unsubstantiated, is as believable as any other of the witnesses who follow, and is more specific and coherent than most. It is also one of the few to contain an admission by Dunne himself.

A final possibility remains: that Dunne was lying to Martin about the plan's authority in order to obtain his help. Martin reportedly knew nothing beyond what Dunne told him. It seems to be true that Dunne hoped his actions would reunite the warring factions of the I.R.A. (see below), so that part of Martin's story seems to have an authentic ring, but why would Dunne choose to confide in an untried pro-Treaty volunteer (Martin said he joined in 1921)? On the other hand, if the story is true, it

---

[28] *Evening Press*, 18 July 1958.

[29] His story was also published in a peculiarly roundabout manner. Cathal O'Shannon, who reported it, was given Martin's statement in 1958 by a professor at University College Galway, who was himself given it in London in 1935. I cannot find any mention of Martin in I.R.A. memoirs or correspondence. Denis Kelleher cannot remember him either—see Taylor, *Assassination*, 80–1. Michael Hopkinson's notes mention evidence given by Martin, but he does not disclose the source (*Green Against Green*, 293, n. 6).

[30] NLI, Count Plunkett Papers, MS 11,410.

raises the intriguing possibility that Dunne told others about a fictional order—perhaps from Michael Collins.

The earliest attempts to implicate Collins came from anti-Treaty republicans in the 1920s and 1930s, who charged their perennial scapegoat, the I.R.B., with the murder. In fact, they were not the first to do so. The day after Wilson was shot, a Conservative M.P., Lieutenant-Colonel Martin Archer-Shee, claimed that 'the leaders of the Irish Republican Brotherhood...are the people who send the murderers here', but he did not name Collins and his accusation was lost amid the rumour-mongering tumult that gripped the House of Commons.[31]

Dorothy Macardle wrote in *The Irish Republic* that 'popular belief attributed the assassination to the I.R.B. It was thought that Michael Collins ordered it.'[32] M. J. MacManus said much the same in his biography of de Valera.[33] Sean MacConnell, a Dublin republican, was more forthright when he spoke at the unveiling of a monument to Dunne and O'Sullivan erected by their London comrades: 'suffice it to restate what is common knowledge—that the killing was ordered by the Irish Republican Brotherhood.'[34]

The most detailed of these charges came from Diarmuid O'Crowley, a former supreme court judge in the revolutionary legal system. In a remarkably detailed lecture, he accused an unnamed cabal within the Provisional Government of engineering Wilson's death in order to break the Treaty and keep the I.R.A. united:

On June 9 a special messenger came from London to Dublin. He came from the members of the Provisional Government in London to the members in Dublin. The messenger's name was Reginald Dunn [*sic*]. The messenger returned to London accompanied by the Chairman of the Provisional Government [Collins]. Two Scotland Yard men saw them alight at Euston Station and followed them. Dunn and another man, O'Sullivan, met the members of the Provisional Government in London. The order to shoot Wilson was given in London by two members of the Provisional Government, who were members of the I.R.B. Supreme Council [of which Collins was chairman].[35]

---

[31] *Hansard*, vol. 155, col. 1537 (see also *The Times*, 24 June 1922). Archer-Shee also claimed that Dunne and O'Sullivan only came to London the previous week. He was unable to provide any more concrete information to the Special Branch, who were deluged with conspiracy theories after the fact. See Asst. Comm., S.B., to Comm., Metropolitan Police, n.d. (MEPO 2/1974).

[32] Dorothy Macardle, *The Irish Republic* (London, 1937), 737.

[33] M. J. MacManus, *Eamon de Valera* (Dublin, 1947), 216.

[34] *An Phoblacht*, 17 Aug. 1929.

[35] Ibid., 10 Feb. 1934.

O'Crowley's reconstruction of events, while remarkably circumstantial (it fits with the movements of Collins and other Irish ministers as recorded in the *Irish Times*), is completely unsubstantiated. O'Crowley also charged the British government with complicity in the cover-up in return for the Provisional Government's promise to crush the I.R.A., thus neatly tying together all the chief villains in the republican pantheon.[36] The idea of a British cover-up was revived by Michael Maguire in a 1982 article in the *Sunday Tribune*, but he failed to offer any new evidence.[37]

After Fianna Fail came to power in Ireland in 1932, a group of London republicans, led by Pat O'Sullivan (Joe's brother) and Sean McGrath, a veteran I.R.B. and I.R.A. organizer, began a campaign to have Dunne and O'Sullivan officially recognized as soldiers of the I.R.A., contrary to the Provisional Government's damning denial. They also wanted the hanged men's parents to receive pensions and to have their bodies returned to Ireland.

The campaign, fought privately and publicly—most notably in the pages of the *Irish Democrat* and the *Irish Press*—lasted into the 1950s and was highly successful. Its main argument, repeated many times with slight variations, was summed up as follows by Patrick Sullivan and Frank Lee: 'The execution of Sir Henry Wilson was ordered by I.R.A. H.Q., Dublin, previous to the Truce. It was never cancelled—indeed, it was confirmed during the Treaty negotiations. The order was issued by Michael Collins, *chief of the staff*, and the direct order was conveyed to Commandant Dunne as battalion commander of the London I.R.A.'[38]

Lee, Sullivan and their allies were primarily concerned with rehabilitating Dunne's and O'Sullivan's reputations and refuting Mulcahy's dismissal of them as mere assassins. They thus concentrated on establishing Dunne's and O'Sullivan's I.R.A.—i.e. 'soldierly'—credentials, and on

---

[36] We know from Home Office and Special Branch documents, however, that the British government knew nothing of Dunne or O'Sullivan before the murder, and concluded that they acted alone, thus contradicting this part of O'Crowley's account. See nn. 25 and 26 above.

[37] Michael Maguire, 'Did Collins Have Wilson Shot?', *Sunday Tribune*, 27 June 1982.

[38] Patrick Sullivan and Frank Lee, 'The Execution of Field Marshal Sir Henry Wilson: The Facts', *Sunday Press*, 10 Aug. 1958. A few errors in the quotation should be pointed out: Collins was never chief of staff, and there never was a London battalion of the I.R.A. For the campaign, see the 1938 open letter from the 'Late Intelligence and Arms Officer, London Units I.R.A.' [Sean McGrath] (O'Brien Papers, MS 8461) and 'Shooting of Sir Henry Wilson', *Irish Democrat*, Feb. 1948. These arguments are found in their most complete form in Sullivan and Lee, 'The Execution', and in *Remembrance*, a pamphlet published by the London Memorial Committee of ex-I.R.A. and Cumann na mBan. This can be found in the Florence O'Donoghue Papers (NLI, MS 31,285) and is reprinted in *Assassination*.

proving the existence of a previous legitimate order to eliminate Wilson. What they did not do is prove that Collins ordered the killing in the summer of 1922. To imply as they did that the absence of a direct cancellation meant that the order was still in force is ludicrous; the plan was only supposed to be put into effect in the event of renewed fighting. Dunne may well have convinced himself and O'Sullivan that the original order somehow made Wilson a legitimate target, but that is a separate issue.

The only public statements by a subordinate of Collins relating to the matter have come from Joe Dolan. In 1953 he stated that Collins, in his capacity as Director of Intelligence, gave the order to kill Wilson to Sam Maguire—described as 'O/C Britain'—who turned the matter over to Dunne. The operation was meant as a reprisal for Wilson's alleged encouragement of Protestant violence in Northern Ireland.[39] In 1960, in a letter to Rex Taylor, Dolan added that the order was given 'about a fortnight before Wilson was removed from the scene'.[40] Dolan, like O'Crowley, is gratifyingly precise in identifying the date and chain of command, although his letters do contain some factual errors. For example, Collins was no longer Director of Intelligence in June 1922, and Rory O'Connor, not Maguire, was 'O/C Britain'.

The only other detailed account of the origins of the order was given by Sean McGrath:

A meeting was held in December [1921] in Shaftesbury Avenue of the I.R.B. [and] Officers of Companies in London. Dunne was then O/C I.R.A. [Sam] Maguire i/c I.R.B. He had been appointed Intelligence and Arms Officer while I was away. At that meeting it was decided to sink our differences and to carry out the execution of three people. 1) Bowen Colthurst 2) a woman who had betrayed people in Cork but who had been traced 3) Sir Henry Wilson.[41]

McGrath's account was positively denied by Denis Kelleher, Dunne's second-in-command, who attended this and other I.R.B. meetings. It is implicitly denied by the accounts of other I.R.B. men on the spot, who make no mention of this apparently crucial decision.[42] In addition to this, McGrath's testimony, given to Ernie O'Malley, seems odd in light of the

---

[39] *Sunday Press*, 27 Sept. 1953.       [40] Taylor, *Assassination*, 219.

[41] Sean McGrath (O'Malley Papers, P17b/100). Bowen Colthurst was the officer responsible for the shooting of Francis Sheehy-Skeffington in the Dublin Rising of 1916.

[42] Denis Kelleher (O'Malley Papers, P17b/107) and Denis Brennan (P17b/37, 100). See also Art O'Brien's memoir of the London I.R.B. (O'Brien Papers, MS 8427).

fact that, as part of the campaign to rehabilitate Dunne and O'Sullivan, he repeatedly stated for many years that the orders came from Dublin.[43] McGrath's son also seemingly contradicted his father after his death by endorsing Joe Dolan's version of events.[44]

No other witness has claimed to have such precise knowledge of the affair, but there are others who refer to specific times and places, and so can be checked against alternate claims. One key pair of witnesses is Mick Murphy and Con Neenan, both veteran officers of the Cork City I.R.A. and frequent visitors to London. Murphy told Ernie O'Malley that he was in London with Neenan just before the assassination and that Dunne and Joe Carr, another London activist, asked for help in killing Wilson, for which they had instructions from Collins.[45] Joe Carr consistently denied any knowledge of the killing, a claim which, since he was a gun-runner rather than a gunman, rings true.[46] For his part, Con Neenan has stated that he was in Cork at the time, and other witnesses have placed both him and Murphy in their home city then.[47] Neenan has given three separate accounts of his connection with the affair, each of them different from Murphy's. He told O'Malley that he was in London in the first week of December 1921 trying to trace an informer from Cork, and during his stay encountered Sam Maguire: 'They were tracking Wilson and they were very bitter about him. Sam discussed with me the shooting of Henry Wilson. I think D[unne] and S[ullivan] made up their minds to do the job. Sam was here in Ireland at the time. They used to visit Murray a Dublin lad there, a volunteer, and they decided to get it over... I have a feeling that Sam Maguire knew that these two lads would do the Wilson job.[48]

Nearly thirty years later he told a very different story:

I knew both Reggie Dunne and Joe O'Sullivan well; I had met them with Sam Maguire. Sometime in May [1922?], I had bumped into him one night at Mooney's when I called in for cigarettes. He emerged with me; he was with Frank Thornton, one of Collins' men, *the job on Wilson is on*, said he. I was not to breathe a word. I could not. It was a profound secret. And I did not breathe it.

[43] *Irish Democrat*, Feb. 1948.

[44] Proinsias MacAonghusa, 'The Day a Field-Marshal Died', *Sunday Independent*, 2 July 1967.

[45] Mick Murphy (O'Malley Papers, P17b/112).

[46] Notes of a conversation with Sean MacGrath and Denis Carr, 18 Feb. 1935 (O'Brien Papers, MS 8427); Joe Carr to Art O'Brien, 31 May 1938 (MS 8461).

[47] Uinseann MacEoin (ed.), *Survivors* (Dublin, 1980), 243; Pat Sullivan [no relation to Joe](O'Malley Papers, P17b/111).

[48] Con Neenan (O'Malley Papers, P17b/112).

Sean O'Hegarty had sent me and Mick Murphy over to London, to track down and shoot a famous spy we had here [in Cork].[49]

Here Neenan apparently places himself and Murphy, and the hunt for the spy, five months later and suggests Collins's direct involvement. The first account, although confusing as to timing (when did they decide to get it over and when did Maguire know?), suggests they acted on their own. It might jibe with McGrath's story, but the contradictions between these two accounts are difficult to reconcile.

Neenan also wrote a third, anonymous, account in which his first knowledge of the Wilson plot, and his encounter with Frank Thornton and Sam Maguire, is backdated to the spring of 1921. He returned to England in December on another spy-hunt, thereby 'resuming the contact' with Dunne and O'Sullivan. No mention is made of the plan to kill Wilson at this date, nor is there any reference to a visit in May 1922.[50] Apart from the absence of a Wilson plot in December 1921, this would fit with both of the other accounts if Neenan, in the second quotation, meant May of 1921 rather than 1922. What does seem likely is that Neenan was quite unreliable as to when he heard about the Wilson plot.

Frank Thornton, a member of Collins's 'squad', has said only that 'the order to kill Wilson was carried out by these two soldiers of the I.R.A. on the direct orders of their H.Q.'[51] This seems to be a rather formulaic endorsement of Sullivan, Lee, and McGrath's campaign to rehabilitate Dunne's and O'Sullivan's reputations: it stresses the fact that the pair were soldiers and that there was an official order, but it tells us nothing about who was involved or when the order was given.

Another Cork witness was Billie Aherne, who was also active in London and knew Dunne well:

D[unne] and S[ullivan] came to Dublin and I was with them for a holiday. They intended to stay, but Collins or whoever was in charge ordered them back... Then they decided to shoot Wilson. They had instructions to shoot Wilson before the Truce, but the order was never countermanded. So they got on to him...They saw S[am] M[aguire] at Mooney's Pub the night before. The Cumann [na mBan] were attacking D and S. Dunne said 'I'll show you that we'll do something yet.'[52]

[49] MacEoin (ed.), *Survivors*, 243–4.    [50] O'Donoghue Papers, MS 31,337.
[51] O'Malley Papers, P17b/100.    [52] William Aherne (O'Malley Papers, P17b/99).

Aherne also gave a lengthy account to Maurice (Moss) Twomey:

Billie is sure that nobody, from any side, gave an order for the shooting at the time it took place, but that Dunne and others would or might take up the attitude—the order was never cancelled, therefore it stood . . . one theory B. has why Dunne acted is that he knows such people as Cumann na mBan at the time in London were saying Dunne was no good, that the I.R.A. was doing nothing, etc. and that he believes D. reacted to this kind of criticism. Billie says he knows that D. decided on the shooting without much thought or plan. That the night before he read in the newspapers that Wilson was to unveil a war memorial next day, and he saw Sullivan and told him that he was going to shoot Wilson after he left the unveiling place (he gave me some details of this which it is not necessary to go into). Billie says he is certain there were no officers in London from Dublin before the shooting, in connection with it.[53]

Ulick O'Connor has also reported that Aherne told him he 'met RD in Dublin a week before the affair and he remembered clearly how angry Dunne was that Collins would not allow him proceed with the killing'.[54] And finally, Pat O'Sullivan once referred to a 1939 statement from Aherne confirming 'that the order was official', but this probably referred to the pre-Treaty order, as mentioned in the first Aherne quotation above.[55]

P. A. (Pa) Murray, our last witness from the Cork I.R.A., said that he met Dunne and O'Sullivan in London in May (on his way back from shooting an informer in New York), and that they told him of their intention to shoot Wilson. In another statement he declared that 'the shooting of Henry Wilson was official. Collins knew of it and Sam Maguire also.'[56] Murray, who was put in charge of the I.R.A. in Britain during the Civil War, did not reveal how he knew this.

Denis Kelleher, the adjutant of the London I.R.A., has given us a particularly confusing set of statements. In 1953, in a letter to the *Sunday Press*, he confined himself to the Sullivan and Lee line: 'I state emphatically that the instructions for the liquidation of Sir Henry Wilson was contingent on the break down of the peace negotiations. The order was not subsequently cancelled.'[57] At roughly the same time however, he told Ernie O'Malley that:

[53] Moss Twomey to Florence O'Donoghue, 10 Sept. 1953 (O'Donoghue Papers, MS 31,421).
[54] From a review in the *Sunday Independent*, 2 Nov. 1980, as quoted in Meda Ryan, *The Day Michael Collins was Shot* (Swords, 1989), 20.
[55] *Sunday Press*, 10 Aug. 1958.
[56] Pa Murray (O'Malley Papers, P17b/88, 89).
[57] *Sunday Press*, 15 Oct 1953.

Collins and Rory O'Connor were concerned in the Wilson affair. Men were sent North to contact Wilson, but they failed. [Liam] Tobin and [Tom] Cullen were in London. George White came over to me from R. O'C. about the shooting of Wilson. Tobin and Cullen came over afterwards about a rescue... There was no discussion about Wilson until three or four months before he was shot. I never heard that Wilson was to have been shot in London in December of 1921.[58]

These two accounts clearly contradict one another. To complicate matters even further, several years later he told Rex Taylor that he believed Dunne acted on his own, and showed Taylor a letter purportedly written by Dunne to prove it.[59] Kelleher is clearly not a trustworthy witness.

George White, a member of the Dublin Brigade, claimed that he had nothing to do with the shooting but did take part in the abortive rescue plan: 'Kelleher told us all about the Dunne and O'Sullivan business. He said there was an order for Wilson's execution. The London crowd didn't want to do the job; they wanted men from Dublin; but Kelleher himself was very keen.'[60]

White elaborated on this in another statement: 'I believe that Collins' side shot Wilson. I was told that the order to shoot Wilson had been issued twelve months previously. The men who shot him thought that his shooting would clarify the situation which was then confused.'[61]

These statements could be interpreted in different ways. In the first it is unclear whether the order referred to was the pre-Treaty one or of more recent origin. In the second, White is again confusing: he points to 'Collins' side', but then seems to support Aherne's belief that the killers acted on their own on the basis of the earlier instruction. It may be that O'Malley's interview notes are to blame for this lack of clarity rather than White himself.

Liam Tobin and Tom Cullen were two of Collins's most valued intelligence men. The only other suggestion of their involvement comes from Tim Pat Coogan in his recent biography of Collins. He reports the deathbed statement (to her son) of Peig ni Braonain, a republican courier in Dublin. A week before Wilson's murder she carried a message to a 'tall

[58] Denis Kelleher (O'Malley Papers, P17b/107).

[59] Taylor, *Assassination*, 181–5. See also Denis Kelleher to Rex Taylor, 20 April 1961 (O'Donoghue Papers, MS 31,285), which casts doubt on Taylor's presentation of the letter. Taylor is now deceased and his papers cannot be located, so his copy of this letter cannot be checked (information from Mrs Taylor).

[60] George White (O'Malley Papers, P17b/105).

[61] 2d. (O'Malley Papers, P17b/99).

man called Tobin' in London. She 'sensed', but was never told, that the message was from Collins, and Coogan concludes that the Tobin mentioned was Liam.[62] Even if we accept this third-hand evidence and ni Braonain's and Coogan's conclusions as to the identities of the people involved, however, there is no proof that this letter referred to Wilson. Collins, Arthur Griffith, and other Irish leaders were in London at about this time, so the message could have been about almost anything.

Tobin himself spoke to Ernie O'Malley, who wrote down what he said sometime afterwards: 'when Tobin told Mulcahy that our lads had shot Wilson, Mulcahy did not at first believe him, then he said he was going to resign.'[63]

Here we must tread with care as this is an after-the-fact paraphrase of Tobin's remarks.[64] The phrase 'our lads' seems to implicate the pro-Treaty side, but it probably only meant that the assassins were members of the I.R.A., contrary to what Mulcahy had believed and said publicly (he knew very little about the I.R.A. in Britain, despite his being Chief of Staff in 1921). Mulcahy may well have threatened to resign because he felt betrayed by being kept in ignorance or because he felt his honour was at stake. It should also be remembered that a deep animosity existed between Tobin and Mulcahy.[65]

Finally, someone signing himself 'One of the 22' (he claimed he was one of twenty-two men assigned to the task of rescuing Dunne and O'Sullivan from prison) wrote in the *Sunday Press* that 'the job was to be done in April, but Wilson was going away on business, and thus was not done until June'.[66] This provides yet another account of the timing of the supposed plan, though it says nothing of its origin.

## Cross Examination

What are we to make of this mass of conflicting and confusing evidence? The first thing to keep in mind is that these events were the subject of

[62] Tim Pat Coogan, *Michael Collins*, 375–6.     [63] Liam Tobin (O'Malley Papers, P17b/94).

[64] This point is underlined by the fact that this statement is followed by: 'Dunne and O'Sullivan had hoped it would bring about unity between the two sides', which, if Tobin said it, would seem to support the idea that they acted on their own. However, it is probable that these are O'Malley's words, inserted when he recopied his notes.

[65] See Hopkinson, *Green Against Green*, 62. Mulcahy's discomfort with the subject of the Wilson assassination may be indicated by the fact that his notes and writings, so informative on every other subject, avoid the question altogether.

[66] *Sunday Press*, 11 Oct. 1953.

rumour and speculation on all sides of Irish politics, and that the debate was politically charged. Michael Collins remained a powerful symbol after his death, the origins of the Civil War were still a bitter source of contention in the 1920s and 1930s, and the main vehicles of the debate, *An Phoblacht*, the *Sunday Press*, and the *Irish Democrat*, were partisan newspapers. Thus, by the 1950s the accounts of those concerned had undoubtedly been influenced by what they read and heard and by their political allegiances. For example, Con Neenan's statement published in 1980 seems to have been prompted by Rex Taylor's book on the assassination.

Another problem evident in the quotations given above is that most accounts are very brief and fragmentary. Not one witness has ever been thoroughly questioned, and no one has supplied a full account. In each case we have to puzzle over what a few words or sentences may mean, so most of our interpretations are clouded by considerable uncertainty.

When was the order given? Joe Dolan says that Collins acted around 8 June. Diarmuid O'Crowley comes very close to this by dating it about 10 June. Frank Martin was approached to help in June and even Frank O'Connor suggests June as the time.[67] Billie Aherne (according to Ulick O'Connor) remembers Dunne being told by Collins not to carry out the killing in mid-June. At one point Denis Kelleher said that 'discussions' about killing Wilson began in February or March, but not in December. 'One of the 22' places the plan in April, while Pa Murray and one of Con Neenan's statements have it under way in May. Sean McGrath declares that the idea originated in December, and another of Neenan's accounts concurs.

Some of these accounts can be reconciled but others cannot, unless we assume an extraordinarily convoluted series of orders, discussions and false starts. Moreover, if the motive behind the conspiracy was to reunite the I.R.A. or was part of Collins's Northern Ireland strategy, as various writers have suggested, then the question of timing becomes crucial. Neither aim would have been likely to push Collins into such an extreme action in December, February, or March of 1922, since only by May or June did negotiations on these two fronts look hopeless. The conspiracy theories do not start to make political sense until the month before the actual assassination.

Who gave the order and how was it given? McGrath says the I.R.B. in London, with Dunne present, decided to kill Wilson in December. Dolan

---

[67] Frank O'Connor, *The Big Fellow* (1965 edn.), 203.

says Collins gave the order to Maguire who passed it on to Dunne. O'Crowley thinks two members of the Provisional Government cabinet (who were also I.R.B. supreme council members) gave the order in London. Martin was told that it came from the anti-Treaty rebels in the Four Courts. Kelleher claims (among other things) that Collins and Rory O'Connor acted together and sent their own men over to help. Frank O'Connor and Billie Aherne believed that Dunne met with Collins in Dublin, although they report different outcomes. To make matters even more complicated, Reggie's father, Robert Dunne, told the police that Reggie had not been in Dublin since 1921.[68] Who should we believe?

Beyond the fact that these various statements are riddled with factual errors or inconsistencies on their own, they contradict and discredit one another in nearly every respect. For one of these versions to be accepted as true, almost all the others must be dismissed as false. As a result, although the sheer number of reports seems to indicate some sort of conspiracy, they only support one another if they are used selectively to build a composite—and hence fictional—picture of events. Unfortunately, this is what some writers have done.

One problem with the conspiracy theories is the lack of a 'smoking gun', a confession by one of the principals or else some documentary proof connecting Michael Collins with the murder. Joseph Sweeney, a pro-Treaty I.R.A. commander from Donegal, appeared to provide such a link when he reported in the early 1980s that: 'I met Mick [Collins] on the day that Field-Marshal Wilson was shot in a doorway in London, and I said to him, "Was that an official job?" "Yes", he said. I never went any further than that with him, but this is a thing that has been in dispute several years. I've never said anything about it before, but I think the time has come for not holding out on these things.'[69] Sweeney had said something before, however. He had told Ernie O'Malley that: 'I met Collins in Dublin the day after Wilson was shot. "It was two of our men did it" he said. He looked very pleased... "How do we stand about the shooting of Wilson" I asked Collins, and that was his reply.'[70] He subsequently also confided to Richard Mulcahy (in two separate remarks): 'Mick also told me later on when I was in Dublin that it was our fellows who shot Sir Henry Wilson', and 'He told me it was a couple of our lads

---

[68] Statement of Robert Dunne (Lloyd George Papers, F/97/1/30).

[69] Kenneth Griffith and Timothy O'Grady (eds.), *Curious Journey: An Unfinished History of Ireland's Unfinished Revolution* (London, 1982), 281.

[70] Joseph Sweeney (O'Malley Papers, P17b/97).

that did it, that they had had sanction for it. He didn't say from where they had sanction.'[71]

What *did* Collins say exactly—and when? As it stands, these remembered conversations could support a range of possible interpretations. 'Our men', 'our lads', and 'our fellows' could simply be an admission that, contrary to what Mulcahy had told the press, the men were members of the I.R.A. or I.R.B. 'An official job' and a 'sanction' could have referred to the earlier plans to kill Wilson in 1921. And, since Sweeney has given us four different versions of this fleeting conversation, perhaps Collins said something else altogether.

Another colleague who spoke to Collins soon after the shooting was Emmet Dalton, a senior officer in the new Irish army. He told Meda Ryan that 'Collins was angry that the London I.R.A. had taken an irresponsible attitude "at this time"'. Dalton believed Collins had nothing to do with it.[72] Ernest Blythe, a Provisional Government cabinet minister, echoed this conclusion. He too saw Collins shortly after Wilson's death and thought he was as shocked as anybody (Blythe also felt Collins was hiding something, which he was: the fact that Dunne and O'Sullivan were I.R.A. men).[73]

One explanation for Collins's apparently contradictory confidences was his habit of telling people what they wanted to hear. Perhaps with the sympathetic Ulsterman, Sweeney, he suggested he had been associated with the shooting, but with Dalton, as with Griffith and Mulcahy, he completely distanced himself. It is with such nudges and winks that he may have convinced a number of people that he had given the order, and perhaps even convinced Dunne that he favoured the killing of Wilson.

Indeed, it may be wrong to frame the question as narrowly as: did Michael Collins order the assassination? In the welter of cliques, rumours, and misinformation which engulfed the Irish republican movement in 1922, there was probably an enormous grey area between 'yes' and 'no'. Collins was faced with a barrage of crises, demands, and decisions and was pulling every available lever to maintain some kind of control. He was simultaneously juggling the I.R.B., the various pro-Treaty factions of the I.R.A., and the new National Army headquartered in Beggar's Bush, not to mention his personal loyalists. He also continued to deal with—and tried

[71] Notes of conversations with Joseph Sweeney, 1962 and 1964 (Mulcahy Papers, P7D/43).
[72] Ryan, *The Day Michael Collins Was Shot*, 20.
[73] Leon O'Broin, *Michael Collins* (Dublin, 1980), 133 and Ryan, *The Day Michael Collins Was Shot*, 18.

to manipulate—elements of the anti-Treaty I.R.A. on issues such as Northern Ireland. It would not be surprising if, amidst all this, Collins or one of his men sent a message or made a remark which Dunne interpreted too literally or over-zealously as giving him the authority to shoot Wilson.

One puzzle still remains. If, rightly or wrongly, Dunne and O'Sullivan did think they were following orders, why did they not say so? The usual I.R.A. procedure in England and Ireland was to declare oneself a soldier of the I.R.A. upon capture, and this the assassins did not do. The *Irish Times* correspondent in London reported that the men called themselves soldiers but refused to give their regiments.[74] No other newspaper carried this report. Presumably it could be argued that Collins, or whoever gave the order, also told the two men to keep silent no matter what, and then covered it up at their end as well. Would Dunne and O'Sullivan have been willing to go it alone in this fashion? Perhaps, but it does add yet another twist to the story.

A number of red herrings have been dragged across the trail over the years. The first variety are documentary. Rex Taylor makes much of the following entries in Collins's personal diary:

January 26 1922: 'Work for Paddy Dunne.'
February 2 1922: 'Notify Paddy D. Spencer of Cork St., Ross and W. also.'
April 18 1922: 'Mrs. Dunne.'[75]

These have no apparent bearing on the case. As an only child, Reggie Dunne did not have a brother named Patrick. There were many other Dunnes active in both the I.R.A. and Sinn Féin to whom Collins's notes could have referred. Several people have also claimed to have seen a written order to kill Wilson signed by Michael Collins. If so it has never been made public, and cannot be considered until it is.[76]

Another oft-evoked 'clue' is the attempt on the part of Collins to rescue or reprieve the killers. However, if this is to be taken as an indication of prior involvement, then it indicts all sections of the I.R.A., as the southern rebels headed by Liam Lynch, the Four Courts faction under Rory O'Connor, and Collins's men were all concerned in the rescue plans. Whether or not he planned the assassination, Collins probably did approve of the act—he was certainly as enraged at events in Belfast as

---

[74] *Irish Times*, 23 June 1922.     [75] Taylor, *Assassination*, 83.

[76] See e.g. Maguire, *Sunday Tribune*, 27 June 1982. I myself have been told by several people that they have seen such a document, but no one has been able to produce it.

anybody.[77] Despite his dealings with the British government, he was still a dedicated republican, and Reggie Dunne and Joe O'Sullivan were colleagues whom he felt bound to help. It may be that his activities at this stage served to convince many of those around him of his complicity.

Michael Hopkinson believes that Wilson's assassination was a part of Collins's policy towards Northern Ireland, and that it fits in with Collins's other attempts to attack and weaken the new government there.[78] While this does provide a plausible context for the murder, it does not explain the earlier plots to kill Wilson in 1921. If the murder was a considered act, why was it not better planned or prepared? Dunne and O'Sullivan had no one to help them, had to find and buy their own guns, and did not even use the morning of 22 June to prepare (O'Sullivan went to work that day as usual, and helped carry out the assassination during his lunch break).[79]

The murder does fit another pattern, however. Political violence in Ireland was driven, not by conspiracies and grand strategies, but by a tit-for-tat logic of reprisal and revenge adhered to by all sides. Early 1922 had seen a proliferation of armed parties accompanied by a loss of central control, both north and south. In this vacuum, local gunmen, whether I.R.A., Special Constabulary, or others, pursued their own little wars. Sectarian violence and revenge killings flourished in the north and spread across the south. Reprisals against unionists became commonplace. It was, in fact, a season of assassinations all across Europe. Just two days after Wilson's death, for example, Walter Rathenau, the German minister for foreign affairs, was shot to death in Berlin. His killers considered him a threat to German nationalism and declared 'We die for our ideals! Others will follow us!'—sentiments which could just as well have been uttered by Wilson's assassins.[80]

## Motives

Let us now turn to the one explanation still to be accounted for: that put forward by Reggie Dunne and Joe O'Sullivan themselves. In contrast to his exceedingly quiet home life after he returned from the war, Dunne had proved to be an erratic and very strong-willed commander of the London

[77] See O'Connor, *The Big Fellow* (1965 edn.), 200–4 and Coogan, *Michael Collins*, 354.

[78] Hopkinson, *Green Against Green*, 112–14.

[79] Statements of A. W. Watson and Ernest John Jordan (Lloyd George Papers, F/97/1/30).

[80] Robert L. G. Waite, *Vanguard of Nazism* (New York, 1952), 218–20.

I.R.A. He was jealous of his own authority and reluctant to take advice or orders. After the Truce was declared in July 1921, and without the war to enforce unity, Dunne's relations with his fellow republicans quickly reached a crisis point. He offended and alienated the leaders of the London Cumann na mBan, the women's auxiliary, as well as those of the Irish Self-Determination League, from whom he tried forcibly to extract money and support. These actions and attitudes exasperated Art O'Brien, the leading London republican and a confidant of Michael Collins. O'Brien referred to Dunne as 'a young fellow with such muddled notions', and to the city's I.R.A. unit as a 'farce', a 'fiasco', and a 'Gilbert and Sullivan Opera'.[81] Dunne was also frustrated with his position in the I.R.A. Neither the London organization nor Dunne's rank had ever been officially recognized, a fact which he attributed in part to nationalist snobbery over his English birth.[82] At the same time, unemployment and inaction were undermining the organization itself, and its members appealed constantly to Dunne for help. He, in turn, looked to Dublin but received no aid.

Then came the Treaty, which divided and weakened the Irish republican community in London. Some I.R.A. men crossed the sea to join the new army, but most simply dropped out of the movement altogether. Dunne's command began to wither away, and he was torn between anti-Treatyites like O'Brien and McGrath, who dominated the London scene, and the pro-Treaty side led by Michael Collins, to whom he felt a strong sense of loyalty.[83] The urban guerrillas of the city's I.R.A. tended to be against the Treaty, while many in the I.R.B. were willing to accept Collins's assurances that he was still working towards a republic.

Apparently pulled both ways, Dunne tried to stay neutral, an attitude which did not sit well with hard-line republicans. He (and perhaps O'Sullivan as well) was mocked and challenged by members of Cumann na mBan and his authority was questioned.[84] All around him his world was falling apart—his only world, as he had dropped out of college, could not find a job, and had no money. Meanwhile he, like most Irish nationalists, was growing more and more outraged by the continuing attacks on

[81] O'Brien to Collins, 10 Feb., 20, 26 July 1921 (O'Brien Papers, MS 8430).

[82] Dir. of Engineering [Rory O'Connor] to C/S [Richard Mulcahy], 31 Oct. 1921 (Mulcahy Papers, P7/A/27).

[83] See Denis Kelleher (O'Malley Papers, P17b/100), Denis Brennan (P17b/107), and Art O'Brien's memoir of the I.R.B. (O'Brien Papers, MS 8427).

[84] Michael Cremins (O'Malley Papers, P17b/89), Robert Briscoe (P17b/97), and William Aherne (P17b/99).

Catholics in Northern Ireland. Dunne had told his critics that 'I'll show you that we'll do something yet'. It is not difficult to see how he might have sought to resolve his pressures and anxieties in some dramatic and patriotic way. Northern Ireland provided a natural focus—the one issue which united all his former comrades—and Wilson, whose assassination had been planned at least once before, provided an obvious target.

Whatever personal motives may have lain behind the assassination, the political motive was crystal clear. Reggie Dunne described his act as 'ridding the human world of a scourge'. His father, Robert, told the police that 'he [Reggie] has read deeply in the papers about his co-religionists, and the pogroms in Belfast, and I have seen the tears run down his face as he has been reading this. He has very fine feelings.'[85] Reggie closed his final letter to his mother by saying: 'I was very glad that you heard from the women of Falls Road. That is one of the fruits of my achievement for Ireland.'[86]

What little direct knowledge we have of Dunne's thinking supports this theory.[87] His letters reveal a Pearse-like martyrological obsession (not unusual in fervent young republicans), replete with references to himself as Christ. He was also a great admirer of Terence MacSwiney, who starved himself to death in the belief that such self-sacrifice would advance the revolution. Dunne clearly saw his actions in these terms. If Reggie Dunne sought to vindicate himself and be a hero, he succeeded. It is striking how many conflicts were put to rest by his action. Art O'Brien and other anti-Treatyites went from criticism to extravagant praise. The Cumann na mBan members who had previously reviled him became instant supporters. I.R.A. men now thought him a hero rather than a failure. He had taken a political stand and he was assured that his parents would be well provided for.

We know almost nothing about O'Sullivan's motives. He was a shy, quiet man and his only surviving letter is largely a collection of political and religious pieties. We do know that O'Sullivan had always been close to Dunne, that he had killed before, and that he was probably the only I.R.A. man in London willing to join with Dunne in an assassination pact. He remains an enigmatic figure, although this does not necessarily mean that there was much more to be revealed.

---

[85] Statement of Robert Dunne (Lloyd George Papers, F/97/1/30).

[86] NLI, MS 2653 contains Dunne's prison letters.

[87] Several of Dunne and O'Sullivan's comrades also believed they acted on their own for these reasons. See William Aherne (O'Malley Papers, P17b/99) and Mick Cremins (P17b/89).

Was the murder premeditated? At what point the idea occurred to them, or to Dunne, is unknown. They apparently bought their guns only a week before the shooting.[88] The plan seems to have originated the night before the murder, when O'Sullivan read about Wilson's scheduled appearance at Liverpool Street station the next day.

On 22 June Dunne and O'Sullivan went to the unveiling of the station's war memorial, but it was very crowded. They decided to wait for Wilson outside his home in Eaton Place.[89] The fact that they carried loaded guns suggests they were out to kill, but they obviously had not devoted any thought or preparation to the plot. O'Sullivan had gone to work that morning and Dunne was carrying incriminating (albeit curiously dated) I.R.A. documents. No escape routes or hiding places had been readied, contrary to their experiences in the 1921 campaign.

According to Denis Kelleher and J. H. MacDonnell, Dunne's and O'Sullivan's lawyer (and a prominent pro-Treaty republican), Dunne confessed that he had not intended to kill Wilson but rather that the shots were fired without prior arrangement, in the heat of the moment.[90] This may have been so, but it does not accord with the determination with which the attack was pressed home, with the self-assurance displayed by the pair after their capture, or with the principled and coherent justification they offered. In addition, this story conflicts with Dunne's official report of the incident, as quoted at the beginning of this article. Here is yet one more aspect of the case where the evidence points in several directions.

## The Verdict

To understand the prevalence of conspiracy theories about Sir Henry Wilson's death, it would be useful to follow the course of this controversy once more. In the aftermath of the killing, the truth about the killers was hidden. Although many people knew about Dunne's and O'Sullivan's personal histories and their close ties with Michael Collins, Rory O'Connor, the I.R.A., and the I.R.B., no one, including the accused men

[88] See the statement of Ernest Jordan (Lloyd George Papers, F/97/1/30).

[89] See Dunne's report in the *Sunday Press*, 14 Aug. 1955. He mentions meeting another, unnamed officer the night before. This could have been Dennis Brennan, who says Dunne made no mention of Wilson (O'Malley Papers, P17b/37 and 100), or possibly Sam Maguire. Billie Aherne reports that the latter saw them the night of 21 June but he never knew if they discussed the murder (P17b/99).

[90] Taylor, *Assassination*, 182–4.

themselves, said anything. Chief of Staff Eoin O'Duffy's denial that they were even I.R.A. members, almost certainly made in good faith, was allowed to stand uncontradicted. However, it is important to remember that any suggestion of a cover-up implicates Rory O'Connor as much as Michael Collins.

Speculation flourished on both sides of the Irish Sea, particularly as the killing did not remain an isolated event. Six days later Provisional Government troops attacked Rory O'Connor's followers in the Four Courts with British guns, and civil war had begun. The assassination had helped trigger the war, and it now became inextricably entangled with its emotional and political legacies. The stage was now set for the first series of 'revelations' about the assassination by anti-Treaty republicans, which might better be described as rumours (with the possible exception of Diarmuid O'Crowley's detailed account). None of these people had any personal involvement in the affair, but they had undoubtedly heard something of Dunne and O'Sullivan's past and their connection with Collins and the hated I.R.B. This organization was widely blamed for the betrayal of the republic, so it was naturally also blamed for Wilson's death.

The second wave of conspiracy theories came with the campaign on the part of Patrick O'Sullivan, Joe's brother, and others to set the record straight. The history of the London I.R.A., the role of Dunne and O'Sullivan in it, and the existence of plans to shoot Wilson in 1921 were all revealed, but absolutely no proof was offered that Collins or any other Irish leader was involved in the 1922 murder.

The subsequent confusion, accusations, and misinterpretations flowed from two basic errors, which became entrenched in the debate at this time:

First, there *was* a cover-up of sorts—but of Dunne's and O'Sullivan's active membership in the I.R.A. and involvement in earlier assassination plots, not of a conspiracy to kill Wilson in 1922. Moreover, it was a passive rather than an active cover-up (no doubt at least partly the result of the distraction and deaths caused by the Civil War), which involved people on all sides of Irish politics.

Second, there *was* a plot to murder Wilson—but in 1921, not 1922, and Rory O'Connor and others were almost certainly just as involved in its planning as Michael Collins.

There is no solid evidence to support a conspiracy theory linking Michael Collins or anyone else to the murder. In the absence of such evidence, we must accept the assertions of the murderers that they acted alone, in the (grossly mistaken) belief that Wilson was responsible for Catholic deaths in Belfast. My own hypothesis as to Dunne's and O'Sullivan's motives cannot be definitely proven, but it fits not only with what we know of them and the London I.R.A. and I.R.B., but also with the general anarchy and proliferation of revenge killings in Ireland at the time.

Although this chapter has probed the supposed riddles of plots and secret societies, the reality was, ultimately, not very 'mysterious'. For two young Irish idealists to take matters into their own hands and shoot a hated foe was not a particularly unusual political act in the summer of 1922.

# PART IV
# Minorities at Bay

# 9

# The Protestant Experience of Revolution in Southern Ireland

Between 1911 and 1926 the twenty-six counties that became the Irish Free State lost 34 per cent of their Protestant population.[1] To put this number into context, over the same period the Catholic populations in both the north and south fell by 2 per cent and the Protestant population in Northern Ireland rose by 2 per cent. Over the previous thirty years, the two groups within the twenty-six counties had declined at almost exactly the same—gradually decreasing—rate (Protestants by 20 per cent, Catholics by 19 per cent).[2] So this catastrophic loss was unique to the southern minority and unprecedented: it represents easily the single greatest measurable social change of the revolutionary era. It is also unique in modern British history, being the only example of the mass displacement of a native ethnic group within the British Isles since the seventeenth century. Did the political and demographic upheavals coincide? How voluntary was this migration, and what were its causes? How sectarian was the Irish nationalist revolution?

Protestant experiences of the revolution in southern Ireland ranged from massacre and flight to occasional inconvenience and indifference, from outraged opposition to enthusiastic engagement. Even within the

[1] By 'Protestants' I refer to Protestant episcopalians, Presbyterians, and Methodists, not including those described as 'others' in the census. For a discussion of the statistics of Protestant population loss, see R. E. Kennedy, *The Irish: Emigration, Marriage and Fertility* (Berkeley, 1973), 110–38.

[2] *Census of Ireland*, vol. III, part 1, Table 1.

small, troubled district of Kilbrittain in West Cork—a hot zone of republicanism and violence—the conflict could mean radically different things
to different people.

Dorothy Stopford had a good revolution. A recent graduate of Trinity
College, she spent part of 1921 and 1922 as the dispensary doctor in
Kilbrittain. As a pipe-smoking woman wearing riding breeches and an
eyeglass, she caused a minor sensation, but neither her politics (republican) nor her religion (Church of Ireland) prevented her from getting
along with her neighbours.[3] To the local republican activists, her Protestantism was merely a curiosity: 'I sternly refuse all efforts to be converted
and say I prefer to go to Hell. Then they all exclaim that they know it's
wrong but they can't believe I will go to Hell—we have great sport.'[4] At
the same time, 'I am on excellent terms with all the gentry and Protestants,
they are very nice and broadminded.'[5] Her life did not lack variety: 'I went
to a work party at the Rectory the other day and sewed an apron and we
had prayers and sang hymns. I was much amused... I met all the ladies of
the parish. Next minute I am out fishing or ferreting with the I.R.A. You
can guess which I prefer.'[6]

For Dorothy Stopford, the guerrilla war raging in West Cork merely
added the spice of adventure to a pleasant life ('it is always fun here,
something happening every minute'). For John Bolster Barrett, also living
in Kilbrittain, the same period was one of unrelenting fear:

I had to sleep or try to sleep many nights in the open sometimes unable to
protect myself from rain and cold... I was unable to get provisions for my house
except by long, secretive journeys to loyal shops in Bandon. Many of my friends
and neighbours of the same political adherence were murdered in West Cork,
some in their beds, a few more shot on the way to and from Bandon whither
they had gone for food. I am a member of the Church of Ireland and I was told
on two occasions by Sinn Féiners that all the Protestants in West Cork were
going to be shot. During this time my house was raided several times at
night... I had therefore to sleep in the fields, my wife bringing me food secretly.
These are only a few of the experiences I have gone through... I have never

---

[3] Dorothy (Stopford) Price, 'Kilbrittain' (NLI, Dorothy Price Papers, MS 15,343[2]). See also
León Ó Broin, *Protestant Nationalists in Revolutionary Ireland: The Stopford Connection* (Dublin,
1985).

[4] Dorothy Stopford letter, 9 Nov. 1921 (NLI, Dorothy Price Papers, MS 15,341[8]).

[5] Ibid., 8 July 1921.

[6] Ibid., 9 Nov. 1921.

been restored to the health I enjoyed previous to 1920. Sometimes I suffer from long fits of depression, also from loss of memory.[7]

How representative were Stopford, Barrett, and Kilbrittain? What follows is an exploration in outline of the Protestant experience of revolution in the three southern provinces of Munster, Leinster, and Connaught. I am stopping at the border of Ulster rather than Northern Ireland because, although the minority communities of Cavan, Monaghan, and Donegal shared the general demographic fate of their fellow Free State counties, their political history had far more in common with the rest of Ulster than with their southern neighbours. For the purposes of this chapter, therefore, 'southern' means what it meant before Ireland was partitioned.

## When Did the Protestants Leave?

To understand why Protestants left, we must first ask when. Clearly, if much of the decline took place before 1919—before or during the Great War—or if it was spread evenly over the whole sixteen years between 1911 and 1926, this fact would call for a very different interpretation than otherwise. Fortunately, the change can be dated using church records. Unfortunately, neither national nor diocesan membership or attendance records exist for the Church of Ireland—by far the largest Protestant denomination in the south—but observers within the church do consistently point to late 1920 as the turning-point. 'It is the bare truth to say that we have lost more of our people during the last three years than in the fifty-three years since disestablishment', wrote one in 1923.[8] This impression is supported by the annual reports of the Board of Education of the united dioceses of Cork, Cloyne, and Ross. These reveal a 30 per cent drop in the number of pupils between 1911 and 1926, nearly three-quarters of which took place in 1920-2.[9]

My analysis of nineteen complete parish Preachers' Books in West Cork—including the Kilbrittain area—confirms this pattern.[10] Attendance

---

[7] John Bolster Barrett statement (PRONI, Southern Irish Loyalist Relief Association Papers, D989B/3/8). See also his file in the Irish Grants Committee Papers (PRO, CO/762/165).

[8] *Church of Ireland Gazette*, 26 Oct. 1923.

[9] Reports of the Diocesan Board of Education, 1911–1926 (Cork Diocesan Office Library).

[10] These records are located in the Representative Church Body Library and in the Abbeystrewrey, Carrigrohane, Fanlobbus, and Moviddy Parish Unions. I am grateful to their custodians for giving me access to them.

at Sunday service, averaged year by year, was higher in 1918 and 1919 than in 1911 or 1914. After 1919, attendance fell by 22 per cent, with more than two-thirds of the decline taking place in a single year—1922. Methodist congregations in Cork district followed an almost identical path, as did congregations throughout the three southern provinces. Methodist membership was higher in 1918, 1919, and 1920 than in 1914, but fell precipitously thereafter. Once again, 1921–3 were the crucial years, accounting for 74 per cent of the lost population.[11]

The suddenness and scale of this movement eliminates any long-term demographic explanations. These have frequently been advanced, most recently by Enda Delaney in his important study *Demography, State and Society: Irish Migration to Britain, 1921–1971*. He offers a judicious review of various contributing factors, but concludes in part that 'the decline in [Protestant] numbers was a process initiated before the advent of Irish independence in 1921–22'.[12] This is true, but it must be stressed that the same could be said of Catholics; it is relative decline that is at issue. Protestant population loss was relatively greater than that of Catholics in 1901–11, but both rates of decline were decreasing and the difference disappears if previous decades are taken into account. In his equally careful study, *The Aftermath of Revolution: Sligo 1921–23*, Michael Farry has suggested that what happened between 1911 and 1926 was an 'acceleration of already increasing decline' due to an 'accumulation of disappointments and dashed hopes during the whole second decade of the century'.[13] This argument may fit Sligo (where Farry's research is clearly authoritative), but does not work for the whole of southern Ireland. As has already been noted, historic Protestant and Catholic emigration rates had actually been falling, not rising, before 1911. It also fails to explain the specific timing of the departures and misleadingly lumps this event together with succeeding waves of emigration through the 1920s and 1930s when it was precisely the first shock that precipitated this movement. The outflow of the early 1920s was not part of a greater trend, it was the crisis through which one pattern of behaviour was transformed into another.

The salience of the year 1922 suggests at least a partial explanation for this timing, and for the decline as a whole: the withdrawal of the British

[11] These figures include junior and adult members for Dublin, Waterford, Cork, Limerick, and Sligo Districts, and are derived from the Methodist Church in Ireland Minutes of Conference, 1911–1926 (Wesley Historical Society).

[12] Enda Delaney, *Demography, State and Society* (Liverpool, 2000), 82.

[13] Michael Farry, *The Aftermath of Revolution* (Dublin, 2000), 200–1.

army and disbandment of the Royal Irish Constabulary early that year. And indeed, departing soldiers, sailors, policemen, and their families (assuming all of the latter did leave) do account for about one-quarter of the emigrants, a significant contributing factor, although ultimately a minor one.[14] They played no part in the West Cork figures discussed above, for example. Indeed, this transfer accounts for a much greater proportion of the Catholic population loss recorded in this period. Moreover, Irish-born Protestants left at almost exactly the same rate as those born outside the country.[15] Since almost all members of the armed forces in Ireland were British, it is clear that the movement was far more than that of an alien 'garrison'; these were overwhelmingly Irish men, women, and families that were leaving.

These figures also eliminate another common explanation for the decline: the impact of the Great War. As staunch imperial patriots, Irish Protestants were widely believed to have served and died in disproportionately large numbers, thus crippling their home communities.[16] Many families were shattered by the loss of their sons ('Hardly a week passed without news of a casualty, a brother, a cousin, an older sister's fiance, or a friend'[17]). The rural gentry, true to their martial traditions, suffered heavily as a class ('The world we had known had vanished. We hunted again, but ghosts rode with us'[18]). This mattered little in demographic terms. At most, the war induced a slight, temporary decrease in overall numbers in 1915 and 1916, apparently soon compensated for by the stoppage of emigration.

In any case, southern Protestants were no more willing to sacrifice themselves for Britain than their Catholic neighbours. Ulster's enlistment rate far outstripped that of the rest of Ireland, where there was little overall difference in enthusiasm between Catholics and non-Catholics. In many southern counties Protestants were actually less likely to enlist in either the army or navy than their Catholic neighbours, and made up a much smaller proportion of reservists. Occupation, not religion, determined the pattern of recruitment. Farmers and their sons made particularly reluctant soldiers, no matter what their denomination.[19] Thus, while

[14] *Census of Ireland*, vol. X, 46–7. Most British soldiers and sailors were unmarried, and of those who were many were married to Catholic women, with Catholic children.

[15] *Census of Ireland*, vol. X, 46.

[16] See W. B. Stanford, *A Recognized Church: The Church of Ireland in Eire* (1944), 16.

[17] Frances Moffett, *I Also Am of Ireland* (London, 1985), 83.

[18] Elizabeth, Countess of Fingall, *Seventy Years Young* (London, 1937), 386.

[19] David Fitzpatrick, 'The Logic of Collective Sacrifice: Ireland and the British Army, 1914–1918'. See also Pauline Codd, 'Recruiting and Responses to the War in Wexford', in

southern Protestants did go to war in considerable numbers, they were in fact one of the least affected communities in the British Isles. It was not the world war that blighted southern Protestantism, but what came after.

## How Loyal Were the Loyalists?

Between 1912 and 1922 Irish politics was transformed by a host of new and renewed organizations: Ulster, National, and Irish Volunteers (later the Irish Republican Army), Sinn Féin and Cumann na mBan, the Ulster Special Constabulary and the National Army, the Irish Transport and General Workers' Union and the Labour Party. Vast, unprecedented numbers of men and women gave their names, money, time, votes, freedom, or lives for the causes these groups represented. Not so the Protestant men and women of Connaught, Leinster, and Munster. In this great era of mass mobilization they produced neither party nor private army, nor did they contribute more than a scattering of members to anyone else's. This set them apart from their co-religionists not only in the six counties of Northern Ireland but also in Cavan, Monaghan, and Donegal, thousands of whom joined the Ulster Volunteer Force in 1913–14 and self-defence associations and the Ulster Special Constabulary in 1920–1.[20]

As John Henry Bernard, the Church of Ireland archbishop of Dublin, wrote to Lloyd George after the Easter Rising, 'the one class in Ireland which has *not* had resort to arms in support of its political opinions in 1913–16 is the Unionist class in the South and West'.[21] The cause of southern unionism was represented by the Irish Unionist Association (and after 1919 by the breakaway unionist Anti-Partition League) and a few unionist clubs, but their membership was drawn from a tiny elite. The former had only 683 members in 1913, and the latter were small in

---

Fitzpatrick (ed.), *Ireland and the First World War* (Dublin, 1986), 18–19; Terence Dooley, 'Monaghan Protestants in a Time of Crisis, 1919–22', in R. V. Comerford, M. Cullen, J. Hill, and C. Lennon (eds.), *Religion, Conflict and Coexistence in Ireland* (Dublin, 1990), 236–7.

[20] For the U.V.F., see Breandán MacGiolla Ghoille, *Intelligence Notes 1913–16*, 8–9, 74–5, 100–2. A few companies of Ulster Volunteers were formed in Leitrim in 1914. For Protestant vigilante groups in the 1920s, see C.I. Monthly Reports for Monaghan and Cavan, July 1920 (CO/904/112) and for Monaghan, Feb., Mar. 1921 (CO/904/116); H. V. Ross, 'Partition and Protestants in Monaghan 1911–26' (UCD MA, 1983), 19–20.

[21] J. H. Bernard to Lloyd George, 3 June 1916 (BL, John Henry Bernard Papers, Add. MS 52781).

number and size at best, at the height of the home rule crisis in 1914.[22] Even these largely disappeared after 1914, and failed to reappear in subsequent crises.[23] There was no need for an electoral machine, as unionist candidates only ran in and around the cities of Dublin and Cork in the general election of 1918 (and only in the University of Dublin in the 1921 election for a southern parliament), and were almost as scarce in the local council elections of 1914 and 1920.

What of Protestant nationalism? Protestant home rulers were a rare but identifiable breed, largely irrelevant after 1918. Protestant republicans such as Dorothy Stopford or Albinia Brodrick were far more exotic creatures, although not confined to any class or area.[24] When a pumpkin bearing the words 'Up Sinn Féin' appeared amidst the Kanturk church harvest festival decorations in 1921, the outrage was traced to the sexton who, it turned out, was 'well in with the rebels'.[25] Rarer still were Protestants in the I.R.A., who could be counted on one hand. Thus, while it would be fair to say that the vast majority of Protestants would have preferred that southern Ireland remain part of the Union, this was for the most part a passive, unexpressed preference. As a group, they were politically inert.

Most importantly, what Protestants—the vast majority of them—did not do during the guerrilla wars was resist the I.R.A. or assist government forces. What the Royal Irish Constabulary and the British army needed above all was information: who the local Volunteers were, where their arms were hidden, when an ambush was being prepared. With the exception of a very few isolated individuals, Protestants did nothing to provide such intelligence, and generally avoided contact with soldiers and policemen. Official reports and memoirs are unanimous in this regard. John Regan, the County Inspector of the Limerick R.I.C., wrote of 'southern loyalists' that, 'for many I had the most profound contempt. Certainly there were some who deserved great praise, but on the whole they were a poor lot...The Government could expect little help from them.'[26] One constable stationed in the west recalled that 'we wouldn't be a bit better in

[22] Patrick Buckland, *Irish Unionism I: The Anglo-Irish and the New Ireland 1885–1922* (Dublin, 1972), 18–21; Fitzpatrick, *Politics and Irish Life 1913–21*, 57–8.

[23] See J. M. Wilson's notes from a tour of Ireland in 1916 (PRONI, D989A/9/7).

[24] For Albinia Brodrick, daughter of Lord Midleton and cousin of Lord Bandon, see Mark Bence-Jones, *Twilight of the Ascendancy* (London, 1987), 107–8, 211.

[25] Royal Gloucestershire Regiment Archives, Lt. R. M. Grazebrook diary, 1 Oct. 1921.

[26] John Regan Memoirs, 157–9 (PRONI, D.3160). For a much more detailed discussion of the I.R.A., intelligence, and informers, see Hart, *The I.R.A. and Its Enemies*, 293–315.

with Protestants than Republicans. We'd be less better in with them...
because they were afraid to be accused of giving us news... they kept away
from us altogether.'[27] In Dublin, the Irish command's official history
noted that 'a considerable minority were professedly loyal but were so
intimidated that they refused to give information even when they themselves had been the sufferers by I.R.A. action'.[28] A military situation report
on the midlands and Connaught in December 1921 described 'active
loyalists' as 'an inconsiderable class'.[29] A survey of army commanders in
Munster in the spring of 1921 produced the same conclusions: 'Personally
I have no very high opinion of the politic value of the loyalist'; 'Few in
these counties are reliable'; 'I can see no sign of any effort to actively help
the government'; 'I would say that their action is very passive... Whether
they know things or not, I cannot say, but I do not think any try to be of
any assistance in the way of intelligence.'[30]

The West Cork Protestants I have interviewed confirm these impres-
sions. 'Even if you knew something, you wouldn't say it.'[31] Several told of
their fathers asking British officers not to talk to them or visit them, to 'go
away or you'll get me shot'.[32] 'There might be the odd one' who informed
on the guerrillas, but for the most part 'people were too afraid to do it'.[33]
'They kept their tongues in their cheeks.'[34] This was felt to be true of any
expression of anti-nationalist or anti-I.R.A. dissent. To rural and small-
town Protestants, 'talk' meant trouble even under normal circumstances.[35] During the revolution it could be terrifyingly dangerous. 'You
could get into trouble from anything—without thinking.'[36] As one man
told me: 'they kept quiet because they were afraid; I mean if I said
something to you tonight you would say something to somebody else
and somebody else and it would have got worse every time.'[37] 'You'd get

[27] J. D. Brewer, *The Royal Irish Constabulary: An Oral History* (Belfast, 1990), 82.

[28] G.H.Q. Ireland, Record of the Rebellion in Ireland in 1920–21, vol. ii, p. 16 (IWM, Sir Hugh Jeudwine papers).

[29] 'A History of the 5th Division in Ireland', App. XIV (Jeudwine Papers).

[30] Extracts from reports quoted in Gen. Macready to Miss Stevenson, 20 June 1921 (HLRO, Lloyd George Papers, F/36/2/19).

[31] Interview with C.R., 25 Oct. 1993.

[32] Interview with B.T., 9 Nov. 1994.

[33] Interviews with R.G and G.D., 17, 18 Apr. 1993.

[34] Interview with W.M., 17 Apr. 1993.

[35] See C. G. Bloodworth, 'Talking Past Differences: Conflict, Community and History in an Irish Parish', Ph.D. dissertation, Cornell University (1988), 260–2.

[36] Interview with R.G.

[37] Interview with G.H., 17 Apr. 1993.

into trouble very quickly and when you got into trouble it was hard to get out of it. We couldn't say a word anyway.'[38] W. B. Sanford wrote of the southern Church of Ireland as a whole that, 'the general policy adopted was "Lie low and say nothing", "Wait and see."'[39]

Despite this strong communal consensus that 'you didn't speak out if you had any sense', there were those who were 'outspoken' or 'stern' or who 'passed remarks'.[40] Such people were considered 'stupid' and 'foolish' troublemakers, dangerous not only to themselves but to the whole Protestant community. Those who did proclaim or act on their loyalty in this way did so knowing they were on their own. James McDougall, a businessman who had to flee Cork, stated bitterly that he 'wasn't like the spineless so-called "loyalists" I knew there'.[41] Tom Bradfield, another devout unionist (shot by the I.R.A.), declared that he was 'not like the rest of them round here'.[42] Even among Irish Grants Committee claimants, who had to demonstrate their loyalty to the Crown to receive compensation from the British government, only fifteen out of approximately 700 Cork applicants (or 2 per cent) said that they had provided information to the authorities.[43]

This withholding of support was not prompted by self-preservation alone, but also by alienation from British forces and methods themselves. Southern Protestants of all classes were repelled by British counter-insurgency tactics and by the new police recruits, the notoriously undisciplined Black and Tans and Auxiliaries. 'Those awful men! Everyone hated them, Roman Catholics and Protestants alike.'[44] Nor did this indignation stop at the Ulster border.[45] Protestants were probably less likely to be mistreated or to be singled out as the objects of retaliation, but they were far from immune. The only known Protestant I.R.A. Volunteers in Munster were two young Tipperary men who joined after being beaten by the police.[46]

[38] Interview with G.D.   [39] Stanford, *Recognized Church*, 16.

[40] Interviews with K.O., 20 Apr. 1993, R.G. and T.N., 17 Nov. 1994.

[41] James McDougall statement (PRO, Irish Grants Committee Papers, CO/762/112).

[42] Ó Broin, 177.

[43] The complete files can be found in the Irish Grants Committee Papers (CO/762).

[44] Interview with F.B., 6 Dec. 1993. For similar opinions, see Brian Inglis, *West Briton* (London, 1962), 31; Moffett, *I Also*, 102–5; Edith Somerville diary, 12–13 Dec. 1920 and 24 June 1921 (Queen's University Special Collections, Somerville and Ross Papers); E. M. Ussher, 'The True Story of a Revolution', 36, 58 (TCD, Ms. 9269).

[45] Rosemary Harris, *Prejudice and Tolerance in Ulster: A Study of Neighbours and 'Strangers' in a Border Community* (Manchester, 1972), 188–9.

[46] W. G. Neely, *Kilcooley: Land and People in Tipperary* (1983), 140.

Active resistance to I.R.A. raids and demands was as unusual as collaboration with the authorities, and even more dangerous. When it did occur
it was spontaneous, unorganized, and almost always punished with the
utmost severity. Tom Sweetnam of Ballineen became one of the first
Protestants to be driven out of Ireland by the I.R.A. after he fired on a
group of Volunteers trying to break into his house in 1918.[47] Most
Protestants, however, had neither the arms nor the inclination to engage
in self-defence. Even non-violent resistance—the simple refusal of
demands—often met with a harsh response. Survival depended upon
submission. 'Loyalism', like unionism, was a matter of preference rather
than practice, and most southern Protestants were loyalists in name only:
a name usually applied by others in any case.

## How Sectarian Was the Revolution?

It was the home rule crisis that first raised the spectre of sectarian violence
in the south, just as it did in Ulster. A survey of resident magistrates in
early 1914 gathered predictions and fears from all three provinces. The
Sligo R.M. warned that 'it is idle to suppose, if trouble comes, good
fellowship can be upheld or that it is really now more than superficial'.[48]
In Ballinrobe there was 'some apprehension of attacks on houses of
Protestants who are taking such steps as are possible to protect themselves'. In Ballinasloe it was feared that 'the minority might be in danger of
suffering if the Volunteers were not properly controlled'. In Kerry, 'the
spirit of religious intolerance is stronger than for the past three years'. In
West Cork, 'old sores have been reopened during recent years and religious bigotry has been revived. On the part of the minority there is a
widespread fear of possible outrages against their lives and property.'
Many R.M.s believed that fighting in the north would precipitate reprisals
against Protestants in the south. When publicly expressed, such appre-
hensions or accusations of Catholic intolerance (the stock-in-trade of
unionist propagandists) produced not reassurance but an angry backlash.
Members of the Limerick County Council condemned Munster Protestants for not contradicting such reports, and warned: 'the worm may

---

[47] C.I. Monthly Reports for Cork [East Riding], Apr.–Nov. 1918 (CO/904/105–7).

[48] This and following quotations are from R.M. precis 1914 (CO/904/227). Not every
respondent was so pessimistic: the Wexford R.M. reported that 'if anything, there is a disposition
among Catholics to go out of their way to be fair'.

turn ... and those people who may remain silent now may have reason to regret it.'[49]

These fears vanished practically overnight with the outbreak of war, and were not revisited until the conscription crisis of 1918 (the Easter Rising having had no great impact on communal relations[50]). Thus we move from one might-have-been to another. What might have occurred if the British government had attempted to enforce conscription in Ireland? Sinn Féin and the Irish Volunteers would undoubtedly have resisted, with massive popular support—including from some Protestants. In this eventuality, Volunteer plans called for 'persons known or suspected to be in sympathy with the enemy to be confined to their houses, under penalty of being shot at sight'.[51] Heading this list were those who refused to sign the anti-conscription pledge or subscribe to the campaign fund.[52] Many Protestants both signed and gave when asked, out of conviction or prudence. Many did not and were threatened and harassed. 'They are making the Protestants join in now, or if not, they will be boycotted, or have to go to England's war', wrote one correspondent from Drinagh, county Cork, in May 1918.[53] The County Inspector of the Longford R.I.C. reported in June that the breach between the communities was 'wider than it ever has been in my experience'.[54] One Church of Ireland clergyman wrote from King's County that: 'the Protestant people are being terrified into signing the pledge against conscription under threats of fire and sword ... A higher up Sinn Féiner came here with the list and threatened me that I would be treated just like the British soldiers they would be fighting against if I did not sign it, murder for me and my family and my place would be burned down.'[55] Protestant homes were also frequent targets for nocturnal raids, as much to intimidate as to acquire arms.

This crisis, too, passed without the augured confrontation, but the conscription debacle did launch the I.R.A.'s insurrection. By the end of

---

[49] *Cork Constitution*, 19 Jan. 1914. See also Fitzpatrick, *Politics and Irish Life*, 57–8.

[50] Except possibly in Enniscorthy, where the rector dated the population decline from the Volunteer occupation during Easter week: H. C. Lyster, *An Irish Parish in Changing Days* (London, 1933), 117–8. See also S. F. Glenfield, 'The Protestant Population of South-East Leinster, 1834–1981', M.Litt. thesis, TCD (1991).

[51] *Cork Examiner*, 19 Dec. 1918. See also *Irish Times*, 2 Jan., 2 Apr., 30 Oct. 1919.

[52] Irish Command Weekly Intelligence Survey, 11 June 1918 (IWM, Lord Loch Papers).

[53] Letter from Drinagh 20 May 1918 (Censorship summaries, CO/904/169).

[54] C.I. Monthly Report, June 1918 (CO/904/106). See also C.I. Monthly Reports, Wicklow, Apr. 1918; Galway [East Riding], Cork [East Riding] and Kerry, June, July 1918; Longford, Aug. 1918 (CO/904/105–7). Also *Irish Times*, 15 June, 21 Aug. 1918; 7 Jan. 1919.

[55] Revd Jasper Joly to Canon Jesson, 1 May 1918 (HLRO, Bonar Law Papers, 83/3/7).

1920 the guerrillas were engaged in an escalating struggle for mastery throughout southern Ireland, with their survival depending on the silence and acquiescence of the civilian population. As British forces came to grips with the new threat, fast-rising republican casualties bred suspicion and fear, and a mounting desire for revenge. Each British success would produce a frantic search for informers and a desperate need to hit back at their enemies.

As revolutionary violence spiralled upwards, more and more of its victims were civilians, and more and more of them were Protestant. Scores of Protestant men and women were shot in the winter and spring of 1920–1, throughout the south. Perhaps hundreds of others barely escaped the same fate and were driven from their homes. Not all of those shot were Protestant, but they numbered far in excess of their share of the population. In county Cork, for example, the I.R.A. deliberately shot over 200 civilians between 1920 and 1923, of whom over seventy (or 36 per cent) were Protestant: five times the percentage of Protestants in the civilian population.[56]

An even greater bias can be seen in the I.R.A.'s arson campaign over the same months, their response to British reprisals against property. The guerrillas struck back against private homes, hundreds in all, the great majority of which were owned by Protestants. This also reflected a class bias, as many were country houses of the gentry or aristocracy. By no means all, or even most, fell into this category: the common factor was religion. Of 113 houses burned by the guerrillas in Cork, seventeen (or 15 per cent) belonged to Catholics. Similarly, none of the more than two-dozen farms seized from 'spies' in that county were owned by Catholics.

These attacks had little or nothing to do with the victims' actual behaviour. Although almost all of those shot were accused of being 'spies' or 'informers', this label covered a wide range of 'anti-National' or 'anti-Irish' offenses. Simple dissent or non-cooperation with I.R.A. demands condemned many. Many were condemned by nothing more than 'talk'. As suggested above, very few were actually guilty of aiding the enemy. A large number seem to have been killed simply as a warning to others. Moreover, despite the near-complete absence of political organization, I.R.A. units commonly believed themselves to be opposed by a loyalist underground, and these conspiracy theories multiplied as the war

---

[56] These figures have been assembled from a wide variety of sources, most importantly the *Cork Examiner*, *Irish Times*, and R.I.C. British, National and Irish Republican army reports. For a further discussion of sources and the nature of I.R.A. violence, see *The I.R.A. and Its Enemies*.

progressed. The Freemasons, perennial nationalist and Catholic bogey-men, were felt to be particularly menacing, followed at a distance by the Y.M.C.A.[57]

Most Protestants were thus faced with an acute dilemma for which there was no solution. 'The Protestants were caught, you see, in the middle of the road.'[58] With the escalation of the war came political polarization, a harsh division (at least in republican eyes) between 'us' and 'them'—Protestants and Catholics, British and Irish, nationalist or unionist. 'They became not only different from us,' recalled Lionel Fleming, 'they were against us.'[59] Neutrality and passivity could not overcome past divisions and abiding ethnic and political stereotypes. In the Irish revolution, an unobtrusive unionist was still a unionist, as Richard Williams found out when the I.R.A. burned his house outside Macroom in June 1921. As described by the local reporter for the *Southern Star* (with considerable candour), his situation could stand for that of thousands of others. 'Whether Mr. Williams gave offence to Sinn Féin or endangered any of its adherents in the military sense, one would be very slow to believe.' Nevertheless:

Mr. R. C. Williams has been a consistent Unionist in his politics, though he never openly identified himself with politics. He has always held his opinions quietly but firmly, and though at times, when the cry of intolerance was raised by Southern Protestants, to damage the National cause, he might have done a little more to 'nail the lie to the mast'; still he always enjoyed a large amount of popularity, esteem and respect... The nation was engaged in a life and death struggle and there was little possibility of success adopting a neutral attitude.

Or, as a friend of Williams told me: 'They could have left him alone, I suppose, but they didn't leave anyone alone, that's the point.'[60]

The war continued to escalate right up to the July 1921 Truce, and anti-Protestant violence rose right along with it. Indeed, just before the fighting stopped the Munster I.R.A. had begun to seize Protestants to use as hostages. The County Inspector for South Tipperary commented that 'it looks as if a religious war was about to develop'.[61] The Truce brought comparative peace, along with the prospect of far worse if it failed. 'One of them', a correspondent to the *Irish Times* from Limerick, lamented 'the

---

[57] See *The I.R.A. and Its Enemies.*        [58] Interview with B.T.
[59] Lionel Fleming, *Head or Harp* (London, 1965), 52.
[60] Interview with G.D., 19 Apr. 1993.
[61] C.I. Monthly Report, Tipperary [South Riding], Apr. 1921 (CO/904/115).

state of paralysis into which they [the southern Protestants] have allowed themselves to fall . . . All of them have not yet experienced such pogroms as that of West Cork; but few have been without distinct intimation in some shape or form that they stand selected for special attention.'[62]

If hostilities had resumed, British commanders planned to pursue a far more ruthless course of action, and expected the I.R.A. to follow suit. Willing Protestants (and any other 'loyalists') would have been evacuated into concentration centres—towns and villages emptied of 'rebel sympathizers'—and organized and armed as a 'civil guard'. In other words, they would be expected to participate in the reconquest of the country.[63] I.R.A. intentions may be gauged by Sean Moylan's declaration that, 'if there is a war of extermination on us . . . by God, no loyalist in North Cork will see its finish'.[64] It is hard to imagine anything other than the most terrible—and terminal—consequences for the southern minority under these circumstances.

What did happen after the Anglo-Irish Treaty in many areas still exceeded all but the worst expectations. In effect, the guerrillas (most of whom opposed the Treaty) picked up where they had left off six months earlier, pursuing the same imagined enemies, ex-soldiers and policemen as well as Protestants. Anyone suspected of collaborating with the enemy was in danger. This drive for revenge was fuelled by anger at anti-Catholic violence in the north, heavily publicized in southern newspapers. The Belfast boycott was reapplied, mainly against Protestant traders, and Protestant houses were seized throughout the south, ostensibly to provide shelter for northern refugees. The following letter, sent to scores—possibly hundreds—of homes in the spring of 1922 by western I.R.A. units, illustrates the logic of reprisal:[65]

I am authorised to take over your house and all property contained therein, and you are hereby given notice to hand over to me within one hour from the receipt of this notice the above land and property. The following are reasons for this action:

(1) The campaign of murder in Belfast is financed by the British Government.

(2) As a reprisal for the murder of innocent men, women and children in Belfast.

[62] *Irish Times*, 4 Oct. 1921.

[63] See G.H.Q. memo on the protection of loyalists, 31 Oct. 1921, and associated correspondence in PRO, WO/35/180B.

[64] *Dáil Éireann Official Report: Debate on the Treaty Between Great Britain and Ireland* (Dublin, n.d.), 146.

[65] Proceedings of the House of Lords, vol. 51, col. 889 (11 May 1922).

(3) You, by supporting the union between England and Ireland, are in sympathy with their murder.

(4) In order to support and maintain the Belfast refugees.

It was not merely individual families that were to be 'deported', but whole communities.[66] The Church of Ireland Bishop of Killaloe wrote in June of north Tipperary: 'There is scarcely a Protestant family in the district which has escaped molestation. One of my Clergy has had his motor car and a portion of his house burned. Some other houses have been burned. Cattle have been driven off farms. Protestant families have been warned to leave the neighbourhood. Altogether a state of terrorism exists.'[67] In Ballinasloe:

If the campaign against Protestants which has been carried on there since the end of last month is continued in similar intensity for a few weeks more, there will not be a Protestant left in the place. Presbyterians and members of the Church of Ireland, poor and well-to-do, old and young, widows and children, all alike have suffered in intimidation, persecution and expulsion.

The campaign is carried out in the nighttime, by unnamed persons, who give no reason for their action. The system which usually is followed is, first, the despatch of an anonymous letter giving the recipient so many days, or hours, to clear out. If this notice is disregarded, bullets are fired at night through his windows, bombs are thrown at his house, or his house is burned down (as in the case of Mr. Woods). In one case, an old man who had not left when ordered to do so was visited by a gang, who smashed everything in his cottage—every cup and every saucer, and then compelled him to leave the town, with his crippled son, the two of them destitute...The list of those proscribed is added to constantly, and every Protestant is simply waiting for his turn to come.[68]

Similar campaigns of what might be termed 'ethnic cleansing' were waged in parts of King's and Queen's Counties, South Tipperary, Leitrim, Mayo, Limerick, Westmeath, Louth, and Cork.[69] Worst of all was the massacre of fourteen men in West Cork in April, after an I.R.A. officer had been killed breaking into a house.[70] Such events were often prompted by an unwavering belief in loyalist intrigue. The West Cork massacre was partly

[66] A word used in some letters of this type. See Adj., West Mayo Bde. to Major Browne, 29 April 1922 (Dept. of Taoiseach General Files, S565).

[67] Revd T. Stirling Berrym to Min. of Home Affairs, 10 June 1922 (NA, Dept. of Justice Papers, H5/372).

[68] *Church of Ireland Gazette*, 16 June 1922.

[69] See *Irish Times*, 2, 4, 19, 27 May, 13, 15, 17, 22 June, 8 July 1922; *Belfast News-Letter*, 13 June 1922; *Morning Post*, 1 May 1922.

[70] For a detailed reconstruction of this massacre, see *The I.R.A. and Its Enemies*, 273–92.

animated by the conviction that the victims had been plotting against the republic. Protestant houses in Mullingar were attacked by gunmen and arsonists and their inhabitants ordered to leave after a rumour was spread that 'the Protestant young men of the town have been drilling in fields in the neighbourhood'.[71] In each case, and in hundreds of lesser incidents, the language and intent was explicit: 'It is time they and their sort were out of the country!'[72] The simultaneous onset of civil war in the south and comparative peace in the north removed much of the pressure from Protestant communities in the south, but they continued to be favourite targets for anti-Free State reprisals up until the 1923 ceasefire.

Several points need to be made about the 1920–3 period as a whole. First, murder, arson, and death-threats were a very small part of a much wider pattern of harassment and persecution. For every such case, there were a hundred raids, robberies, or other attacks. Most rural and small-town Protestants spent these years in a constant state of anxiety, waiting for the next knock at the door. Would they want food, shelter, money, a horse or car—or something worse? Thousands of Protestant households had guerrillas billeted upon them for days or weeks at a time, even between the Truce and the Civil War. Some families maintained squatters on and off for years—a kind of I.R.A. *dragonnade*.

This everyday violence went far beyond the I.R.A. Not all the members of that organization—'the three letter word', as it was cautiously known— were involved in robbery and extortion, but by no means all those who were so involved were members. The revolution made Protestants 'fair game' to any of their neighbours, whether angry or covetous. While survivors of this period stress the number of Catholics who remained good neighbours, and it is clear that many disapproved of these attacks, it was Protestants and not their neighbours who were singled out for attention.

Attacks on churches, cemeteries, rectories, and public buildings provide a further index of the growing sectarianism of nationalist violence. Almost beneath notice amidst the whirl of rebellion were the frequent acts of minor vandalism and harassment, as when 'young toughs' in Dublin stoned a Methodist church on the first anniversary of the Rising.[73] Beginning in the conscription crisis, however, churches were marked for destruction in order to intimidate or punish their congregations. Such was the case

---

[71] *Belfast News-Letter*, 13 June 1922.

[72] Memo: 'Land agitation in the Queen's County', n.d. (Dept. of Taoiseach General Files, S566).

[73] *Irish Times*, 10 Apr. 1917.

in Kilbonane, county Cork, when two Church of Ireland families refused to sign the anti-conscription pledge, and in nearby Mallow after a recruiting meeting.[74] Many later attacks appear to have no motive other than religious or ethnic animosity. At least three churches in Clare and at least one in Sligo were burned before the Truce, for example.[75] These were not 'official' acts of the I.R.A., but it is very likely that its members were involved. Other denominational targets included schools, orphanages, and Freemasons' and Orange halls. At least nine Masonic lodges were burned, and a greater number were seized, looted, and wrecked in the course of the 'troubles'.[76] Such acts were far more than an incidental aspect of the military struggle; they formed an integral part of the revolution. To a great many Protestants, the 'troubles' meant persecution and random terror because of who they were, not what they did.

## The Protestant Exodus

The timing and context of population loss turn the census figures into a political and social event, and turn Protestant decline into a Protestant exodus. Almost all of the people who left did so between 1921 and 1924, in a sudden, massive upheaval. The Protestant response, in many cases, was flight. Police and other observers first noticed unusual levels of emigration and property sales in the spring and summer of 1921, in Leitrim, Sligo, Tipperary, Cork, and King's County.[77] These continued through the year, and rose dramatically in 1922, causing a minor refugee crisis in Britain.[78] The rate of departures apparently began to slow again in 1924, but by early 1926 nearly 40 per cent had gone for good.[79]

This statistic captures only a fraction of the displacement caused by the revolution, however. From the winter of 1920 onwards, thousands of men spent many nights away from home, sleeping in barns or fields. While

[74] C.I. Monthly Report, Cork [East Riding], July 1918 (CO/904/106); *Cork Examiner*, 28, 30 Oct. 1918.

[75] For Clare, see Fitzpatrick, *Politics and Irish Life*; for Sligo see *Irish Times*, 31 July, 27 Aug. 1920. See also Farry, *Aftermath of Revolution*, 193.

[76] See the Annual Reports of the Grand Lodge of Freemasons of Ireland, 1920–23; *Irish Times*, 20 May 1922.

[77] C.I. Monthly Reports, Leitrim, Sligo, Kerry, Tipperary [South Riding], Apr. 1921; Cork [East and West Ridings], June 1921; King's, August 1921 (CO/904/115–6). See also *Irish Times*, 22 Oct. 1921.

[78] See *First Interim Report of the Irish Distress Committee* (HMSO, 1922) and the Report of the Irish Grants Committee, 1930 (CO/762/212).

[79] The population loss for Leinster, Munster, and Connaught alone was 37%.

I.R.A. volunteers were going on the run from their enemies, these people were on the run from the I.R.A. 'I know people—they never used sleep inside their houses at all anytime, they just slept outside, and they were people minding their own business I'd say, they had no politics, no nothing.'[80] Hundreds of men and families left home altogether, for days, weeks, or even years, returning when it seemed safe. Many did so more than once. One such was George Applebe Bryan, a Dunmanway merchant. He barely escaped being murdered in the West Cork massacre of April 1922, when his assassin's gun jammed. He hid and attempted to leave town next day by train (along with hundreds of other men throughout the region), but was prevented by an I.R.A. picket. 'He took refuge in various friend's houses, changing every night, and eventually crossed to England.'[81] Bryan suffered a nervous breakdown but recovered enough to start a guest house in Bristol with his wife, supported by several relief agencies. His main concern throughout was to return home, which he attempted to do in June 1922 and finally did after the end of the Civil War in 1923. Bryan's case can stand for many. These people did not leave quickly or easily; they clung to their land or businesses for as long as possible. As remarkable as the number who left, therefore, is the number who stayed or returned.

All of the nightmare images of ethnic conflict in the twentieth century are here: the massacres and anonymous death squads, the burning homes and churches, the mass expulsions and trains filled with refugees, the transformation of lifelong neighbours into enemies, the conspiracy theories and the terminology of hatred. Munster, Leinster, and Connaught can take their place with fellow imperial provinces, Silesia, Galicia, and Bosnia, as part of the post-war 'unmixing of peoples' in Europe. We must not exaggerate. The Free State government had no part in persecution. Cork was not Smyrna, nor Belfast. Nevertheless, sectarianism was embedded in the vocabulary and the syntax of the Irish revolution, north and south. Any accounting of its violence and consequences must encompass the dreary steeples of Bandon and Ballinasloe as well as those of Fermanagh and Tyrone.

---

[80] Interview with D.J., 21 Apr. 1993.

[81] George Applebe Bryan statement (Dunedin Committee Papers, CO//905/17). See also 'Compensation for Southern Irish Loyalists: Typical Cases for the Committee of Enquiry' (SILRA Papers, D989B/2/11) and C. Albert Paine to Sec., Min. of Fin., 20 June 1922 (NA, Dept. of Fin. Records, FIN 665/6).

# 10

# Ethnic Conflict and Minority Responses

All of Europe's new post-war states had minority problems: hostile or vulnerable populations offering at least a potential threat—directly or by proxy—to new-found sovereignty.[1] Such groups often ended up as other states' problems, in the form of exiles, refugees, or irredentists. Anglo-Irish relations were not ultimately thus affected, but Ireland certainly was. As a result of revolution and regime change, both northern Catholics and southern Protestants were harassed, persecuted, and terrorized by virtue of their ethnicity and perceived loyalties. Both groups were cut off from their preferred states and tended to see their new government as an alien imposition. However similar their dilemmas, though, northern and southern minority responses were strikingly different. While Protestants left the twenty-six counties in large numbers (falling by 34 per cent), the Catholic population of Northern Ireland stayed about the same (falling by 2 per cent—the same proportion as in the Free State).

To gauge the importance of this set of outcomes, imagine they had been reversed. Instead of the southern minority, it is the northern Catholic population that falls by one-third: from 33 to 22 per cent of Northern

[1] See Aviel Roshwald, *Ethnic Nationalism and the Fall of Empires: Central Europe, Russia and the Middle East, 1914–1923* (London, 2001); Panikos Panayi, *Outsiders: A History of European Minorities* (London, 1999); Karen Barkey and Mark von Hagen (eds.), *After Empire: Multiethnic Societies and Nation-Building* (Boulder, Col., 1997); Carol Skalnik Leff, *National Conflict in Czechoslovakia: The Making and Unmaking of a State, 1918–1987* (Princeton, 1988); Michael Marrus, *The Unwanted: European Refugees in the Twentieth Century* (Oxford, 1985).

Ireland. Local majorities in Fermanagh and Tyrone are gone. Belfast enclaves shrink and their expansion into north Belfast is halted. Over large stretches of countryside, Catholic families are no more. Schools are closed, parishes are amalgamated, and church budgets decline. The impact echoes on through the decades as new waves of migrants follow the first, compounding the loss. Politically, safe nationalist seats become even scarcer and the cause more hopeless. Altering the border according to the wishes of the adjacent inhabitants would no longer have been a nationalist aspiration; the absence of plebiscites no longer a grievance (to be replaced, perhaps, by the plight of the displaced). Unionist fears of the internal threat recede and loyalist extremists lose credibility, leading possibly to a more open system and more opportunities for a cross-community labour party. Eventually, perhaps, the scene would have been set for a labour-based civil rights movement.

In the south, the change would be less striking, as Protestants would still have been outnumbered many times over and Free State politics did not revolve around issues of religion and ethnicity. Still, a stronger minority operating in elections by proportional representation might have had considerable clout, especially in border counties and south of Dublin. Third parties based on farmers or businessmen would likely have profited most, at least at first. This would not have halted the rise of Fianna Fail, but it might have polarized politics further, especially during the economic war. If ethnic votes had swung a close election (in 1932, for example), the losers might well have been embittered. If 100,000 or so northern refugees had settled in the south, they might have added further volatility to the scene. The consciousness of such victimization—leading perhaps to demands for compensation or repatriation—could well have affected Anglo-Irish relations. Considering what might have happened, it is worth asking: why did events turn out the way they did?

## Violence

The best starting-point in addressing this problem is with the worst part of these peoples' predicaments. Did the differing responses of northern Catholics and southern Protestants reflect varying levels of loss, fear, and uncertainty? In the south, the approximately 300,000-strong Protestant population (as of 1911) lost over 100 people killed and another thirty or so wounded in political shootings (not including native policemen and soldiers). At least 400 Protestant-owned homes and businesses were burned, along with numerous Masonic, Orange, and church halls and other identifiably Protestant property.[2] These major incidents can be counted in a way that theft, vandalism, boycotts, and unarmed assaults cannot. The latter must have numbered in the thousands over the course of the revolution, affecting thousands of Protestant families.[3]

In Northern Ireland, 420,000 Catholics suffered well over 300 civilian deaths and hundreds more wounded by bullets or bombs, and perhaps 600 houses and businesses destroyed. So in either relative or absolute terms, northern Catholics were far worse off than their southern Protestant counterparts. This was especially the case in Belfast, where 96,000 Catholics—less than 25 per cent of the city population—absorbed two-thirds of these casualties and 80 per cent of the property damage. Thousands of homes and livelihoods were also lost due to residential flight and workplace expulsions (8,000 of the former and 6,000 of the latter[4]). The northern minority may not have suffered the same levels of daily predation by gunmen, squatters, thieves, and bullies, but the scale of the onslaught upon them was obviously greater. Common sense would suggest that they should be more likely to leave, not the other way around.

If not scale, then perhaps intent. Did the perpetrators of violence intend to drive their victims out? Were they targeted because of their religion? Or were they merely a kind of collateral damage, as was often claimed by apologists for the southern I.R.A. and Northern Ireland police alike? Southern Protestant victims were almost always shot by members of the I.R.A., who usually claimed military necessity, alleging that their targets were collaborators or informers.[5] Most shootings were motivated by revenge or fear, in response to republican deaths or British successes. The fact that the attacks resumed after the Treaty and British withdrawal indicates the salience of religion or ethnicity as a determinant of violence.

---

[2] These figures are approximate, calculated from newspaper, police, and military reports. They do not include cases where the religion of the victim is uncertain.

[3] Some indication of the scale of such incidents can be found in the thousands of files of the Irish Grants Committee (PRO, CO 762) and of malicious injury claims in Irish Department of Justice records (NA).

[4] For the number of residential expulsions, see the excellent and exhaustive study by Declan Martin, 'Migration Within the Six Counties of Northern Ireland, with Special Reference to the City of Belfast, 1911–37', MA thesis, Queen's University of Belfast (1977), 155–63. For workplace expulsions, see Henry Patterson, *Class Conflict and Sectarianism: The Protestant Working Class and the Belfast Labour Movement 1868–1920* (Belfast, 1980), 115–142, Austen Morgan, *Labour and Partition: The Belfast Working Class 1905–23* (London, 1991), 265–84.

[5] See my *The I.R.A. and Its Enemies*, 293–315.

Sectarian language was frequently used, and wholesale threats were issued to whole communities in some locales.[6] It is significant, however, that no Protestants—north or south, as far as I know—were killed by angry mobs (the same cannot be said for northern Catholics), but Donald Horowitz's work on ethnic riots is still relevant. Horowitz identifies only two general aims that such events have in common: to humiliate or put down the target group—to 'teach them a lesson'; and the reduction of ethnic heterogeneity—to drive them away.[7] If we take these drives to be thematically central to ethnic violence in general, it must be noted that one or the other were frequently present in attacks on southern Protestants. The bottom line for understanding the reasons for mass departure is that many Protestants felt themselves to be just such a target group, under deadly threat.

This perception, and the arguments presented in the previous chapter, raise a question: if it was so bad, why did so many Protestants stay? After all, while one-third may have left, two-thirds stayed. Answering this requires an assessment of what might have happened and what did not happen. A whole parallel narrative of the revolution can be constructed from these what-ifs and what-might-have-beens. What if civil war rather than a foreign war had come in 1914? What if the 1918 German offensive had been more successful and the British government had implemented conscription? What if negotiations had failed and all-out war had been declared instead of a Truce in the summer of 1921? What if there had been no Anglo-Irish Agreement in December 1921? What if the Treaty had failed to pass the Dáil? What if the Provisional Government had collapsed or the British government had reintervened in 1922? All in all, the Protestant population may have been fairly—even spectacularly— lucky in the sequence of cards they were dealt and in the way other hands were played. Of course, everyone in Ireland would probably have suffered if these alternative events had come to pass, but it is not surprising that Protestants believed that they narrowly escaped something far worse. It should also be pointed out that, while the built-in peacefulness and neighbourliness of Irish society may have played a part in damping sectarian friction, the same attitudes and structures existed in other multi-ethnic societies before they fell apart. If violence in Ireland had continued to escalate, there is no reason to expect Irish people of any denomination to act with greater restraint than Bosnians or Kosovars.

---

[6] See Ch. 9.      [7] Donald Horowitz, *The Deadly Ethnic Riot* (Berkeley, 2001), 424.

If we turn to examine the actors involved, it can once more be argued that what did not happen was as important as what did. The British government never played the ethnic card. It is a common ploy when waging guerrilla wars to arm a native militia to do the dirty work. While this was contemplated in the south in 1921 if the Truce had broken down, it was only reluctantly carried out in Ulster with the Special Constabulary, who were never deployed elsewhere. There was no repeat of the brutal Yeomanry and Militia campaigns of the 1790s.

Equally importantly, the Irish Free State was in no way implicated in any attacks on, or discrimination against, its minority. It did not seek their property or their departure, thereby setting itself above a great many other post-war and post-revolutionary regimes. No political party suggested or endorsed such a programme and the Catholic Church was committed to tolerance and peaceful coexistence (unlike in Yugoslavia or Rwanda). It must also be stressed once again that southern Protestants themselves as a group were not politically active. If any unionist organizations had fought the I.R.A. as in Ulster—or even contested elections against Sinn Féin— this would certainly have polarized community relations to a much greater extent.

So the only organization directly implicated in sectarian violence or intimidation was the I.R.A. itself, which brings us back to the question of intent. The key point here is that, despite the violence, there was no plan, no ideology, and no institutional support for continental-style ethnic cleansing. Neither Sinn Féin nor the I.R.A. were ever officially committed to the idea of expulsion. In fact, quite the opposite. Both were formally non-sectarian in membership and constitution. Sinn Féin did have a scattering of Protestant members, including several in leadership positions. Nor were any killings or burnings officially ordered or condoned if based purely on religion: that anything of the sort took place was vigorously denied. And this nondenominational rhetoric was taken seriously and believed sincerely by a great many republican activists. It was not unusual to find Volunteers protecting Protestants and their property in early 1922, at least during labour disputes.

On the other hand, many guerrillas—including some senior officers— were very suspicious of Protestants in general and harboured a sense of historical grievance against their very presence. They were willing to act on their own in this regard, or to let others have their way. It is certainly significant that almost no one in the I.R.A. was ever punished for a sectarian attack. The rules, hierarchy, and ideology of the I.R.A. did act as something of a brake on outright ethnic attacks or 'hate crimes'. They also rendered a systematic campaign of such violence unlikely without great provocation. Nevertheless, the loose, localized nature of the organization, and the radicalizing pressures of a guerrilla war, provided a permissive environment for low-level but widespread, and occasionally intense, persecution.

Finally, it has to be said that this persecution rarely rose to outright murder—let alone mass murder. In comparative terms, the hundred-odd fatalities in sectarian shootings in southern Ireland rank very low on the scale of twentieth-century atrocities. Protestants were a minority—albeit a disproportionate minority—of civilians killed by the I.R.A. in the south, and civilians made up a minority of its total victims. Sustained runs of ethnic murders were confined to the first six months of 1921 and of 1922. The scale of the violence was such as to reach into a great many households and create massive fear and flight, but it provided nowhere near enough leverage to move an entire population. Of course, if events had unfolded differently in 1921 or 1922, their intensity and momentum might have been greatly multiplied.

What happened in southern Ireland did not constitute 'ethnic cleansing', and there were at least four necessary factors missing to make this so:

(1) a state with its resources and authority, in the hands of one group directed at another;
(2) a plan or an enabling or mobilizing racial or sectarian ideology;
(3) any real threat or provocation on the part of the target group; and
(4) violence at totalizing or eliminationist levels.

In the absence of all these potential fuses and explosives, it is sobering that a harmless, passive minority could be so quickly turned on or left to their fate by so many neighbours; that so much irrevocable damage could be done by so few people, if given guns and power. On the other hand, what is also striking is the insufficiency of 'ancient hatreds' or 'quarrels', even combined with ardently maintained ethnic boundaries and guerrilla war, to push things any farther. These elements did produce a kind of chemical reaction precipitating ethnically targeted violence. For ethnic cleansing to occur, however, the materials have to be refined and processed. It requires a whole apparatus of propaganda, parties, prisons, and camps. The nightmare images were there, but they should not be confused with very different realities elsewhere.

In the south, Cork was a particular centre of sectarian trouble; in the north, it was Belfast that generated by far the majority of such fatalities. The usual label for what happened to Catholics in Belfast and Lisburn in 1920–2 is 'pogrom'. This was the term used at the time and ever since, an obvious contemporary analogy with communal attacks on Russian Jews, particularly in the revolutionary years of 1903–6 and 1917–21. These events were defined by massacres of helpless civilians, looting, and residential expulsions, often with apparent official connivance. Nineteenth-century Odessa, where the modern pogrom was invented, even resembled Belfast in its segregated neighbourhoods, Jewish–Greek divide, and accompanying ritualized crowd violence (at Easter rather than in July). Both cities shared a lengthy back catalogue of popular eruptions.[8]

Table 21(A and B) demonstrates that the victims in Belfast were indeed overwhelmingly civilian—at least, they were never identified with, or claimed by, any official or paramilitary group. Less than ten men known to be or claimed as members of the I.R.A. were killed in the city, few of whom were killed in action.[9] Most Catholic victims were adult men though (about 80 per cent), so if we use the victimization of women and children as a rough index of indiscriminate violence, we can conclude that loyalists and security forces were somewhat discriminating in their choice of target. Some of the victims might have been communal combatants as well.

Belfast also saw a lot of crowd violence, of course, sometimes aimed at ethnic or religious targets like Catholic churches and convents, but mostly at homes and businesses (particularly bars). With this came a systematic campaign of intimidation—and occasionally direct expulsion—intended to drive Catholics out of areas seen by Protestants as their own territory, street by street. These efforts were absolutely unambiguous in intent, widespread, and repeated throughout the 1920–2 period. The pattern was always the same: Catholic families would be removed from the Protestant enclave, and adjoining Catholic areas would be pushed back in order to consolidate the majority's territory.[10]

---

[8] For an overview of Russian pogroms, see John Klier, 'The Pogrom Paradigm in Russian History', in Klier and Shlomo Lambroza (eds.), *Pogroms: Anti-Jewish Violence in Modern Russian History* (Cambridge,1992), 13–38.

[9] See Jim McDermott, *Northern Divisions: The Old I.R.A. and the Belfast Pogroms 1920–22* (Belfast 2001) and National Graves Association, *The Last Post* (Dublin, 1985).

[10] See Martin, 'Migration', 41–135 for a very detailed description and analysis of the anti-Catholic violence.

## TABLE 21. *Victims of violence in Belfast, 1920–1922*

### A. *Newspaper/police reports survey*

| | R.I.C. | | U.S.C. | | Military | | I.R.A. | | Civilians | | Total | |
|---|---|---|---|---|---|---|---|---|---|---|---|---|
| | K | W | K | W | K | W | K | W | K | W | K | W |
| **1920** | | | | | | | | | | | | |
| Jan.–Mar. | o | 1 | | | o | o | o | o | o | 2 | | |
| Apr.–June | o | 1 | | | o | o | 1 | o | o | o | | |
| July–Sept. | 1 | 3 | | | o | 1 | 1 | o | 59 | 256 | | |
| Oct.–Dec. | o | 5 | o | o | o | o | 1 | o | 4 | 17 | | |
| TOTAL | 1 | 10 | o | o | o | 1 | 3 | o | 63 | 275 | 67 | 286 |
| **1921** | | | | | | | | | | | | |
| Jan.–Mar. | 5 | 1 | o | o | o | o | o | o | 4 | 2 | | |
| Apr.–June | 5 | 4 | o | o | o | o | 3 | o | 11 | 58 | | |
| July–Sept. | 2 | 7 | o | 3 | o | o | o | o | 46 | 189 | | |
| Oct.–Dec. | 1 | 1 | o | 1 | o | o | o | 4 | 32 | 109 | | |
| TOTAL | 13 | 13 | o | 4 | o | o | 3 | 4 | 93 | 358 | 109 | 379 |
| **1922** | | | | | | | | | | | | |
| Jan.–Mar. | 3 | 1 | 2 | 2 | 1 | 7 | o | o | 85 | 262 | | |
| Apr.–June | 2 | 9 | 3 | 7 | o | 4 | o | o | 122 | 210 | | |
| July–Sept. | o | o | o | 2 | o | 1 | o | o | 15 | 26 | | |
| Oct.–Dec. | o | o | o | o | o | o | o | o | o | 7 | | |
| TOTAL | 5 | 10 | 5 | 11 | 1 | 12 | o | o | 222 | 505 | 233 | 538 |
| TOTALS | 19 | 33 | 5 | 15 | 1 | 13 | 6 | 4 | 378 | 1,138 | 409 | 1,203 |

*Note*: K = killed; W = wounded

### B. *Identified dead, July 1920–July 1922*

| | Civilian | | Military | R.I.C. | U.S.C. | I.R.A. |
|---|---|---|---|---|---|---|
| | Catholic | Protestant | | | | |
| 1920 | 35 | 31 | 5 | 2 | | 3 |
| 1921 | 74 | 45 | 1 | 12 | 1 | 5 |
| 1922 | 150 | 88 | 2 | 7 | 9 | o |
| TOTALS | 259 | 164 | 8 | 21 | 10 | 8 (3 killed in action) |
| % of total | 56 | 35 | 2 | 4 | 2 | |
| Women/children | 50 | 14 | | | | |
| % of total | 19 | 9 | | | | |
| 7 deaths | | | | | | |

## C. Snapshots

| | Official | | G. B. Kenna (Father Hassan) | | Michael Collins | | *Freeman's Journal* | |
|---|---|---|---|---|---|---|---|---|
| | 23–31 Aug. 1920 | | 6–25 Feb. 1922 | | 1–27 Apr. 1922 | | Jan.–June 1922 | |
| **Catholics** | | | | | | | | |
| killed | | | 27 | (63%) | 24 | (69%) | 170 | (64%) |
| wounded | | | 69 | | 41 | | 345 | |
| TOTAL | 134 | (48%) | 96 | (70%) | 65 | (59%) | 515 | (63%) |
| **Protestants** | | | | | | | | |
| killed | | | 16 | (37%) | 11 | (31%) | 95 | (36%) |
| wounded | | | 26 | | 34 | | 210 | |
| TOTAL | 145 | (52%) | 42 | (30%) | 45 | (41%) | 305 | (37%) |

*Sources*: (A): *Irish Times* and *Freeman's Journal*, 1920–2; (B): G. B. Kenna [Fr. John Hassan], *Facts and Figures: The Belfast Pogroms 1920–22* (Dublin, 1922), 101–12, and, for *The* I.R.A. figures, *Last Post* (National Graves Association, 1986); (C): *Irish Times*, 4 Sept. 1920; Kenna, *Facts and Figures*, 69, 133–8 (used by Michael Collins in communications with the British government); *Freeman's Journal*, Jan.–June 1922. Kenna's figures for those killed are the most reliable but the differences between them and those drawn from newspaper and police reports in (A) are likely due to the fact that many of those listed as wounded in (A) subsequently died.

With very few exceptions, then, Belfast's experience of ethnic trouble differed in degree and kind from the rest of Ireland, north and south. Elsewhere, intended civilian casualties generally occurred due to their identification with one side or another in a guerrilla war. Both the I.R.A. and the various government forces themselves absorbed a lot of the punishment. In Belfast, the designated combatants suffered little. They certainly dished it out, but they didn't take it. This was primarily a communal war and a sectarian war, fought on the basis of ethnic mobilization rather than paramilitary organization. As such, it was part of a great tradition of rioting and territorial struggle going back through 1912, 1886, 1872, 1864, and 1857, and forward to the present day. The moves, the repertories of action, were more or less pre-programmed, automatic, down to the timing of major outbreaks in the Orange marching season.[11] What moved the violence to another level of destruction was the simultaneous struggle between states—British, republican, and Northern

[11] See S. E. Baker, 'Orange and Green: Belfast 1832–1912', in H. J. Dyos and M. Wolff (eds.), *The Victorian City: Image and Reality* (London, 1973), 789–814; Ian Budge and Cornelius O'Leary, *Belfast: Approach to Crisis: A Study of Belfast Politics, 1613–1970* (London, 1973), 73–100; and Frank Wright, *Two Lands on One Soil: Ulster Politics Before Home Rule* (Dublin, 1996), 241–83.

Irish—that raised the stakes to winner-take-all. Nationalists were making unprecedented political advances, especially in Ulster, where proportional representation gave them command of many local governments and a strong presence on the Belfast Corporation. Republican guerrillas were increasingly active through 1920 and 1921, and, while ineffective in Belfast, were a powerful presence elsewhere in Ulster.[12] Northern unionists inevitably countered with their own paramilitary revival, and then acquired state power for the first time—and with it the ability to enforce their rule.

This mutually threatening dynamic inevitably produced a two-sided conflict whose victims were Protestant as well as Catholic. Something like a thousand Protestants lost their homes in Belfast, fleeing from nationalist-controlled areas (although there is no evidence of a systematic campaign to achieve this).[13] Thousands of Protestant shipyard and factory workers were expelled from their jobs alongside Catholics, on account of their socialism or insufficient loyalism.[14] And, as Table 21B demonstrates, over a third of all murder victims were Protestant civilians, rising even higher in some periods—notably in August 1920 (Table 21C).

In this regard it is often pointed out as a measure of Catholic suffering that they represented 23 per cent of the Belfast population but made up 56 per cent of murder victims, three-quarters of those expelled from workplaces, and 80 per cent of those displaced from their homes. This is absolutely true, but not quite the whole picture. If we turn things around and look at agency rather than victimization, the Catholic 23 per cent of the population (and a significantly smaller proportion of adult males) inflicted 44 per cent of the casualties (assuming that all I.R.A. members were Catholic, and that they or other nationalist gunmen were responsible for all the police and military casualties) and 20 per cent of the residential displacements. Per capita—and especially considering that many Catholics were killed by members of the security forces—Catholics were as or more violent than their Protestant neighbours, despite having fewer weapons.[15] Since (by Donald Horowitz's estimate) aggressors usually

[12] See Chs. 2 and 3.      [13] Martin, 'Migration', 136–54.

[14] See Morgan, *Labour and Partition*, 265–70.

[15] This assumes that all I.R.A. members were Catholic and that they or other nationalist gunmen were responsible for all the military, police, and Protestant casualties. In fact, some Protestants were probably shot by co-religionists or security forces, and some Catholics were likely shot by the I.R.A. It is impossible to say for sure in many cases, but the numbers were not large and would have cancelled each other out to some degree.

inflict 85–95 per cent of the losses in ethnic riots and suffer correspondingly little on their own account, this is a remarkable record.[16]

Both sides saw their actions as being defensive. Catholic gunmen, many of whom were not members of the I.R.A., saw themselves as protecting their homes and neighbourhoods, holding back the onslaught. There were enough massacres of Catholic men to maintain the most extreme fears of what loyalists might do if they failed. But from the Protestant side, these same men were automatically perceived as snipers and bombers threatening Protestant heartlands, who had to be removed or pushed back. Many I.R.A. operations, authorized or not, took the form of indiscriminate revenge attacks, and so were indistinguishable from intended aggression. The typical Belfast gun battle saw grenades and shots exchanged between streets over many hours, with any man a possible target. Protestant aggression was an objective reality, but both sides got caught up in the same tit-for-tat battle of reprisals that drove the southern guerrilla war and attendant ethnic killings. In the south, however, the minority was defenceless and had no communal territory to protect. The reciprocity of northern violence does not fit the pogrom model or imagery so well.

Although loyalist vigilantes did set out to 'cleanse' Protestant areas and firms, this was a limited war for territorial security and political mastery, not an absolute war of extermination or elimination. Again, as with southern republicanism, the vital ingredients of ethnic cleansing were lacking. There was no grand plan, just time-tested and traditional local initiatives. There was no truly destructive intent, more a coercive re-establishment of an unequal status quo; no enabling institutions or ideology, although the Protestant churches and Northern Ireland government shamefully did nothing to discourage popular sectarianism, and the Unionist Party often encouraged it. The battle for Belfast started off in June 1920 as a pogrom with a massive assault on defenceless Catholics in their homes and workplaces, but subsequent resistance and counter-attacks turned the situation into something more like a miniature civil war.

## States

So in neither the northern or southern cases can we say that ethnically targeted violence amounted to full-scale ethnic cleansing. And neither the

---

[16] Horowitz, *Ethnic Riot*, 385–6.

scale nor the intent of the violence explains the variant outcomes. Perhaps, then, it was the new state's relationship with the minority—hostile, supportive, or indifferent—that determined the popular response. In the twenty-six separatist counties, attitudes within the Provisional Government and the Free State towards Protestants as a group ranged from indifference to support. There was certainly no institutional discrimination or constraints on identity, employment, economic activity, education, or movement. There were no purges of the civil service, and Protestants were free to take part in politics. There were even minority safeguards built into the new constitution, although largely on behalf of the social elite.[17]

On the other hand, the new regime categorically refused to recognize the victimization of Protestants past or present, and therefore did nothing specifically to counter it. British journals, such as the *Spectator*, that reported sectarian incidents were censored. Most importantly, the government was greatly distracted and unable to function properly until well into 1923, so its attitudes were practically irrelevant. The primary problem in 1922 and 1923 was not hostile or indifferent government, but no government.

The Catholic experience in Northern Ireland was very different. The unionist regime ranged from indifferent at best, to systematically and deeply hostile at worst. A lot of anti-Catholic violence was perpetrated by members of the security forces, including some of the worst murders.[18] The Ulster Unionist Party and the Orange Order, inextricably linked to the new government, were explicitly anti-nationalist and anti-Catholic respectively. Many of their leaders and activists, including Edward Carson, encouraged or condoned violence and discrimination. The East Belfast death squad, the Ulster Protestant Association, had close ties to the Party.[19] Even some Protestant church leaders implicitly defended such actions by publicly denying they were taking place.[20]

---

[17] For a general overview of the position of the Protestant minority, see F. S. L. Lyons, 'The Minority Problem in the 26 Counties', in F. MacManus, *The Years of the Great Test* (Cork, 1967), and Kurt Bowen, *Protestants in a Catholic State: Ireland's Privileged Minority* (Dublin, 1983).

[18] This seems indisputable, and would fit with the general pattern of reprisals and assassinations carried out by policemen and soldiers—including those of the Provisional Government and Free State—throughout Ireland. See Michael Farrell, *Arming the Protestants: The Formation of the Ulster Special Constabulary 1920–27* (London, 1983), chs. 3–5.

[19] See Morgan, *Labour and Partition*, 215–28, 265–314.

[20] See Mary Harris, *The Catholic Church and the Foundation of the Northern Irish State* (Cork, 1993), 126–7.

To keep things in perspective, though, neither government nor party nor loyal order organized the expulsion campaigns. There was no overt official persecution on religious grounds as the Northern Irish constitution forbade it. It should also be noted that the northern security regime was actually much more lenient than that operating in the south, which not only had its own death squads but also jailed and executed its opponents with far greater enthusiasm. All in all, once again we would expect this factor to favour northern Catholic emigration. As it produced no such effect, it has no independent explanatory power.

What of the minorities' relationships with outside states or forces? In the south, it was important that the British government never tried to mobilize southern Protestants against the I.R.A. as had been done in the north.[21] There was no intervention on behalf of the minority from Britain or Northern Ireland after the Treaty and partition, despite the urgings of some Conservative politicians and newspapers. The British government did grant compensation to loyalists for losses inflicted after the Truce, but most of this went to people who had already left Ireland.[22] So: no real outside support for Protestants to stay in place. For some, this produced a feeling of abandonment, a demoralizing incentive to leave.

In the north, the British government also withdrew as far as possible and as quickly as possible. After the Truce it tried to adopt a position of neutrality. The Lloyd George administration did attempt to negotiate in order to resolve north–south conflicts—hence the Craig–Collins Pacts—but there would be no reintervention to protest the besieged minority.[23]

Michael Collins's Provisional Government was opposed to Northern Ireland in principle, blamed it for the 'pogroms', and quickly became aggressively involved. Money and guns were sent to northern I.R.A. units. Rebel local governments and schools that refused to recognize the authority of the new regime were encouraged and supported financially. Collins himself assumed the leadership of northern nationalism and negotiated on behalf of northern Catholics. However, once the southern Civil War began, most of these efforts were abandoned, permanently so

---

[21] See Ch. 9.

[22] Niamh Brennan, 'A Political Minefield: Southern Loyalists, the Irish Grants Committee and the British Government, 1922–31', *Irish Historical Studies*, 30 (May 1997), 406–19.

[23] Patrick Buckland, *The Factory of Grievances* (Dublin, 1979), ch. 12.

once Collins died. This left the northerners with much the same withdrawal symptoms as those felt by southern Protestants.[24]

In addition to a temporarily sympathetic outside state, northern Catholics also had the aid of a number of relief agencies. The Irish White Cross in particular, as well as other secular and religious charities, channelled huge amounts of money (especially American money) into Belfast to support expelled workers and displaced families.[25] Again, this dwindled rapidly once the Civil War broke out and violence in Belfast subsided. Northern Catholics might have been encouraged to stay up to 1922, but by the end of that year the collapse of outside support should have had the opposite effect. Nor can it be reasonably argued that they might have been waiting for the Boundary Commission to transfer large areas into Free State jurisdiction. Even if this were so, it would not have affected the position of Belfast, where the Catholic population actually rose in spite of it all.


## Minority Responses

Three options were available for these people as individuals and communities: resistance, accommodation, and flight. Resistance first. Apart from a very few individuals, no southern Protestants resisted the I.R.A. or collaborated with the British or Free State forces. Unlike their northern co-religionists, they were inert, unarmed, unorganized, and crucially lacked any tradition of defiance or confrontation.[26] Moreover, they lacked real leadership, the southern unionist grandees being both divided and unrepresentative.[27] They lacked solidarity and they lacked their own territory to defend or where they might feel safe. The Protestant population was scattered, divided by class, and nowhere a majority. The absence of resistance was not just a matter of choice but also of simple capacity to mount any meaningful challenge.

---

[24] For Collins's 'northern policy', see Eamon Phoenix, *Northern Nationalism: Northern Politics, Partition, and the Catholic Minority in Northern Ireland, 1890–1940* (Belfast, 1994), 167–251, and John Regan, *The Irish Counter-Revolution 1921–1936: Treatyite Politics and Settlement in Independent Ireland* (Dublin, 1999), 61–5.

[25] See the *Report of the Irish White Cross to 31st August 1922*, 125–39. Belfast received approximately £363,000 in personal relief funds from this source.

[26] See Ch. 9.

[27] On southern unionist politics, see Patrick Buckland, *Irish Unionism 1: The Anglo Irish and the New Ireland 1885 to 1922* (Dublin, 1972).

Northern Catholics, on the other hand—and southern Catholics, for that matter—were a highly mobilized and competitive community. The circumstances of the early twentieth century produced a surfeit of activists and leaders within the Irish Party, the Ancient Order of Hibernians, the United Irish League, the Irish Volunteers, and Sinn Féin—although many were eventually drawn to Dublin by the centripetal demands of nation and state. The Catholic Church provided a unitary institutional backbone and further leadership and organization, with its command of schools, hospitals, property, and jobs. At the neighbourhood level, Catholic enclaves in Belfast and elsewhere shared a great tradition of solidarity: the habit and practice of self-help and self-defence (shared with many northern Protestant communities as well).[28] All in all, Catholics and nationalists had at their command a very sophisticated repertoire of collective action.

Underpinning or even enabling this activity was the fact of Catholic concentration in territorial blocs. Catholics were a minority in Ulster and Northern Ireland as a whole, but many or most actually lived as part of a local majority, in west Ulster, south Down and Armagh, and in the Falls and adjacent districts of West Belfast. Within these boundaries people were relatively secure from attack, providing safe havens for those beyond in times of trouble. So, with a strong geographical base and an array of social and organizational resources, the Catholic community's capacity for resistance and perseverance was formidable.

If resistance is of no avail and leaving is undesirable, the only option left is to transfer loyalty—or at least accommodate oneself—to the new regime. The majority of southern Protestants chose one or other of these options. In the Church of Ireland, for example, some local vestries declared their acceptance of the Free State at its outset, and the *Church of Ireland Gazette* encouraged its readers to do the same.[29] Even before the Treaty, many individuals had accepted the republic as the will of the majority—if only from a position of practical neutrality and because they had no other choice. Protestant preferences may still have lain with

---

[28] See A. C. Hepburn, 'The Catholic Community of Belfast, 1850–1940', 'Ulster or the North of Ireland? Belfast Catholics from Ethnicity to Nationalism, 1880–1900', and 'Catholic Ulster and Irish Politics: The Ancient Order of Hibernians, 1905–14', in Hepburn, *A Past Apart: Studies in the History of Catholic Belfast 1850–1950* (Belfast, 1996). For comparative figures on membership in nationalist organizations, see Fitzpatrick, 'The Geography of Irish Nationalism'—although it must be remembered that per capita figures refer to the whole population, not just to the Catholic minority.

[29] See *Church of Ireland Gazette*, 13 Jan.; 21 Sept. 1922.

a united kingdom, but their priorities were law, order, and economic stability.

Most northern Catholics were nationalists of one kind or another.[30] Even if they didn't care for full-blown independence, they wanted all-Ireland home (i.e. majority) rule and an end to Protestant privilege. Thus, reluctant and hopefully temporary accommodation was the most enthusiastic response any could muster to the unionist state. And in border areas even this didn't come until after the Boundary Commission reported in 1925. In 1920, 1921, and 1922 the dominant attitude was one of non-recognition and non-cooperation. Nationalist councils rejected the government's authority, as did MPs elected to Stormont, and even Catholic schools. The Church itself was adamantly opposed to partition, and worked with local politicians and the Provisional Government in Dublin first to stop it and then to reverse it.[31]

However, when Catholic representatives did attempt to negotiate with unionists, they were frequently rebuffed. Such was the case with the two Craig–Collins pacts of 1922. While James Craig and some of his colleagues may have wanted to reconcile moderate nationalist opinion, these efforts lacked commitment and were undercut by more militant elements within his party.[32] In general, the governing principle of Northern Ireland was one of hostility to nationalism and even to the minority population as a whole. They were to be excluded from any real power. Catholic accommodation with such attitudes could only be uncomfortable. Loyalties remained firmly alienated, fused with unrelieved grievances. The same resources sustaining opposition worked to uphold this segregated 'state within a state' for decades to come.

The final option, then, was flight—which brings us back to our starting-point. To understand the decisions involved, though, they have to be broken down further. Flight could be forced or voluntary, permanent or temporary, local or long-distance, and people could choose these options for different reasons. The Catholic population in the six counties fell by about 10,000 people between 1911 and 1926, or by 2 per cent. In Belfast, where most of the murders occurred, the Catholic population actually rose slightly, most likely due to in-migration from rural areas. The Catholic proportion of the city population did decline, but this was due more to faster Protestant growth and a lower Catholic marriage rate

---

[30]  See Hepburn, 'Ulster or the North of Ireland?'; Phoenix, *Northern Nationalism*, 1–56.

[31]  See Harris, *The Catholic Church*, chs. 3–5.

[32]  See Phoenix, *Northern Nationalism*, 167–212.

than to expulsions.[33] Some northern refugees went south in 1922, perhaps 1,500, perhaps even more, but most of these probably returned to their homes.[34]

Catholic refugees were not a myth, of course, but they largely stayed within Belfast. Here there was mass displacement of families and households. At least 8,000 people were forced from their homes between the summers of 1920 and 1922. Ten per cent or more of the entire Catholic population was affected, even if some only moved a few streets away and very few were actually home-owners. Typically, these people left vulnerable or mixed areas to go to predominantly Catholic neighbourhoods. In most cases they had been attacked, threatened, or found themselves residing in a crossfire. Few were literally expelled but they certainly felt that they had little choice at that particular moment. It is likely that some thought the move might only be temporary, and planned to go back to their homes once the violence had subsided. The unprecedented duration of the fighting made their relocation permanent, however, as did the loyalist habit of burning or wrecking the vacant dwellings. Perhaps a quarter of that number of Protestants in Catholic areas did the same, although without experiencing the same intimidation or subsequent home-wrecking.

Such movement was made possible by the existence of a large and compact Catholic zone in West Belfast and a population capable of absorbing the migrants and solidaristic enough to support them (the houses vacated by Protestants allowed something of a trade to take place as well). In fact, not only was housing found or built for the refugees, but thousands of expelled workers and their dependants were also maintained by their neighbours, the Church, and the greater ethnic community outside Northern Ireland. In retrospect, in the midst of a deep economic recession, this was a remarkable achievement.

For Protestants in the southern provinces there were no internal heartlands or comparable support networks—and no real tradition of self-help. They simply did not think and act collectively to anywhere near the same extent. The exceptions to this rule were those who lived in the three Ulster counties on the Free State side of the border: Cavan, Monaghan, and Donegal. Here there was a strong recent unionist tradition, an active U.V.F. membership (in 1912–14), and a solid Orange Order. This

33 Martin, 'Migration', 36–7.
34 Brennan, 'A Political Minefield', 408.

produced two effects. First, the decline in population was lower than the overall Free State average. Second, those who left did have a nearby Protestant heartland across the border. How many went to Northern Ireland as opposed to Britain or Canada is unknown, and has probably been exaggerated for political reasons. Stories of Protestant refugees in unionist newspapers at the time were as dubious as similar stories about Catholic evacuees in their nationalist opposite numbers.[35] Still, it can reasonably be assumed that thousands of border Protestants moved north or east into perceived secure areas, just as Catholics did in Belfast. Interestingly, Catholics on the 'wrong' side of the border in Fermanagh or Tyrone did not follow suit and move south.

While the key distinction to be made in the northern experience is between internal and external flight, for the southern minority it is between temporary and permanent departure. Many Protestant men left with the intention of returning, and many did return, but often only to leave again so that, by default, they made new lives elsewhere. As in Belfast, the sheer duration of the violence became a factor in itself. In both cases, it must be noted, the evidence suggests that most people concerned maintained a clear preference to remain. These were Irish people who wished to remain so.

What do these events reveal about the structure and dynamics of the Irish revolution? That ethnicity was central to both: as a framework for solidarity and polarization; as a political marker, willing or unwilling; and as a vector of violence. One of the mainsprings of revolution (and counter-revolution) was the mobilization of communities against perceived outsiders, infiltrators, traitors, oppressors, and aggressors. Inherent in this process was the urge to suppress dissent and to secure territory and unanimity in order to eliminate danger. Although this process had different forms and outcomes north and south, it was, at heart, the same process. To understand it, historians of the revolution must eschew partitionist history. The revolution happened all over Ireland, and explanations of why and how must be applied in the same way.

---

[35] For an apparently more reliable story of refugees in Belfast, see *Church of Ireland Gazette*, 26 May 1922.

# INDEX